STUDENT SOLUTIONS MANUAL
BY EDW. S. GINSBERG FOR
PHYSICS FOR SCIENTISTS AND ENGINEERS

VOLUME III

RICHARD WOLFSON | JAY M. PASACHOFF

Taken from:

Student Solutions Manual by Edw. S. Ginsberg for
Physics for Scientists and Engineers, Third Edition
by Richard Wolfson, Jay M. Pasachoff

Cover Art *Electr1* by Barry Cronin

Taken from:

Student Solutions Manual by Edw. S. Ginsberg
for
Physics, For Scientists and Engineers, Third Edition
by Richard Wolfson, Jay M. Pasachoff
Copyright 1999 by Addison Wesley Longman, Inc.
A Pearson Education Company
Boston, Massachusetts 02116

Printed in the United States of America

10 9 8 7

ISBN 0-536-17339-7

2005460102

MT

Please visit our web site at *www.pearsoncustom.com*

PEARSON CUSTOM PUBLISHING
75 Arlington Street, Suite 300, Boston, MA 02116
A Pearson Education Company

CONTENTS

PREFACE

The decision to compile a manual of worked-out solutions to the end-of-chapter problems in Wolfson and Pasachoff's textbook arose from a consideration of the crucial importance of homework problems in the learning of physics. The process of applying physical concepts to construct explanations and answer questions is an excellent means of increasing one's understanding and confirming one's knowledge of those very concepts. (Learning physics without doing problems is like learning to swim without going in the water!) These solutions are designed to aid this process by supplementing, reinforcing, and sometimes replacing classroom discussions.

This *Student Solutions Manual* contains solutions to every odd-numbered problem in the text. In order for the reader to achieve the most benefit from using this manual, most of the solutions have been written in a form that requires his or her active participation. Such an actively engaged reader simultaneously reads and works through each solution with pencil and paper, calculator, and open textbook. Intermediate steps, such as algebraic manipulations, substitution of variables or data, diagrams, conversion of units, etc., are frequently and intentionally omitted. They must be supplied by an engaged reader, using the manual's solutions as guideposts and textual materials as references. Wolfson and Pasachoff intended their problems to help readers understand and use concepts presented in their textbook, and develop problem-solving skills. I have integrated references to the text into my solutions in fulfillment of this goal.

My solutions are not necessarily the only ones possible (or even the best, simplest, etc.). In some cases, alternate methods are indicated; in others, a different point of view from the text's is deliberately presented. Students should remember that the logical equivalence of different approaches to a problem has to be demonstrated by means other than just getting the same answer.

Many authors have enumerated helpful suggestions for students to follow when solving problems. My own version of such a list is the following:

- Carefully READ and understand the question. It may be necessary to visualize a situation or device, as described in the text, or as known from personal experience. The context of the question, i.e., the chapter or section in which it occurs, is often of help.

- THINK about how the quantities that determine the sought-for answer are physically related to the quantities that are either given in the question, or obtainable from them and other sources of data. Construction of a simple, physical, conceptual model, to represent the situation in the problem, may often be necessary.

- Write down physical equations involving the relevant quantities and relations, perhaps using approximations where appropriate, and SOLVE for the desired variables. For some problems, this is the most difficult step.

- CONSIDER the reasonableness of your answer. Does it make sense? Is it consistent with your initial expectations? Does it change suitably when the conditions in the problem are altered? If not, the previous steps may require repetition or verification.

In the real world of experimental science, numerical results reflect the precision of actual measurements and theoretical uncertainties in their interpretation. Such subjects are probably more appropriate to laboratory or advanced courses. By default, I have adopted the once-standard convention of regarding most numbers in problems as accurate to three significant figures, unless otherwise indicated by the context. I think common sense is a better guide than consistency at this level. On a different aspect of accuracy, I must admit to the responsibility for any errors which inevitably are present in a work of this size, and will make any corrections brought to my attention.

Although I personally have solved every problem in this manual, I acknowledge a great debt to other authors, my colleagues, former teachers, and students. Wolfson and Pasachoff have produced a scholarly, interesting, and well-written textbook with problems to match. I have tried to emulate their high standards in this accompanying manual of solutions, which I hope will be a practical aid to both students and instructors.

Edw. S. Ginsberg
University of Massachusetts Boston
Boston, MA 02125-3393
edw.ginsberg@umb.edu

Additional Supplements to Wolfson and Pasachoff,
Physics for Scientists and Engineers, Third Edition

Student Study Guide Volume 1, with *ActivPhysics1* (ISBN: 0-321-05148-3)
Student Study Guide Volume 2, with *ActivPhysics2* (ISBN: 0-321-05147-5)

CHAPTER 16 WAVE MOTION

ActivPhysics can help with these problems:
Activities 10.1, 10.2, 10.7, 10.10

Section 16-2: Wave Properties

Problem

1. Ocean waves with 18-m wavelength travel at
   5.3 m/s. What is the time interval between wave
   crests passing under a boat moored at a fixed
   location?

Solution

Wave crests (adjacent wavefronts) take a time of one
period to pass a fixed point, traveling at the wave
speed (or phase velocity) for a distance of one
wavelength. Thus $T = \lambda/v = 18$ m/(5.3 m/s) = 3.40 s.

Problem

3. An 88.7-MHz FM radio wave propagates at the
   speed of light. What is its wavelength?

Solution

From Equation 16-1, $\lambda = v/f = (3 \times 10^8$ m/s)$\div$
$(88.7 \times 10^6$ Hz) = 3.38 m.

Problem

5. A 145-MHz radio signal propagates along a cable.
   Measurement shows that the wave crests are spaced
   1.25 m apart. What is the speed of the waves on the
   cable? Compare with the speed of light in vacuum.

Solution

The distance between adjacent wave crests is one
wavelength, so the wave speed in the cable (Equa-
tion 16-1) is $v = f\lambda = (145 \times 10^6$ Hz)(1.25 m) = $1.81 \times$
10^8 m/s = $0.604c$, where $c = 3 \times 10^8$ m/s is the wave
speed in vacuum.

Problem

7. Detecting objects by reflecting waves off them is
   effective only for objects larger than about one
   wavelength. (a) What is the smallest object that
   can be seen with visible light (maximum frequency
   7.5×10^{14} Hz)? (b) What is the smallest object that
   can be detected with a medical ultrasound unit
   operating at 5 MHz? The speed of ultrasound
   waves in body tissue is about 1500 m/s.

Solution

(a) The wavelength of light corresponding to this
maximum frequency is $\lambda = c/f = (3 \times 10^8$ m/s)$\div$
$(7.5 \times 10^{14}$ Hz) = 400 nm, violet in hue (see Equation 16-1). (b) The ultrasonic waves described have
wavelength $\lambda = v/f = (1500$ m/s)/(5 MHz) = 0.3 mm.

Problem

9. In Fig. 16-28 two boats are anchored offshore and
   are bobbing up and down on the waves at the rate
   of six complete cycles each minute. When one boat
   is up the other is down. If the waves propagate at
   2.2 m/s, what is the minimum distance between the
   boats?

Solution

The boats are $180° - \pi$ rad out of phase, so the
minimum distance separating them is half a
wavelength. (In general, they could be an odd number
of half-wavelengths apart.) The frequency is 6/60 s =
0.1 Hz, so $\frac{1}{2}\lambda = \frac{1}{2}v/f = \frac{1}{2}(2.2$ m/s)/(0.1/s) = 11 m.
(Fig. 16-28 shows the answer, not the question.)

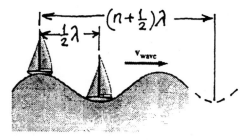

FIGURE 16-28 Problem 9 Solution.

Section 16-3: Mathematical Description of
Wave Motion

Problem

11. An ocean wave has period 4.1 s and wavelength
    10.8 m. Find (a) its wave number and (b) its
    angular frequency.

Solution

From Equations 16-3 and 4, (a) $k = 2\pi/10.8$ m =
0.582 m^{-1}, and (b) $\omega = 2\pi/(4.1$ s) = 1.53 s^{-1}.

Problem

13. A simple harmonic wave of wavelength 16 cm and amplitude 2.5 cm is propagating along a string in the negative x direction at 35 cm/s. Find (a) the angular frequency and (b) the wave number. (c) Write a mathematical expression describing the displacement y of this wave (in centimeters) as a function of position and time. Assume the displacement at $x = 0$ is a maximum when $t = 0$.

Solution

(b) Equation 16-4 gives $k = 2\pi/16$ cm $= 0.393$ cm^{-1}, and (a) Equation 16-6 gives $\omega = kv = (0.393$ cm$^{-1})\times$ $(35$ cm/s$) = 13.7$ s^{-1}. (c) Equation 16-5, for a wave moving in the negative x direction, becomes $y(x, t) = (2.5$ cm$) \cos[(0.393$ cm$^{-1})x + (13.7$ s$^{-1})t]$.

Problem

15. What are (a) the amplitude, (b) the frequency in hertz, (c) the wavelength, and (d) the speed of a water wave whose displacement is $y = 0.25 \sin(0.52x - 2.3t)$, where x and y are in meters and t in seconds?

Solution

Comparison of the given displacement with Equation 16-5 reveals that (a) $A = 0.25$ m, (b) $f = \omega/2\pi = (2.3$ s$^{-1})/2\pi = 0.366$ Hz, (c) $\lambda = 2\pi/k = 2\pi/(0.52$ m$^{-1}) = 12.1$ m, and $v = \omega/k = (2.3$ s$^{-1})/0.52$ m$^{-1} = 4.42$ m/s. (Note: The presence of a phase constant of $\phi = -\pi/2$ in the expression for $y(x, t) = A \sin(kx - \omega t) = A \cos(kx - \omega t + \phi)$ does not affect any of the quantities queried in this problem.)

Problem

17. At time $t = 0$, the displacement in a transverse wave pulse is described by $y = 2(x^4 + 1)^{-1}$, with both x and y in cm. Write an expression for the pulse as a function of position x and time t if it is propagating in the positive x direction at 3 cm/s.

Solution

From the shape of the pulse at $t = 0$, $y(x, 0) = f(x)$, a pulse with the same waveform, traveling in the positive x direction with speed v, can be obtained by replacing x by $x - vt$, $y(x, t) = f(x - vt)$. For the given $f(x)$ and v, $y(x, t) = 2[(x - 3t)^4 + 1]^{-1}$, with x and y in cm and t in s.

Problem

19. Figure 16-30a shows a wave plotted as a function of position at time $t = 0$, while Fig. 16-30b shows the same wave plotted as a function of time at position $x = 0$. Find (a) the wavelength, (b) the period, (c) the wave speed, and (d) the direction of propagation.

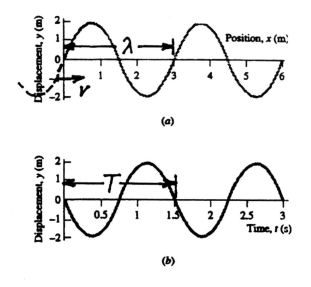

FIGURE 16-30 Problem 19.

Solution

(a) The wavelength is the distance between successive maxima at the same time (say $t = 0$), so Fig. 16-30a gives $\lambda = 3$ m. (b) The period is the time interval between successive maxima (or some other specific phases differing by 2π) at the same point (say $x = 0$), so Fig. 16-30b gives $T = 1.5$ s. (c) $v = \omega/k = \lambda/T = 2$ m/s. (d) Fig. 16-30b shows that as t increases from 0, the displacement at $x = 0$ first becomes negative. The waveform in Fig. 16-30a must therefore move to the right, in the positive x direction. [For the sinusoidal wave pictured, $y(x, 0) = A \sin kx$ and $y(0, t) = -A \sin \omega t = A \sin(-\omega t)$, so $y(x, t) = A \sin(kx - \omega t)$.]

Section 16-4: Waves on a String

Problem

21. The main cables supporting New York's George Washington Bridge have a mass per unit length of 4100 kg/m and are under tension of 250 MN. At what speed would a transverse wave propagate on these cables?

Solution

$v = \sqrt{F/\mu} = \sqrt{(2.5\times10^8 \text{ N})/(4100 \text{ kg/m})} = 247$ m/s (from Equation 16-7).

Problem

23. A transverse wave with 3.0-cm amplitude and 75-cm wavelength is propagating on a stretched spring whose mass per unit length is 170 g/m. If the wave speed is 6.7 m/s, find (a) the spring tension and (b) the maximum speed of any point on the spring.

Solution

(a) Equation 16-7 gives $F = \mu v^2 = (0.17 \text{ kg/m}) \times (6.7 \text{ m/s})^2 = 7.63$ N. (b) The unnumbered equation for the vertical velocity of the medium in Section 16.5 gives $u_{max} = (dy/dt)_{max} = \omega A = (2\pi v/\lambda)A = 2\pi(6.7 \text{ m/s})(3 \text{ cm})/(75 \text{ cm}) = 1.68$ m/s.

Problem

25. A 3.1-kg mass hangs from a 2.7-m-long string whose total mass is 0.62 g. What is the speed of transverse waves on the string? *Hint:* You can ignore the string mass in calculating the tension but not in calculating the wave speed. Why?

Solution

The tension in the string is approximately equal to the weight of the 3.1 kg mass (since the weight of the string is only 2% of this). Thus, $v = \sqrt{F/\mu} = \sqrt{(3.1 \text{ kg})(9.8 \text{ m/s}^2)(2.7 \text{ m})/(0.62 \text{ g})} = 364$ m/s. (0.62 g is small compared to 3.1 kg, but not small compared to zero!)

Problem

27. The density of copper is 8.29 g/cm^3. What is the tension in a 1.0-mm-diameter copper wire that propagates transverse waves at 120 m/s?

Solution

The linear mass density of copper wire with diameter d is $\mu = m/\ell = \rho \frac{1}{4}\pi d^2 = (8.29 \text{ g/cm}^3)\frac{1}{4}\pi(1 \text{ mm})^2 = 6.51 \times 10^{-3}$ kg/m, so $F = \mu v^2 = (6.51 \times 10^{-3} \text{ kg/m}) \times (120 \text{ m/s})^2 = 93.8$ N.

Problem

29. A 25-m-long piece of 1.0-mm-diameter wire is put under 85 N tension. If a transverse wave takes 0.21 s to travel the length of the wire, what is the density of the material comprising the wire?

Solution

From the length of wire, travel time, and Equation 16-7, $v = 25 \text{ m}/0.21 \text{ s} = \sqrt{85 \text{ N}/\mu}$, so $\mu = 6.00 \times 10^{-3}$ kg/m. But for a uniform wire of length ℓ and diameter d, $\rho = \mu/\frac{1}{4}\pi d^2 = (6.00 \times 10^{-3} \text{ kg/m}) \div \frac{1}{4}\pi(1 \text{ mm})^2 = 7.64$ g/cm^3 (see solution to Problem 27).

Problem

31. A steel wire can tolerate a maximum tension per unit cross-sectional area of 2.7 GN/m^2 before it undergoes permanent distortion. What is the maximum possible speed for transverse waves in a steel wire if it is to remain undistorted? Steel has a density of 7.9 g/cm^3.

Solution

The linear density is the (volume) density times the cross-sectional area (see solution to Problem 27), whereas the maximum tension is 2.7 GN/m^2 times the same cross-sectional area. Therefore $v_{max} = \sqrt{(2.7 \text{ GN/m}^2)/(7.9 \text{ g/cm}^3)} = 585$ m/s. (Recall that the prefix giga equals 10^9 and that 1 g/cm$^3 = 10^3$ kg/m^3.)

Section 16-5: Wave Power and Intensity

Problem

33. A rope with 280 g of mass per meter is under 550 N tension. A wave with frequency 3.3 Hz and amplitude 6.1 cm is propagating on the rope. What is the average power carried by the wave?

Solution

The average power transmitted by transverse traveling waves in a string is given by Equation 16-8, $\bar{P} = \frac{1}{2}\mu\omega^2 A^2 v = \frac{1}{2}(0.28 \text{ kg/m})(2\pi \times 3.3 \text{ Hz})^2(0.061 \text{ m})^2 \times \sqrt{550 \text{ N}/(0.28 \text{ kg/m})} = 9.93$ W. (We used Equation 16-7 for v.)

Problem

35. A 600-g Slinky is stretched to a length of 10 m. You shake one end at the frequency of 1.8 Hz, applying a time-average power of 1.1 W. The resulting waves propagate along the Slinky at 2.3 m/s. What is the wave amplitude?

Solution

We assume that the elastic properties of a stretched string are shared by the Slinky, so Equation 16-8 applies. Then $A = \sqrt{2(1.1 \text{ W})/(0.06 \text{ kg/m})(2.3 \text{ m/s})}/(2\pi \times 1.8 \text{ Hz}) = 35.3$ cm.

Problem

37. Figure 16-32 shows a wave train consisting of two cycles of a sine wave propagating along a string. Obtain an expression for the total energy in this wave train, in terms of the string tension F, the wave amplitude A, and the wavelength λ.

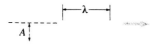

FIGURE 16-32 Problem 37.

Solution

The average wave energy, $d\bar{E}$, in a small element of string of length dx, is transmitted in time, dt, at the same speed as the waves, $v = dx/dt$. From Equation 16-8, $d\bar{E} = \bar{P}dt = \frac{1}{2}\mu\omega^2 A^2 v\, dt = \frac{1}{2}\mu\omega^2 A^2 dx$, so the average linear energy density is $d\bar{E}/dx = \frac{1}{2}\mu\omega^2 A^2$. The total average energy in a wave train of length $\ell = 2\lambda$ is $\bar{E} = (d\bar{E}/dx)\ell = \frac{1}{2}\mu\omega^2 A^2(2\lambda)$. In terms of the quantities specified in this problem (see Equations 16-1 and 7) $\bar{E} = \frac{1}{2}(F/v^2)(2\pi v/\lambda)^2 A^2(2\lambda) = 4\pi^2 F A^2/\lambda$. (Note: The relation derived can be written as $\bar{P} = (d\bar{E}/dx)v$. For a one-dimensional wave, $\bar{P}$ is the intensity, so the average intensity equals the average energy density times the speed of wave energy propagation. This is a general wave property, e.g., see the first unnumbered equation for S in Section 34-10.)

Problem

39. A loudspeaker emits energy at the rate of 50 W, spread in all directions. What is the intensity of sound 18 m from the speaker?

Solution

The wave power is spread out over a sphere of area $4\pi r^2$, so the intensity is $50\text{ W}/4\pi(18\text{ m})^2 = 12.3\text{ mW/m}^2$. (See Equation 16-9.)

Problem

41. Use data from Appendix E to determine the intensity of sunlight at (a) Mercury and (b) Pluto.

Solution

Equation 16-9 gives the ratio of intensities at two distances from an isotropic source of spherical waves as $I_2/I_1 = (r_1/r_2)^2$. If we use the average intensity of sunlight given in Table 16-1 and mean orbital distances to the sun from Appendix E, we obtain (a) $I_{\text{Merc}} = I_E(r_E/r_{\text{Merc}})^2 = (1368\text{ W/m}^2)(150\div 57.9)^2 = 9.18\text{ kW/m}^2$, and (b) $I_{\text{Pluto}} = (1368\text{ W/m}^2)\times(150/5.91\times10^3)^2 = 0.881\text{ W/m}^2$. (Alternatively, the luminosity of the sun, $\bar{P} = 3.85\times10^{26}$ W, from Appendix E, could be used directly in Equation 16-9, with only slightly different numerical results.)

Problem

43. Light emerges from a 5.0-mW laser in a beam 1.0 mm in diameter. The beam shines on a wall, producing a spot 3.6 cm in diameter. What are the beam intensities (a) at the laser and (b) at the wall?

Solution

If we assume that the power output of the laser is spread uniformly over the cross-sectional area of its beam, then $I = \bar{P}/\frac{1}{4}\pi d^2$. (a) When the beam emerges, $I = 5\text{ mW}/\frac{1}{4}\pi(1\text{ mm})^2 = 6.37\text{ kW/m}^2$, while (b) after its diameter has expanded by 36 times, at the wall, $I' = I(1/36)^2 = 4.91\text{ W/m}^2$.

Problem

45. Use Table 16-1 to determine how close to a rock band you should stand for it to sound as loud as a jet plane at 200 m. Treat the band and the plane as point sources. Is this assumption reasonable?

Solution

To have the same loudness, the soundwave intensities should be equal, i.e., $I_{\text{band}}(r) = I_{\text{jet}}(200\text{ m})$. Regarded as isotropic point sources, use of Equation 16-9 gives $\bar{P}_{\text{band}}/r^2 = \bar{P}_{\text{jet}}/(200\text{ m})^2$. The average power of each source can be found from Table 16-1 and a second application of Equation 16-9, $\bar{P}_{\text{band}} = 4\pi(4\text{ m})^2(1\text{ W/m}^2)$ and $\bar{P}_{\text{jet}} = 4\pi(50\text{ m})^2(10\text{ W/m}^2)$. Then $r^2 = (\bar{P}_{\text{band}}/\bar{P}_{\text{jet}})(200\text{ m})^2 = (200\text{ m})^2(4\text{ m})^2\times(1\text{ W/m}^2)/(50\text{ m})^2(10\text{ W/m}^2)$, or $r = 5.06$ m. The size of a rock band is several meters, nearly equal to this distance, so a point source is not a good approximation. Besides, the acoustical output of a rock band usually emanates from an array of speakers, which is not point-like. Moreover, the size of a jet plane is also not very small compared to 50 m.

Section 16-6: The Superposition Principle and Wave Interference

Problem

47. Two wave pulses are described by

$$y_1(x,t) = \frac{2}{(x-t)^2 + 1}, \quad y_2(x,t) = \frac{-2}{(x-5+t)^2 + 1},$$

where x and y are in cm and t in seconds.
(a) What is the amplitude of each pulse?
(b) At $t = 0$, where is the peak of each pulse, and in what direction is it moving? (c) At what time will the two pulses exactly cancel?

Solution

(a) The absolute value of the maximum displacement for each pulse is 2 cm, a value attained when the denominators are minimal ($x - t = 0$ for the first pulse and $x - 5 + t = 0$ for the second). (b) At $t = 0$, the peak of the first pulse is at $x = 0$ moving in the positive x direction. ($x - t = 0$ represents the peak, so if t increases so does x. This is why a wave traveling in the positive x direction is represented by a function of $x - vt$.) For the second pulse, the peak is at $x = 5$, moving in the negative x direction, when $t = 0$ ($x - 5 + t = 0$ implies $x = 5 - t$ and $dx/dt = -1 < 0$). (c) $y_1(x,\ t) + y_2(x,\ t) = 0$ for all values of x implies $(x - t)^2 = (x - 5 + t)^2$. This is true for all x, only if $(x - t) = +(x - 5 + t)$ or at $t = \frac{5}{2} = 2.5$ s. (The other root, $(x - t) = -(x - 5 + t)$, shows that $x = 2.5$ cm is always a node, i.e., the net displacement there is zero at all times.)

Problem

49. You're in an airplane whose two engines are running at 560 rpm and 570 rpm. How often do you hear the sound intensity increase as a result of wave interference?

Solution

As mentioned in the text, pilots of twin-engine airplanes use the beat frequency to synchronize the rpm's of their engines. The beat frequency is simply the difference of the two interfering frequencies, $f_{\text{beat}} = (570 - 560)/60$ s $= \frac{1}{6}$ s^{-1}, so you would hear one beat every six seconds.

Problem

51. What is the wavelength of the ocean waves in Example 16-5 if the calm water you encounter at 33 m is the *second* calm region on your voyage from the center line?

Solution

The second node occurs when the path difference is three half-wavelengths, or $AP - BP \equiv \Delta r = \frac{3}{2}\lambda_2$. (A phase difference of $k_2\Delta r = (2\pi/\lambda_2)\Delta r = 3\pi$, or an odd multiple of $\pi = 180°$ in general, insures complete destructive interference.) From Example 16-5, $2\ \Delta r = 16.0$ m, so $\lambda_2 = 2\ \Delta r/3 = 5.34$ m.

Section 16-7:   The Wave Equation

Problem

53. The following equation arises in analyzing the behavior of shallow water:

$$\frac{\partial^2 y}{dx^2} - \frac{1}{gh}\frac{\partial^2 y}{dt^2} = 0,$$

where h is the equilibrium depth and y the displacement from equilibrium. Give an expression for the speed of waves in shallow water. (Here *shallow* means the water depth is much less than the wavelength.)

Solution

The equation given is in the standard form for the one-dimensional linear wave equation (Equation 16-12), so the wave speed is the reciprocal of the square root of the quantity multiplying $\partial^2 y/\partial t^2$. Thus $v = \sqrt{gh}$.

Paired Problems

Problem

55. A wave on a taut wire is described by the equation $y = 1.5\sin(0.10x - 560t)$, where x and y are in cm and t is in seconds. If the wire tension is 28 N, what are (a) the amplitude, (b) the wavelength, (c) the period, (d) the wave speed, and (e) the power carried by the wave?

Solution

The wave has the form of Equation 16-5, with a phase constant of $-\frac{\pi}{2} = -90°$, $y(x,\ t) = A\sin(kx - \omega t) = A\cos(kx - \omega t - \frac{\pi}{2})$. Comparison reveals that $k = 0.1$ cm^{-1}, $\omega = 560$ s^{-1}, and (a) $A = 1.5$ cm (b) $\lambda = 2\pi/k = 2\pi/(0.1$ cm$^{-1}) = 62.8$ cm (Equation 16-4). (c) $T = 2\pi/\omega = 2\pi/(560$ s$^{-1}) = 11.2$ ms (Equation 16-3). (d) $v = \omega/k = 56$ m/s (Equation 16-6). (e) $\bar{P} = \frac{1}{2}\mu\omega^2 A^2 v = \frac{1}{2}(\omega A)^2(F/v) = \frac{1}{2}(560$ s$^{-1}\times 0.015$ m$)^2(28$ N$)/(56$ m/s$) = 17.6$ W (Equation 16-8, and Equation 16-7 to eliminate μ).

Problem

57. A spring of mass m and spring constant k has an unstretched length ℓ_0. Find an expression for the speed of transverse waves on this spring when it has been stretched to a length ℓ.

Solution

The spring may be regarded as a stretched string with tension, $F = k(\ell - \ell_0)$, and linear mass density $\mu = m/\ell$. Equation 16-7 gives the speed of transverse waves as $v = \sqrt{k\ell(\ell - \ell_0)/m}$.

Problem

59. At a point 15 m from a source of spherical sound waves, you measure a sound intensity of 750 mW/m^2. How far do you need to walk, directly away from the source, until the intensity is 270 mW/m^2?

Solution

The intensity of spherical waves from a point source is given by Equation 16-9. At a distance r_1, $I_1 = \bar{P}/4\pi r_1^2$, while after increasing the radial distance by d, $I_2 = \bar{P}/4\pi(r_1 + d)^2$. Dividing and solving for d, one finds $d = r_1(\sqrt{I_1/I_2} - 1) = (15 \text{ m})(\sqrt{(750/270)} - 1) = 10.0$ m.

Problem

61. Two motors in a factory produce sound waves with the same frequency as their rotation rates. If one motor is running at 3600 rpm and the other at 3602 rpm, how often will workers hear a peak in the sound intensity?

Solution

The beat frequency equals the difference in the motors' rpm's, so the period of the beats is $T_{\text{beat}} = 1/f_{\text{beat}} = 1/(3602 - 3600)$ min^{-1} = 30 s. (See also Problem 49.)

Supplementary Problems

Problem

63. For a transverse wave on a stretched string, the requirement that the string be nearly horizontal is met if the amplitude is much less than the wavelength. (a) Show this by drawing an appropriate sketch. (b) Show that, under this approximation that $A \ll \lambda$, the maximum speed u of the string must be considerably less than the wave speed v. (c) If the amplitude is not to exceed 1% of the wavelength, how large can the string speed u be in relation to the wave speed v?

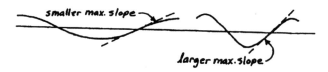

Problem 63 Solution.

Solution

(a) The relative "flatness" or "peakedness" of a sinusoidal waveform is determined by its maximum slope, $|dy/dx|_{\text{max}} = |\partial/\partial x[A\cos(kx - \omega t)]|_{\text{max}} =$

$kA = 2\pi(A/\lambda)$. If $A \ll \lambda$ (or $kA \ll 1$), the slope is nearly horizontal. (b) In terms of the speeds, $kA = \omega A/v = u_{\text{max}}/v$, so the string is nearly flat if $u_{\text{max}} \ll v$. (c) If $A/\lambda < 1\%$, then $u_{\text{max}}/v = 2\pi(A/\lambda) < 2\pi(1\%) = 6.3\%$.

Problem

65. An ideal spring is compressed until its total length is ℓ_1, and the speed of transverse waves on the spring is measured. When it's compressed further to a total length ℓ_2, waves propagate at the *same* speed. Show that the uncompressed spring length is just $\ell_1 + \ell_2$.

Solution

The tension in a compressed spring has magnitude $k(\ell_0 - \ell)$ while its linear mass-density is $\mu = m/\ell$. Therefore, the speed of transverse waves is $v = \sqrt{F/\mu} = \sqrt{k\ell(\ell_0 - \ell)/m}$ (as in Problem 57 for a stretched spring). If $v_1 = v_2$ for two different compressed lengths, then $\ell_1(\ell_0 - \ell_1) = \ell_2(\ell_0 - \ell_2)$ or $(\ell_1 - \ell_2)\ell_0 = \ell_1^2 - \ell_2^2 = (\ell_1 - \ell_2)(\ell_1 + \ell_2)$. Since $\ell_1 \neq \ell_2$, division by $\ell_1 - \ell_2$ gives $\ell_0 = \ell_1 + \ell_2$.

Problem

67. A 1-megaton nuclear explosion produces a shock wave whose amplitude, measured as excess air pressure above normal atmospheric pressure, is 1.4×10^5 Pa (1 Pa = 1 N/m^2) at a distance of 1.3 km from the explosion. An excess pressure of 3.5×10^4 Pa will destroy a typical woodframe house. At what distance from the explosion will such houses be destroyed? Assume the wavefront is spherical.

Solution

The intensity of a spherical wavefront varies inversely with the square of the distance from the central source (see Fig. 16-18b). In general, the intensity is proportional to the amplitude squared, so $A \sim 1/r$ for a spherical wave. (This can be proved rigorously by solution of the spherical wave equation, a generalization of Equation 16-12.) Therefore $A_1/A_2 = r_2/r_1$, or the overpressure reaches the stated limit at a distance $r_2 = (1.4\times10^5$ Pa$/3.5\times10^4$ Pa$)(1.3$ km$) = 5.2$ km from the explosion.

Problem

69. In Example 16-5, how much farther would you have to row to reach a region of maximum wave amplitude?

Solution

In general, the interference condition for waves in the geometry of Example 16-5 is $AP - BP = n\lambda/2$, where

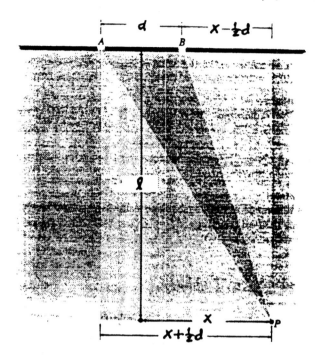

FIGURE 16-36 Problem 69 Solution.

n is an odd integer for destructive interference (a node) and n is an even integer for constructive interference (a maximum amplitude). (In Example 16-5, $n = 1$ gave the first node and in Problem 51, $n = 3$ gave the second node.) If $d = 20$ m is the distance between the openings, $\ell = 75$ m is the perpendicular distance from the breakwater, and x is the distance parallel to the breakwater measured from the midpoint of the openings, the interference condition is $\sqrt{\ell^2 + (x + \frac{1}{2}d)^2} - \sqrt{\ell^2 + (x - \frac{1}{2}d)^2} = n\lambda/2$ (see Fig. 16-36). In this problem, we wish to find x for the first maximum, $n = 2$, and the wavelength calculated in Example 16-5, $\lambda = 16.01$ m. Solving for x, we find:

$$x^2 = \frac{[\ell^2 + (\frac{1}{2}d)^2 - (\frac{1}{4}n\lambda)^2]}{(2d/n\lambda)^2 - 1}$$

$$= \frac{[(75)^2 + (10)^2 - (8.005)^2]\ \text{m}^2}{(40/32.02)^2 - 1} = (100.5\ \text{m})^2.$$

This is 100.5 m $-$ 33 m $= 67.5$ m farther than the first node in Example 16-5. (Note: We rounded off to three figures; if you round off to two figures, the answer is 67 m. Also, if $x = 33$ m is substituted into the general interference condition, one can recapture the wavelengths of the first and second nodes, for $n = 1$ and 3, calculated in Example 16-5 and Problem 51, respectively.)

CHAPTER 17 SOUND AND OTHER WAVE PHENOMENA

ActivPhysics can help with these problems: Activities 10.3, 10.4, 10.5, 10.6, 10.8, 10.9

Sections 17-1 and 17-2: Sound Waves and the Speed of Sound in Gases

Problem

1. Show that the quantity $\sqrt{P/\rho}$ has the units of speed.

Solution

The units of pressure (force per unit area) divided by density (mass per unit volume) are $(\text{N/m}^2)/(\text{kg/m}^3) = (\text{N/kg})(\text{m}^3/\text{m}^2) = (\text{m/s}^2)\text{m} = (\text{m/s})^2$, or those of speed squared.

Problem

3. Find the wavelength, period, angular frequency, and wave number of a 1.0-kHz sound wave in air under the conditions of Example 17-1.

Solution

The value of the speed of sound in air from Example 17-1 was 343 m/s. Therefore (a) $\lambda = v/f = (343 \text{ m/s})/(1 \text{ kHz}) = 34.3$ cm; (b) $T = 1/f = 1$ ms; (c) $\omega = 2\pi f = 6.28 \times 10^3 \text{ s}^{-1}$; and (d) $k = \omega/v = 2\pi/\lambda = 18.3 \text{ m}^{-1}$. (See Equations 16-1, 3, 4, and 6.)

Problem

5. Timers in sprint races start their watches when they see smoke from the starting gun, not when they hear the sound (Fig. 17-25). Why? How much error would be introduced by timing a 100-m race from the sound of the shot?

Solution

The sound of the starting gun takes $(100 \text{ m}) \div (340 \text{ m/s}) = 0.294$ s to reach the finish line. An error of this magnitude is significant in short races, where world records are measured in hundredths of a second. (This problem is almost the same as Problem 2, Chapter 2.)

Problem

7. At standard atmospheric pressure $(1.0 \times 10^5 \text{ N/m}^2)$, what density of air would make the sound speed 1.0 km/s?

Solution

Solving for the density in Equation 17-1, we find: $\rho = \gamma P/v^2 = 1.4(1.0 \times 10^5 \text{ N/m}^2)/(10^3 \text{ m/s})^2 = 0.14 \text{ kg/m}^3$.

Problem

9. A gas with density 1.0 kg/m^3 and pressure $8.0 \times 10^4 \text{ N/m}^2$ has sound speed 365 m/s. Are the gas molecules monatomic or diatomic?

Solution

Solving for γ in Equation 17-1, we find $\gamma = \rho v^2/P = (1.0 \text{ kg/m}^3)(365 \text{ m/s})^2/(8.0 \times 10^4 \text{ N/m}^2) = 1.67$, very close to the value for an ideal monatomic gas. (Actually, $\gamma - 5/3 = -1.35 \times 10^{-3}$ for this gas.)

Problem

11. Saturn's moon Titan has one of the solar system's thickest atmospheres. Near Titan's surface, atmospheric pressure is 50% greater than standard atmospheric pressure on Earth, while the density in molecules per unit volume is one-third that of Earth's atmosphere. If Titan's atmosphere is essentially all nitrogen (N$_2$), what is the sound speed?

Solution

The data and method used in Example 17-1, combined with the numbers given for Titan's atmosphere, yield

$$v = \left[\frac{(1.4)(1.5 \times 1.01 \times 10^5 \text{ N/m}^2)}{(28 \text{ u})(1.66 \times 10^{-27} \text{ kg/u})(\frac{1}{3} \times 2.51 \times 10^{25} \text{ m}^{-3})} \right]^{1/2}$$
$$= 739 \text{ m/s}.$$

Problem

13. You see an airplane straight overhead at an altitude of 5.2 km. Sound from the plane, however, seems to be coming from a point back along the plane's path at a 35° angle to the

vertical (Fig. 17-26). What is the plane's speed, assuming an average 330 m/s sound speed?

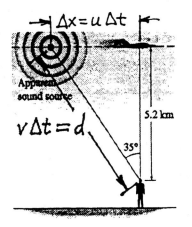

FIGURE 17-26 Problem 13.

Solution

The travel time of the sound from the airplane, reaching you along a line making an angle of 35° with the vertical (from the apparent sound source), is $\Delta t = d/v$. During this time, the airplane moved a horizontal distance $\Delta x = d\sin 35°$, so its speed is $u = \Delta x/\Delta t = d\sin 35°/(d/v) = v\sin 35° = (330 \text{ m/s})\sin 35° = 189$ m/s. (The airplane's altitude, 5.2 km $= d\cos 35°$, was not needed in this calculation.)

Section 17-3: Sound Intensity

Problem

15. Sound intensity in normal conversation is about $1 \mu\text{W/m}^2$. What is the displacement amplitude of air in a 2.5-kHz sound wave with this intensity?

Solution

As in Example 17-2, Equation 17-3c, combined with the atmospheric data in Example 17-1, can be used to calculate the displacement amplitude for sound waves of the specified frequency and intensity:

$$s_0 = \sqrt{2\bar{I}/\rho\omega^2 v} = \left(\frac{1}{2\pi \times 2.5 \times 10^3 \text{ Hz}}\right)$$
$$\times \sqrt{\frac{2(10^{-6} \text{ W/m}^2)}{(1.20 \text{ kg/m}^3)(343 \text{ m/s})}} = 4.44 \text{ nm.}$$

Problem

17. A speaker produces 440-Hz sound with total power 1.2 W, radiating equally in all directions. At a distance of 5.0 m, what are (a) the average intensity, (b) the decibel level, (c) the pressure amplitude, and (d) the displacement amplitude?

Solution

(a) Equation 16-9 gives the average intensity at a given distance from an isotropic point source, $\bar{I} = \bar{\mathcal{P}}/4\pi r^2 = (1.2 \text{ W})/4\pi(5 \text{ m})^2 = 3.82 \text{ mW/m}^2$. (b) From Equation 17-4, this corresponds to a sound level intensity of $\beta = (10 \text{ dB})\log(I/I_0) = (10 \text{ dB}) \times \log(3.82 \times 10^{-3}/10^{-12}) = 95.8 \text{ dB} \simeq 96 \text{ dB}$. (c) The pressure amplitude, for "normal air" of Example 17-1, follows from Equation 17-3b, $\Delta P_0 = \sqrt{2\rho v \bar{I}} = \sqrt{2(1.20 \text{ kg/m}^3)(343 \text{ m/s})(3.82 \times 10^{-3} \text{ W/m}^2)} = 1.77 \text{ N/m}^2$. (d) The corresponding displacement amplitude is $s_0 = \Delta P_0/\rho\omega v = (1.77 \text{ Pa})/(1.20 \text{ kg/m}^2)(343 \text{ m/s})(2\pi \times 440 \text{ Hz}) = 1.56 \mu\text{m}$.

Problem

19. What is the approximate frequency range over which sound with intensity 10^{-12} W/m^2 can be heard? Consult Fig. 17-3.

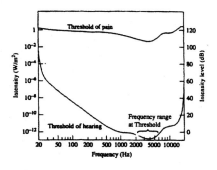

FIGURE 17-3 For reference.

Solution

Inspection of Fig. 17-3 shows that for frequencies approximately between 1 and 6.5 kHz, the threshold of hearing is at or below 10^{-12} W/m^2.

Problem

21. What are the intensity and pressure amplitudes in sound waves with intensity levels of (a) 65 dB and (b) −5 dB?

Solution

The exponentiation of Equation 17-4, to the base ten, relates the intensity to the decibel level, $I/I_0 = 10^{\beta/10 \text{ dB}}$ while Equation 17-3b gives the pressure amplitude, $\Delta P_0 = \sqrt{2\rho v I}$. Here, I is the average intensity, I_0 the threshold level, and we use values of ρ and v for air under the "normal" conditions in Example 17-1. (a) For $\beta = 65$ dB, $I = (10^{-12} \text{ W/m}^2)10^{6.5} = 3.16 \times 10^{-6} \text{ W/m}^2$, and

$\Delta P_0 = \sqrt{2(1.2 \text{ kg/m}^3)(343 \text{ m/s})(3.16\times10^{-6} \text{ W/m}^2)} =$ $5.10\times10^{-2} \text{ N/m}^2$. (b) For $\beta = -5$ dB, $I = I_0 10^{-5/10} = 3.16\times10^{-13} \text{ W/m}^2$ and $\Delta P_0 = 1.61\times10^{-5} \text{ N/m}^2$.

Problem

23. (a) What is the decibel level of a sound wave whose pressure amplitude is $2.9\times10^{-4} \text{ N/m}^2$? (b) Consult Fig. 17-3 to determine the approximate lowest frequency at which this sound would be audible.

Solution

(a) For a sound wave in air under "normal conditions" (see Example 17-1 for values of ρ and v), the average intensity and pressure amplitude are related by Equation 17-3b: $I = \frac{1}{2}\Delta P_0^2/\rho v = (2.9\times10^{-4} \text{ N/m}^2)^2 \div 2(1.20 \text{ kg/m}^3)(343 \text{ m/s}) = 1.02\times10^{-10} \text{ W/m}^2$. Compared to the "normal" threshold for human hearing at 1 kHz, $I_0 = 10^{-12} \text{ W/m}^2$, the sound corresponds to a decibel level (Equation 17-4) of $\beta = (10 \text{ dB})\log(102) = 20.1$ dB. (b) Fig. 17-3 shows approximately $f = 250$ Hz as the lowest audible frequency for this intensity.

Problem

25. Show that a doubling of sound intensity corresponds to very nearly a 3 dB increase in the decibel level.

Solution

If the sound intensity is doubled, $I' = 2I$, Equation 17-4 shows that $\beta' = (10 \text{ dB})\log(I'/I_0) = (10 \text{ dB})\log(2I/I_0) = (10 \text{ dB})\log(I/I_0) + (10 \text{ dB})\log 2 = \beta + 3.01$ dB, or the decibel level increases by about 3 dB.

Problem

27. At a distance 2.0 m from a localized sound source you measure the intensity level as 75 dB. How far away must you be for the perceived loudness to drop in half (i.e., to an intensity level of 65 dB)?

Solution

A change of -10 dB, (i.e., $\beta' - \beta = -10$ dB) corresponds to the intensity decreasing by a factor of one tenth (i.e., $I' = I/10$). To see this, note that Equation 17-4 may be written as $\beta' - \beta = (-10 \text{ dB})\log(I'/I)$, or $I'/I = 10^{(\beta'-\beta)/10 \text{ dB}}$. For an isotropic point source of sound, the intensity falls inversely with the square of the distance (Equation 16-9), so $r'^2 = 10r^2$, or $r' = \sqrt{10}(2 \text{ m}) = 6.32$ m.

Problem

29. Sound intensity from a certain extended source drops as $1/r^n$, where r is the distance from the source. If the intensity level drops by 3 dB every time the distance is doubled, what is n?

Solution

A 3 dB drop corresponds to a drop in intensity by a factor of one half (see Problem 25). Thus, if $I' = \frac{1}{2}I$ when $r' = 2r$, $I'/I = \frac{1}{2} = (1/2r)^n/(1/r)^n = 1/2^n$ implies $n = 1$.

Section 17-4:   Sound Waves in Liquids and Solids

Problem

31. The bulk modulus for tungsten is $2.0\times10^{11} \text{ N/m}^2$, and its density is $1.94\times10^4 \text{ kg/m}^3$. Find the sound speed in tungsten.

Solution

Substitution of the given values of bulk modulus and density for tungsten into Equation 17-6 gives $v = \sqrt{B/\rho} = \sqrt{(2.0\times10^{11} \text{ N/m}^2)/(1.94\times10^4 \text{ kg/m}^3)} = 3.21$ km/s.

Problem

33. The speed of sound in body tissues is essentially the same as in water. Find the wavelength of 2.0 MHz ultrasound used in medical diagnostics.

Solution

From Table 17-2, the speed of sound in water is 1497 m/s, so Equation 16-1 gives the wavelength of 2.0 MHz ultrasound as $\lambda = v/f = (1497 \text{ m/s}) \div (2.0 \text{ MHz}) = 0.749$ mm.

Problem

35. Mechanical vibration induces a sound wave in a mechanism consisting of a 12-cm-long steel rod attached to a 3.0-cm-long neoprene block. How long does it take the wave to propagate through this structure?

Solution

The travel time through each material is its length divided by the speed of sound. With reference to Table 17-2 for the speed of sound in steel and neoprene, the total travel time is $(0.12 \text{ m} \div 5940 \text{ m/s}) + (0.03 \text{ m}/1600 \text{ m/s}) = (20.2 + 18.8)\mu s = 39.0$ μs.

Problem

37. The bulk modulus of the steel whose sound speed is given in Table 17-2 is 1.6×10^{11} N/m^2. A 0.50-mm-diameter wire made from this steel can withstand a tension force of 50 N before it deforms permanently. Is it possible to put this wire under enough tension that the speed of transverse waves on the wire is the same as the sound speed in the wire? Answer by calculating the tension required.

Solution

If the speed of transverse waves (Equation 16-7) equals the speed of sound (Equation 17-6), then $F/\mu = B/\rho$. The ratio of the linear and volume densities of the wire is its cross-sectional area (see solution to Chapter 16, Problem 27), so the required tension would be $F = B(\mu/\rho) = B(\frac{1}{4}\pi d^2) = (1.6 \times 10^{11}$ N/m$^2)\frac{1}{4}\pi(0.50$ mm$)^2 = 31.4$ kN, far greater than the 50 N elastic limit.

Section 17-6: Standing Waves

Problem

39. When a stretched string is clamped at both ends, its fundamental standing-wave frequency is 140 Hz. (a) What is the next higher frequency? (b) If the same string, with the same tension, is now clamped at one end and free at the other, what is the fundamental frequency? (c) What is the next higher frequency in case (b)?

Solution

(a) The frequencies of the standing-wave modes of a string fixed at both ends are all the (positive) integer multiples of the fundamental frequency, $f_m = m f_1$, for $m = 1, 2, \ldots$. (This follows from Equation 17-8 if we use $f_m = v/\lambda_m = m(v/2L) = m(v/\lambda_1) = m f_1$.) Thus, $f_2 = 2 f_1 = 2(140$ Hz$) = 280$ Hz. (b) The velocity of transverse waves is the same (for the same string under the same tension), but when one end is fixed and the other free, the standing-wave wavelengths are $\lambda_m = 4L, 4L/3, \ldots 4L/(2m-1), \ldots$, where $2m-1$ represents any odd integer for $m = 1, 2, \ldots$. (See Fig. 17-13 and its discussion in the text, or the solution to Problem 41.) Therefore, the fundamental frequency for the string fixed at one end is $f_1 = v/4L = \frac{1}{2}(v/2L) = \frac{1}{2}(140$ Hz$) = 70$ Hz, i.e., one half the fundamental frequency of the string fixed at both ends. (c) In this case, the standing-wave frequencies are only the odd multiples of the fundamental frequency, $f_m = (2m-1)f_1$, therefore the second standing-wave mode has frequency $f_2 = 3 f_1 = 3(70$ Hz$) = 210$ Hz for this string.

Problem

41. Show that only odd harmonics are allowed on a taut string with one end tight and the other free.

Solution

For a string free at one end, the amplitude factor in Equation 17-7 is a maximum for $x = L$, i.e., $2 A \sin kL = \pm 2A$. Therefore, $kL = (2m-1)\pi/2$, where $2m-1$ is an odd integer for $m = 1, 2, \ldots$. In terms of standing-wave wavelengths, $kL = (2\pi/\lambda_m)L = (2m-1)\pi/2$, or $L = (2m-1)\lambda_m/4$, as stated on page 428. In terms of frequency, $f_m = v/\lambda_m = (2m-1)f_1$, where $f_1 = v/4L$ is the frequency of the fundamental. Thus, only odd harmonics occur.

Problem

43. Show that the standing-wave condition of Equation 17-8 is equivalent to the requirement that the time it takes a wave to make a round trip from one end of the medium to the other and back be an integer multiple of the wave period.

Solution

The round-trip time for waves on a string of length L, clamped at both ends, is $2L/v = 2L/(\lambda/T) = 2LT/(2L/m) = mT$ (a multiple of the wave period), where we used Equations 16-1 and 17-8.

Problem

45. "Vibrato" in a violin is produced by sliding the finger back and forth along the vibrating string. The G-string on a particular violin measures 30 cm between the bridge and its far end and is clamped rigidly at both points. Its fundamental frequency is 197 Hz. (a) How far from the end should the violinist place a finger so that the G-string plays the note A (440 Hz)? (b) If the violinist executes vibrato by moving the finger 0.50 cm to either side of the position in part (a), what range of frequencies results?

Solution

(a) The fundamental frequency of a string fixed at both ends is $f = v/2L$. Since fingering does not change the tension (and hence v) in a violin string appreciably, $f'/f = L/L'$, or $L' = (197$ Hz$/440$ Hz$)(30$ cm$) = 13.4$ cm. This is the sounding length of the string, so the finger must be placed a distance $(30 - 13.4)$ cm $= 16.6$ cm from the ("nut") end. (b) Alteration of L' by ± 0.5 cm yields frequencies between:

$$f'' = (440 \text{ Hz})(13.4)/(13.4 \pm 0.5) = 424 \text{ to } 457 \text{ Hz}.$$

Problem

47. A bathtub 1.7 m long contains 13 cm of water. By sloshing water back and forth with your hand, you can build up large-amplitude oscillations. Determine the lowest frequency possible for such a resonant oscillation, using the fact that the speed of waves in shallow water of depth h is $v = \sqrt{gh}$. *Hint:* At resonance in this case, the wave has a crest at one end and a trough at the other.

Solution

The distance between a crest and a trough is an odd number of half-wavelengths, so the maximum resonant wavelength of the tub is $L = \frac{1}{2}\lambda$ or $\lambda = 2L = 2(1.7 \text{ m}) = 3.4 \text{ m}$. Thus, the minimum resonant frequency is $f = v/\lambda = \sqrt{gh}/\lambda = \sqrt{(9.8 \text{ m/s}^2)(0.13 \text{ m})}/3.4 \text{ m} = 0.332 \text{ Hz}$. (The period corresponding to this is $T = 1/f = 3.01 \text{ s}$.)

Problem

49. What would be the fundamental frequency of the double bassoon of Example 17-4, if it were played in helium under conditions of Example 17-1?

Solution

The wavelength of the fundamental mode depends on the dimensions of the instrument, so the difference in fundamental frequency, for the bassoon played in helium versus air, is due to the change in the velocity of sound only, $f = v/\lambda$. Thus, if the speed of sound in helium from Example 17-1 is used in place of that in air in Example 17-4, one finds $f = (1000 \text{ m/s}) \div (11 \text{ m}) = 90.9 \text{ Hz}$.

Problem

51. An astronaut smuggles a double bassoon (Example 17-4) to Mars and plays the instrument's fundamental note. If it sounds at 23 Hz, what is the sound speed on Mars?

Solution

Since the wavelength depends only on the dimensions of the bassoon, $v = f\lambda = (23 \text{ Hz})(11 \text{ m}) = 253 \text{ m/s}$. (See Example 17-4 for the fundamental wavelength.)

Section 17-7: The Doppler Effect

Problem

53. A car horn emits 380-Hz sound. If the car moves at 17 m/s with its horn blasting, what frequency will a person standing in front of the car hear?

Solution

From Equation 17-10, with the minus sign in the denominator (car approaching the observer in front), $f' = f/(1 - u/v) = (380 \text{ Hz})(1 - 17/343)^{-1} = 400 \text{ Hz}$.

Problem

55. A fire truck's siren at rest wails at 1400 Hz; standing by the roadside as the truck approaches, you hear it at 1600 Hz. How fast is the truck going?

Solution

One can solve Equation 17-10 for u (with the minus sign appropriate to an approaching source) with the result: $u = v(1 - f/f') = (343 \text{ m/s})(1 - 1400/1600) = 42.9 \text{ m/s} = 154 \text{ km/h}$. (We used the speed of sound in air from Example 17-1.)

Problem

57. The dominant frequency emitted by an airplane's engines is 1400 Hz. (a) What frequency will you measure if the plane approaches you at half the sound speed? (b) What frequency will you measure if the plane recedes at half the sound speed?

Solution

(a) For a 1400 Hz sound source approaching you at half the speed of sound, $u = \frac{1}{2}v$, Equation 17-10 gives a Doppler shifted observed frequency of $f' = f/(1 - u/v) = (1400 \text{ Hz})/(1 - \frac{1}{2}) = 2800 \text{ Hz}$. (b) The same equation for a receding source gives $f' = (1400 \text{ Hz})/(1 + \frac{1}{2}) = 933 \text{ Hz}$.

Problem

59. You're standing by the roadside as a truck approaches, and you measure the dominant frequency in the truck noise at 1100 Hz. As the truck passes the frequency drops to 950 Hz. What is the truck's speed?

Solution

The result of part (a) of the preceding problem gives $u/v = (1100 - 950)/(1100 + 950) = 0.0732$. For sound waves in "normal" air (Example 17-1), this implies a truck speed of $u = 0.0732(343 \text{ m/s}) = 25.1 \text{ m/s} = 90.4 \text{ km/h}$. (From Equation 17-10, the frequency, emitted by the truck is $f = f_1(1 - u/v) = f_2(1 + u/v)$, where f_1 and f_2 are the observed frequencies when the truck is approaching or receding, respectively. The solution of this equation for the source's speed is $u/v = (f_1 - f_2)/(f_1 + f_2)$.)

Problem

61. Use the binomial approximation to show that Equations 17-10 and 17-11 give the same result in the limit $u \ll v$.

Solution

The binomial expansion for $(1 \pm u/v)^{-1}$ is $1 \mp u/v + \cdots$, so Equations 17-10 and 11 are the same, for small u/v. (Note the difference in sign convention for u in these two equations.)

Section 17-8:   Shock Waves

Problem

63. Figure 17-28 shows a projectile in supersonic flight, with shock waves clearly visible. By making appropriate measurements, determine the projectile's speed as compared with the sound speed.

Solution

The half-angle of the shock wave in Fig. 17-28, measured with a protractor, is about 45°, so (with reference to Fig. 17-23b) $u/v = 1/\sin 45° = 1.41$.

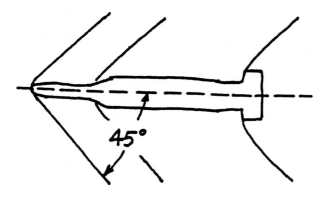

FIGURE 17-28 Problem 63 Solution.

Paired Problems

Problem

65. A 1.0-W sound source emits uniformly in all directions. Find (a) the intensity and (b) the decibel level 12 m from the source.

Solution

(a) The average intensity at any distance from an isotropic sound source is given by Equation 16-9, $\bar{I} = \bar{P}/4\pi r^2 = (1 \text{ W})/4\pi(12 \text{ m})^2 = 5.53{\times}10^{-4} \text{ W/m}^2$. (b) The corresponding decibel level (Equation 17-4) is $(10 \text{ dB})\log(5.53{\times}10^{-4}/10^{-12}) = 87.4 \text{ dB}$.

Problem

67. A pipe 80 cm long is open at both ends. When the pipe is immersed in a gas mixture, the frequency of a certain harmonic is 280 Hz and the next higher harmonic is 350 Hz. Determine (a) the sound speed and (b) the mode numbers of the two harmonics.

Solution

For an open pipe, the frequencies of the harmonics are integer multiples of the fundamental, $f_m = m f_1$, for $m = 1, 2, \ldots$. (b) It is given that $f_m/f_{m+1} = m/(m+1) = 280/350 = 4/5$, therefore $m = 4$ and $m + 1 = 5$ are the mode numbers. (a) Since the wavelengths of the harmonics are given by Equation 17-8, $\lambda_4 = 2L/m = 2(80 \text{ cm})/4 = 40 \text{ cm}$ and $\lambda_5 = 32 \text{ cm}$. From either, $v = f_4\lambda_4 = (280 \text{ Hz})(0.4 \text{ m}) = f_5\lambda_5 = (350 \text{ Hz})(0.32 \text{ m}) = 112 \text{ m/s}$.

Problem

69. Find the wave speed in a medium where a 28 m/s source speed causes a 3% increase in frequency measured by a stationary observer.

Solution

To cause an increase in frequency, the source must be approaching the stationary observer. Solving Equation 17-10 for the wave speed, we find $v = u/(1 - f/f')$. The given increase is 3%, so $f/f' = 1/1.03$ and $v = (28 \text{ m/s})/(1 - 1/1.03) = 961 \text{ m/s}$.

Supplementary Problems

Problem

71. The sound speed in air at 0°C is 331 m/s, and for temperatures within a few tens of degrees of 0°C it increases at the rate 0.590 m/s for every °C increase in temperature. How long would it take a sound wave to travel 150 m over a path where the temperature rises linearly from 5°C at one end to 15°C at the other end?

Solution

The speed of sound is given as a function of the Celsius temperature, $v(T) = 331 \text{ m/s} + (0.590 \text{ m/s/°C})T \equiv v_0 + aT$. The temperature itself varies linearly along the path, from $x_1 = 0$ to $x_2 = 150 \text{ m}$, between the given values $T_1 = 5°C$ and $T_2 = 15°C$, so $T(x) = T_1 + (T_2 - T_1)(x/150 \text{ m}) = 5°C + (1°C/15 \text{ m})x \equiv T_1 + bx$. Thus, the speed, as a function of position along the path, is $v(x) = v(T(x)) = v_0 + aT(x) = v_0 + a(T_1 + bx) = v_0 + aT_1 + abx = dx/dt$. The time for a sound wave to travel an interval dx of path is $dt = dx/v(x)$, so the total time to travel the entire path is

$$t = \int_1^2 dt = \int_{x_1}^{x_2} \frac{dx}{v(x)} = \int_0^{x_2} \frac{dx}{v_0 + aT_1 + abx}$$

$$= \frac{1}{ab} \cdot \ln\left(\frac{v_0 + aT_2}{v_0 + aT_1}\right)$$

$$= \left(0.590\frac{m}{s \cdot {}^{\circ}C}\right)^{-1}\left(\frac{1{}^{\circ}C}{15 \ m}\right)^{-1} \ln\left(\frac{331 + 0.59 \times 15}{331 + 0.59 \times 5}\right)$$

$$= 0.445 \ s.$$

(Note: $v_2 = v(x_2) = v_0 + aT_1 + abx_2 = v_0 + aT_2$, and $v_1 = v_0 + aT_1$.)

Problem

73. A rectangular trough is 2.5 m long and is much deeper than its length, so Equation 16-11 applies. Determine the wavelength and frequency of (a) the longest and (b) the next longest standing waves possible in this trough. Why isn't the higher frequency twice the lower?

Solution

Since the volume of water in the trough is constant, there must be as many "hills" as there are "valleys" in the standing-wave patterns of sinusoidal surface waves. Therefore, there are antinodes at each end, as shown. Since the distance between two antinodes is a multiple of half-wavelengths, $L = m\lambda/2$, so the two longest standing-wave wavelengths are $\lambda_1 = 2L = 5$ m and

$\lambda_2 = L = 2.5$ m. If we use Equation 16-11 for the speed of deep water surface waves, the corresponding standing-wave frequencies are $f_1 = v/\lambda_1 = \sqrt{g/2\pi\lambda_1} = \sqrt{(9.8 \ m/s^2)/2\pi \times 5 \ m} = 0.559$ Hz, and $f_2 = \sqrt{2}f_1 = 0.790$ Hz. These are not multiples of one another because of the way the wave speed depends on the wavelength, i.e., the dispersion relation for these waves is *not* $\omega = (\text{constant})k$.

Problem

75. A supersonic airplane flies directly over you at 6.5 km altitude. You hear its sonic boom 13 s later. What is the plane's Mach number?

Solution

The shock wave trails the airplane (P) with half angle $\theta = \sin^{-1}(v/u)$ as shown (see Fig. 17-23b also). The distance of the closest point on the wavefront (Q) from the observer (O) when the airplane is overhead is $OQ = h\cos\theta$. Since the wavefront travels with the speed of sound, v, the sonic boom reaches O after a time t, given by $OQ = vt = h\cos\theta$. Therefore, we can eliminate θ (from $\sin\theta = v/u$) and solve for u (the plane's speed): $(u/v) = 1/\sin\theta = 1/\sqrt{1 - \cos^2\theta} = 1/\sqrt{1 - (vt/h)^2}$. Suppose $h = 6.5$ km, $t = 13$ s, and $v = 340$ m/s. Then $(u/v) = 1/\sqrt{1 - (340 \times 13/6500)^2} = 1.36$, which is the Mach number.

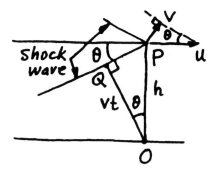

Problem 75 Solution.

Problem

77. Consider an object moving at speed u through a medium, and reflecting sound waves from a stationary source back toward the source. The object receives the waves at the shifted frequency given by Equation 17-11, and when it re-emits them they are shifted once again, this time according to Equation 17-10. Find an expression for the overall frequency shift that results, and show that, for $u \ll v$, this shift is approximately $2fu/v$.

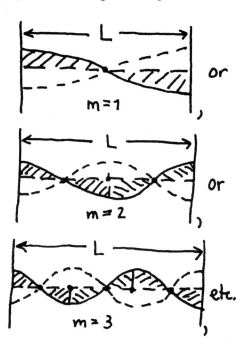

Problem 73 Solution.

Solution

The object receives waves at the frequency of an observer moving toward a stationary source, so $f' = f(1 + u/v)$. (See Equation 17-11.) The reflected waves are re-emitted by the moving object at this frequency, f', and so are received by the original stationary source at frequency $f'' = f'/(1 - u/v) = f(1 + u/v)/(1 - u/v)$. (See Equation 17-10.) The overall frequency shift is $f'' - f = \Delta f = f[(v + u) \times (v - u)^{-1} - 1] = 2uf/(v - u)$. If $u \ll v$, then $\Delta f \approx 2uf/v$. (Note: If the object is moving away from the stationary source, one replaces u with $-u$ in the above treatment.)

Problem

79. What is the frequency shift of a 70-GHz police radar signal when it reflects off a car moving at 120 km/h? (Radar waves travel at the speed of light.) *Hint:* See Problem 77.

Solution

Using the result of Problem 77 for $u \ll v = c$, one finds $\Delta f = 2uf/c = 2(120 \text{ m}/3.6 \text{ s})(7 \times 10^{10} \text{ Hz}) \div (3 \times 10^8 \text{ m/s}) = 15.6$ kHz. (Note that the formula for the Doppler shift for electromagnetic waves is different than for sound, but when $u \ll v$ or c, both formulas are the same.)

CHAPTER 18   FLUID MOTION

Section 18-1:   Describing Fluids: Density and Pressure

Problem

1. The density of molasses is 1600 kg/m^3. Find the mass of the molasses in a 0.75-liter jar.

Solution

The mass of molasses, which occupies a volume equal to the capacity of the jar, is $\Delta m = \rho \, \Delta V = (1600 \text{ kg/m}^3)(0.75 \times 10^{-3} \text{ m}^3) = 1.2$ kg.

Problem

3. The density of atomic nuclei is about 10^{17} kg/m^3, while the density of water is 10^3 kg/m^3. Roughly what fraction of the volume of water is *not* empty space?

Solution

The average density of a mixture of two substances, with definite volume fractions, is $\rho_{av} = \rho_1(V_1/V) + \rho_2(V_2/V)$, where $V_1 + V_2 = V$ is the total volume. (Try this formula in the preceding problem.) The density of water is approximately the average density $(\rho_{av} = 10^3 \text{ kg/m}^3)$ of the nuclei $(\rho_1 = 10^{17} \text{ kg/m}^3)$ and empty space $(\rho_2 = 0)$ provided we neglect the mass of the atomic electrons, so the volume fraction of nuclei in water is $(V_1/V) = \rho_{av}/\rho_1 = 10^3/10^{17} = 10^{-14}$.

Problem

5. A plant hangs from a 3.2-cm diameter suction cup affixed to a smooth horizontal surface (Fig. 18-42). What is the maximum weight that can be suspended (a) at sea level and (b) in Denver, where atmospheric pressure is about 0.80 atm?

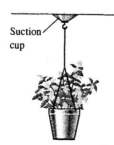

Suction cup

FIGURE 18-42 Problem 5.

Solution

(a) The force exerted on the suction cup by the atmosphere is $F = PA = P_{atm}(\pi d^2/4) = (1.013 \times 10^5 \text{ Pa})\pi(0.016 \text{ m})^2 = 81.5$ N (perfect vacuum inside cup assumed). This is equal to the maximum weight. (b) At Denver, $P = 0.8 P_{atm}$, so the maximum weight is 80% of that in part (a), or 65.2 N (a slight variation in g with altitude is neglected).

Problem

7. Measurement of small pressure differences, for example, between the interior of a chimney and the ambient atmosphere, is often given in **inches of water**, where one inch of water is the pressure that will support a 1-in.-high water column. Express this unit in SI.

Solution

From Equation 18-2, the pressure of 1 in. of water is $\rho_{H_2O} g \, \Delta h = (10^3 \text{ kg/m}^3)(9.81 \text{ m/s}^2)(0.0254 \text{ m}) = 249$ Pa.

Problem

9. The fuselage of a 747 jumbo jet is roughly a cylinder 60 m long and 6 m in diameter. If the interior of the plane is pressurized to 0.75 atm, what is the net pressure force tending to separate half the cylinder from the other half when the plane is flying at 10 km, where air pressure is about 0.25 atm? (The earliest commercial jets suffered structural failure from just such forces; modern planes are better engineered.)

Solution

Consider the skin of the fuselage to be divided into infinitesimal strips, parallel to the cylinder's axis, of area dA (shown in cross-section in the sketch). Because of the pressure difference between the cabin interior and the outside, $\Delta P = (0.75 - 0.25)$ atm at 10 km altitude, there is a net force radially outward on dA of magnitude $dF = \Delta P \, dA$. These forces produce stresses in the skin, i.e., forces of one part of the cylinder on another part, that this problem asks us to estimate. The pressure force on one half of the cylinder is balanced by the stress force exerted by the other half. By symmetry, for every dA located at angle θ

shown, there is a dA' at angle $-\theta$ with opposite y component of pressure force, $dF_y + dF'_y = 0$, so only the x component of dF contributes to the net pressure force on the half cylinder. But $dF_x = \Delta P \, dA \cos\theta = \Delta P \, dA_y$, where dA_y is the projection of the area dA onto an axial plane parallel to the y axis, and the total projected area of the half-cylinder is just the diameter times the length, or $2RL$. Therefore, the net pressure force tending to separate two halves of the fuselage is $F_x = \Delta P(2RL) = (0.75 - 0.25)(101.3 \text{ kPa}) \times (6 \times 60 \text{ m}^2) = 1.82 \times 10^7 \text{ N} \approx 2050$ tons. Note: F_x can be expressed as a surface integral, which for the above area elements, $dA = RL \, d\theta$, reduces to

$$\int_{\text{half-cylinder}} dF_x = \int_{-\pi/2}^{\pi/2} \Delta P \cos\theta \, dA$$

$$= \Delta P \cdot LR \int_{-\pi/2}^{\pi/2} \cos\theta \, d\theta$$

$$= \Delta P \cdot LR \sin\theta \Big|_{-\pi/2}^{\pi/2} = \Delta P \cdot 2RL.$$

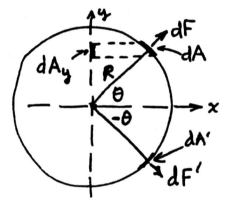

Problem 9 Solution.

Problem

11. A paper clip is made from wire 1.5 mm in diameter. You unbend a paper clip and push the end against the wall. What force must you exert to give a pressure of 120 atm?

Solution

An average pressure of 120 atm over the cross-sectional area of the wire, $\frac{1}{4}\pi d^2$, results in a force of $F = PA = (120 \times 101.3 \text{ kPa})\frac{1}{4}\pi(1.5 \times 10^{-3} \text{ m})^2 = 21.5 \text{ N}$.

Problem

13. When a couple with a total mass of 120 kg lies on a water bed, the pressure in the bed increases by

4700 Pa. What surface area of the two bodies is in contact with the bed?

Solution

The pressure increase times the average horizontal contact surface area equals the weight of the couple, or $A_{\text{av}} = mg/\Delta P = (120 \times 9.8 \text{ N})/(4700 \text{ Pa}) = 0.250 \text{ m}^2$.

Problem

15. The emergency escape window of a DC-9 jetliner measures 50 cm by 90 cm. The interior pressure is 0.75 atm, and the plane is at an altitude where atmospheric pressure is 0.25 atm. Is there any danger that a passenger could open the window? Answer by calculating the force needed to pull the window straight inward.

Solution

The pressure force on the (presumably flat) window is simply $F = \Delta P \cdot A = (0.75 - 0.25)(101.3 \text{ kPa}) \times (0.5 \times 0.9 \text{ m}^2) = 22.8 \text{ kN} = 2.56$ tons. It is unlikely any passenger is this strong.

Section 18-2:   Fluids at Rest: Hydrostatic Equilibrium

Problem

17. What is the density of a fluid whose pressure increases at the rate of 100 kPa for every 6.0 m of depth?

Solution

The increase in pressure with depth, for an incompressible fluid, is given by Equation 18-3. Thus, $\rho = \Delta P/gh = (100 \text{ kPa})/(9.8 \times 6 \text{ m}^2/\text{s}^2) = 1.70 \times 10^3 \text{ kg/m}^3$.

Problem

19. Scuba equipment provides the diver with air at the same pressure as the surrounding water. But at pressures greater than about 1 MPa, the nitrogen in air becomes dangerously narcotic. At what depth does nitrogen narcosis become a hazard?

Solution

In fresh water ($\rho \simeq 10^3 \text{ kg/m}^3$), the pressure is 1 MPa at a depth of $h = (P - P_0)/\rho g = (1 \text{ MPa} - 0.103 \text{ MPa})/(9.8 \times 10^3 \text{ N/m}^3) = 91.7 \text{ m}$, where P_0 is atmospheric pressure at the surface. (See Equation 18-3.) The depth is a little less in salt water since its density is slightly greater.

Problem

21. A vertical tube open at the top contains 5.0 cm of oil (density 0.82 g/cm^3) floating on 5.0 cm of water. Find the *gauge* pressure at the bottom of the tube.

Solution

The pressure at the top of the tube is atmospheric pressure, P_a. The absolute pressure at the interface of the oil and water is $P_i = P_a + \rho_{oil}gh_{oil}$, and at the bottom is $P = P_i + \rho_{water}gh_{water} = P_a + \rho_{oil}gh_{oil} + \rho_{water}gh_{water}$ (see Equation 18-3). Therefore, the gauge pressure at the bottom is $P - P_a = (\rho_{oil}h_{oil} + \rho_{water}h_{water})g = (0.82 + 1.00)(10^3$ kg/m$^3)(0.05$ m$) \times (9.8$ m/s$^2) = 892$ Pa (gauge).

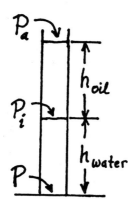

Problem 21 Solution.

Problem

23. A 1500-m-wide dam holds back a lake 95 m deep. What force does the water exert on the dam?

Solution

The pressure varies over the (assumed) vertical and rectangular surface of the dam in the same way as for the wall of the swimming pool in Example 18-2, so $F = P_a wH + \frac{1}{2}\rho gwH^2 = (1500$ m$)(95$ m$)[101.3$ kPa $+ \frac{1}{2}(9.8\times10^3$ N/m$^3)(95$ m$)] = 80.8$ GN.

Problem

25. A U-shaped tube open at both ends contains water and a quantity of oil occupying a 2.0-cm length of the tube, as shown in Fig. 18-45. If the oil's density is 0.82 times that of water, what is the height difference h?

Solution

From Equation 18-3, the pressure at points at the same level in the water is the same, $P_1 = P_2$. Now,

$P_1 = P_{atm} + \rho_{H_2O}g(2$ cm $- h)$ and $P_2 = P_{atm} + \rho_{oil}g(2$ cm$)$, so $h = (2$ cm$)(1 - \rho_{oil}/\rho_{H_2O}) = (2$ cm$)\times (1 - 0.82) = 3.6$ mm (h is positive as shown).

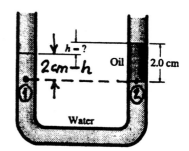

FIGURE 18-45 Problem 25 Solution.

Problem

27. Barometric pressure in the eye of a hurricane is 0.91 atm (27.2 inches of mercury). How does the level of the ocean surface under the eye compare with that under a distant fair-weather region where the pressure is 1.0 atm?

Solution

Equation 18-3 applied at points on the water surface under the hurricane eye and fair-weather region gives 1 atm $= 0.91$ atm $+ \rho gy$, therefore $y = (0.09$ atm$) \times (1.013\times10^5$ Pa/atm$)/(9800$ N/m$^3) = 93.0$ cm.

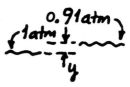

Problem 27 Solution.

Problem

29. A garage lift has a 45-cm diameter piston supporting the load. Compressed air with a maximum pressure of 500 kPa is applied to a small piston at the other end of the hydraulic system. What is the maximum mass the lift can support?

Solution

If we neglect the variation of pressure with height in the hydraulic system (which is usually small compared to the applied pressure), the fluid pressure is the same throughout, or $P_{appl} = F/A$ (for either the small or large cylinders). Thus, $F_{max} = (500$ kPa$)\frac{1}{4}\pi \times (0.45$ m$)^2 = 79.5$ kN, which corresponds to a mass-load of $F_{max}/g = 8.11$ tonnes (metric tons).

Section 18-3: Archimedes' Principle and Buoyancy

Problem

31. On land, the most massive concrete block you can carry is 25 kg. How massive a block could you carry underwater, if the density of concrete is 2300 kg/m^3?

Solution

The 25×9.8 N force you exert underwater is equal to the apparent weight of the most massive block of concrete when submerged, $W_{\text{app}} = W - F_b = W(1 - \rho_w/\rho_c)$, where ρ_c/ρ_w is the ratio of the densities of concrete and water (also known as the specific gravity of concrete). (This relation is derived in Example 18-4, since the buoyant force on an object submerged in fluid is $F_b = W\rho_{\text{fluid}}/\rho$.) Thus, $W = W_{\text{app}}(1 - \rho_w/\rho_c)^{-1}$, or $m = W/g = (25 \text{ kg}) \times (1 - 1/2.3)^{-1} = 44.2$ kg.

Problem

33. The density of styrofoam is 160 kg/m^3. What per cent error is introduced by weighing a styrofoam block in air, which exerts an upward buoyancy force, rather than in vacuum? The density of air is 1.2 kg/m^3.

Solution

The fractorial error is $(W - W_{\text{app}})/W = \rho_{\text{air}}/\rho_{\text{styro}} = 1.2/160 = 0.75\%$ (see Example 18-4).

Problem

35. A partially full beer bottle with interior diameter 52 mm is floating upright in water, as shown in Fig. 18-47. A drinker takes a swig and replaces the bottle in the water, where it now floats 28 mm higher than before. How much beer did the drinker drink?

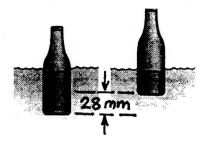

FIGURE 18-47 Problem 35 Solution.

Solution

Archimedes' principle implies that the weight of the beer swallowed equals the difference in the weight of water displaced by the bottle, before and after. Therefore $\Delta m_{\text{beer}} = \rho_{\text{H}_2\text{O}} \Delta V$, where "$g$" was canceled from both sides. The difference in the volume of water displaced equals the cross-sectional area of the bottle times 28 mm. If we ignore the thickness of the walls of the bottle, $\Delta m_{\text{beer}} = (1 \text{ g/cm}^3)\pi(\frac{1}{2} \times 5.2 \text{ cm})^2 \times (2.8 \text{ cm}) = 59.5$ g.

Problem

37. A typical supertanker has mass 2.0×10^6 kg and carries twice that much oil. If 9.0 m of the ship is submerged when it's empty, what is the minimum water depth needed for it to navigate when full? Assume the sides of the ship are vertical.

Solution

If the sides of the hull are vertical, and its bottom flat, the volume it displaces is proportional to its draft (depth in the water), i.e., $V = Ay$, where A is the cross-sectional area. Since the total mass of the full supertanker is $3\times$ that when empty, the draft when full is simply $3\times(9$ m$) = 27$ m.

Problem 37 Solution.

Problem

39. (a) How much helium (density 0.18 kg/m^3) is needed to lift a balloon carrying two people in a basket, if the total mass of people, basket, and balloon (but not gas) is 280 kg? (b) Repeat for a hot air balloon, whose air density is 10% less than that of the surrounding atmosphere.

Solution

The buoyant force must exceed the weight of the load (mass M, including the balloon) plus the gas (mass m), $F_b \geq (M + m)g$. But $F_b = \rho_{\text{air}}gV$, and if we neglect the volume of the balloon's skin etc. compared to that of the gas it contains, $V = m/\rho_{\text{gas}}$, therefore $m = \rho_{\text{gas}}V = \rho_{\text{gas}}(F_b/\rho_{\text{air}}g) \geq (\rho_{\text{gas}}/\rho_{\text{air}})(M + m)$ or $m \geq M\rho_{\text{gas}}/(\rho_{\text{air}} - \rho_{\text{gas}})$. (a) When the gas is helium, $\rho_{\text{air}}/\rho_{\text{He}} = 1.2/0.18$, and $m \geq (280 \text{ kg})(6.67 - 1)^{-1} = 49.4$ kg. (b) For hot air, $\rho_{\text{gas}} = 0.9\rho_{\text{air}}$, and $m \geq (280 \text{ kg})(0.9/0.1) = 2520$ kg. (Note: these masses correspond to gas volumes of 275 m^3 for helium and 2330 m^3 for hot air.)

Sections 18-4 and 18-5: Fluid Dynamics and Applications

Problem

41. A fluid is flowing steadily, roughly from left to right. At left it is flowing rapidly; it then slows down, and finally speeds up again. Its final speed at right is not as great as its initial speed at left. Sketch a streamline pattern that could represent this flow.

Solution

In order to maintain a constant volume rate of flow, in an incompressible fluid, streamlines must be closer together (smaller cross-section of tube of flow) where the velocity is greater, as sketched.

Problem 41 Solution.

Problem

43. A typical mass flow rate for the Mississippi River is 1.8×10^7 kg/s. Find (a) the volume flow rate and (b) the flow speed in a region where the river is 2.0 km wide and an average of 6.1 m deep.

Solution

(a) The mass flow rate and the volume flow rate are related by Equations 18-4b and 5, namely $R_m = \rho v A = \rho R_V$. Therefore, $R_V = (1.8 \times 10^7 \text{ kg/s}) \div (10^3 \text{ kg/m}^3) = 1.8 \times 10^4 \text{ m}^3/\text{s}$ for the Mississippi.
(b) At a point in the river where the cross-sectional area is given, the average speed of flow is $v = R_V/A = (1.8 \times 10^4 \text{ m}^3/\text{s})/(2 \times 10^3 \times 6.1 \text{ m}^2) = 1.48 \text{ m/s}$ ($= 5.31$ km/h $= 3.30$ mph). The actual flow rate of any river varies with the season, local weather and vegetation conditions, and human water consumption.

Problem

45. A typical human aorta, or main artery from the heart, is 1.8 cm in diameter and carries blood at a speed of 35 cm/s. What will be the flow speed around a clot that reduces the flow area by 80%?

Solution

The continuity equation (Equation 18-5) is a reasonable approximation for blood circulation in an artery, so $v' = v(A/A')$. If the cross-sectional area is reduced by 80%, then $A/A' = 100\%/20\% = 5$, so $v' = 5(35 \text{ cm/s}) = 1.75$ m/s.

Problem

47. In Fig. 18-48 a horizontal pipe of cross-sectional area A is joined to a lower pipe of cross-sectional area $\frac{1}{2}A$. The entire pipe is full of liquid with density ρ, and the left end is at atmospheric pressure P_a. A small open tube extends upward from the lower pipe. Find the height h_2 of liquid in the small tube (a) when the right end of the lower pipe is closed, so the liquid is in hydrostatic equilibrium, and (b) when the liquid flows with speed v in the upper pipe.

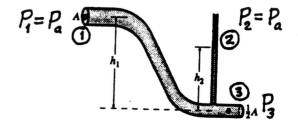

FIGURE 18-48 Problem 47.

Solution

The continuity equation (Equation 18-5) and Bernoulli's equation (Equation 18-6) can be applied to an incompressible fluid whether it is at rest or flowing steadily. (a) In hydrostatic equilibrium, the flow speed is zero everywhere. Since the pressure is P_a at the left end of the upper horizontal pipe and at the top of the liquid in the small vertical tube, Equation 18-6a for these points gives $P_a + 0 + \rho g h_1 = P_a + 0 + \rho g h_2$, or $h_1 = h_2$, where we measured the heights y from the lower horizontal tube. (b) In steady flow, Equation 18-5 gives the flow speed in the lower pipe as $v' = v(A/\frac{1}{2}A) = 2v$, where v is the speed in the upper pipe and the cross-sectional areas are given. Then Equation 18-6a gives $P_a + \frac{1}{2}\rho v^2 + \rho g h_1 = P_3 + \frac{1}{2}\rho(2v)^2 + 0$, where P_3 is the pressure anywhere in the lower pipe. (Since the lower pipe is horizontal, $y = 0$, and uniform in cross-section, $v = $ constant, hence $P_3 = $ constant.) Now, even when liquid flows in the pipes, the liquid in the small vertical tube is stagnant. If we assume the pressure is constant over the cross-section of the lower pipe, then Equation 18-3 gives $P_3 = P_a + \rho g h_2$. Combining these results, we find $P_3 - P_a = -\frac{3}{2}\rho v^2 + \rho g h_1 = \rho g h_2$, or $h_2 = h_1 - 3v^2/2g$.

Problem

49. The water in a garden hose is at a gauge pressure of 140 kPa and is moving at negligible speed. The hose terminates in a sprinkler consisting of many small holes. What is the maximum height reached by the water emerging from the holes?

Solution

The pressure, velocity, and height of the water in the hose (point 1) are $P_1 = P_{atm} + 140$ kPa, $v_1 \approx 0$, and $y_1 = 0$, while at the highest point of a jet of water from a hole (point 2), $P_2 = P_{atm}$, $v_2 \approx 0$, and $y_2 = h$. (We assume that the jets from the holes are the same.) Then Bernoulli's equation (Equation 18-6a) yields $P_{atm} + 140$ kPa $= P_{atm} + \rho gh$, or $h = 140$ kPa$\div$ (9800 N/m^3) $= 14.3$ m.

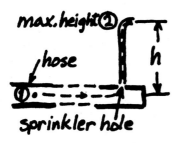

Problem 49 Solution.

Problem

51. The venturi flowmeter shown in Fig. 18-51 is used to measure the flow rate of water in a solar collector system. The flowmeter is inserted in a pipe with diameter 1.9 cm; at the venturi of the flowmeter the diameter is reduced to 0.64 cm. The manometer tube contains oil with density 0.82 times that of water. If the difference in oil levels on the two sides of the manometer tube is 1.4 cm, what is the volume flow rate?

Solution

If we apply Bernoulli's equation (Equation 18-6a) and the continuity equation (Equation 18-5) to points 1 and 2 in the flowmeter, we can calculate the volume rate of flow:

$$P_1 + \frac{1}{2}\rho v_1^2 = P_2 + \frac{1}{2}\rho v_2^2 \quad \text{and} \quad v_1 A_1 = V_2 A_2 \text{ imply}$$

$$P_1 - P_2 = \frac{1}{2}\rho(v_2^2 - v_1^2) = \frac{1}{2}\rho v_1^2 A_1^2 \left(\frac{1}{A_2^2} - \frac{1}{A_1^2}\right),$$

$$\text{or} \quad R_V = v_1 A_1 = \sqrt{\frac{2(P_1 - P_2)}{\rho(A_2^{-2} - A_1^{-2})}}.$$

(This is the same calculation as Example 18-9. Note that pressure variation with height in the flowmeter is assumed negligible.) The pressure difference is related to the difference in height and the density of oil in the manometer (where the fluid is assumed stagnant): $P_1 = P_3 + \rho g y_1$ and $P_2 = P_3 + \rho g y_2 + \rho_{oil}gh$ imply $P_1 - P_2 = (\rho - \rho_{oil})gh$, since $y_1 - y_2 = h$. If we use $A = \frac{1}{4}\pi d^2$ for each part of the flowmeter, we finally obtain $R_V = \frac{1}{4}\pi\sqrt{2gh(1 - \rho_{oil}/\rho)/(d_2^{-4} - d_1^{-4})} = 7.20$ cm^3/s, when the given numerical values are substituted (we used h, d_1, d_2 in cm and $g = 980$ cm/s^2).

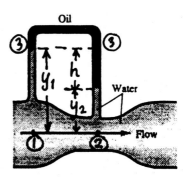

FIGURE 18-51 Problem 51 Solution.

Paired Problems

Problem

53. A steel drum has volume 0.23 m^3 and mass 16 kg. Will it float in water when filled with (a) water or (b) gasoline (density 860 kg/m^3)? Neglect the thickness of the steel.

Solution

An object will float in water if its average density is less than the density of water. (This follows from Archimedes' principle, since the volume of water displaced by an object floating on the surface is less than its total volume, i.e., $V_{dis} < V$. Because the buoyant force equals the weight of a floating object, $F_b = \rho_{H_2O}gV_{dis} = W = \rho_{av}gV$, this implies $\rho_{av} < \rho_{H_2O}$.) (a) Since $\rho_{steel} > \rho_{H_2O}$, when the drum is filled with water, $\rho_{av} > \rho_{H_2O}$ and the drum will sink. (The average density of a composite object is always greater than the smallest density of its components; see solution to Problem 3.) (b) When the drum is filled with gasoline, its average density is $\rho_{av} = (M_{steel} + M_{gas})/V$. If we neglect the volume occupied by the steel compared to the volume of the drum, then $M_{gas} = \rho_{gas}V$ and $\rho_{av} = (16$ kg/0.23 m^3) + 860 kg/m^3 = 930 kg/m^3, which is less than ρ_{H_2O} so the drum floats.

Problem

55. A spherical rubber balloon with mass 0.85 g and diameter 30 cm is filled with helium (density 0.18 kg/m^3). How many 1.0-g paper clips can you hang from the balloon before it loses its buoyancy?

Solution

The buoyant force on the balloon will exceed its weight provided $\rho_{av} < \rho_{air}$ (see solution to Problem 53). If we neglect the volume occupied by the rubber and n paperclips (n is an integer) compared to the spherical volume of the balloon, $V = 4\pi R^3/3$, then $\rho_{av} = (M_{rubber} + nM_{clip} + \rho_{He}V)/V$, where $\rho_{He}V$ is (approximately) the mass of the helium. Thus, the balloon will have excess buoyancy in air of density 1.2 kg/m^3 if 1.2 kg/m^3 > $\rho_{av} = (0.18$ kg/m^3) + $(0.85 + 1.0n) \times 10^{-3}$ kg$/\frac{4}{3}\pi(0.15$ m$)^3$, or $n < \frac{4}{3}\pi(1.5)^3 \times (1.2 - 0.18) - 0.85 = 13.6$. (With $n = 13$ paper clips attached, the balloon will rise until its average density of 1.16 kg/m^3 equals the density of the surrounding air.)

Problem

57. Water at a pressure of 230 kPa is flowing at 1.5 m/s through a pipe, when it encounters an obstruction where the pressure drops by 5%. What fraction of the pipe's area is obstructed?

Solution

Assume horizontal flow in a narrow pipe (so there is no dependence on height). Then $v_1A_1 = v_2A_2$, and $P_1 + \frac{1}{2}\rho v_1^2 = P_2 + \frac{1}{2}\rho v_2^2$ (Equations 18-5 and 18-6a for steady incompressible fluid flow), where subscript 2 refers to the obstruction. Since the pressure at the obstruction is 5% less, $P_1 - P_2 = 0.05P_1 = \frac{1}{2}\rho v_1^2 \times [(A_1^2/A_2^2) - 1]$, where we eliminated v_2. Then $(A_1/A_2)^2 = 1 + (0.1\times230$ kPa$)/(10^3$ kg/m$^3) \times (1.5$ m/s$)^2 = (3.35)^2$. The fraction of area obstructed is $(A_1 - A_2)/A_1 = 1 - (1/3.35) = 70.1\%$.

Problem

59. Find an expression for the volume flow rate from the siphon shown in Fig. 18-52, assuming the siphon area A is much less than the tank area.

Solution

Bernoulli's equation applied between points at the top surface of the water in the tank and at the mouth of the siphon (where both pressures are atmospheric pressure) gives $P_a + \frac{1}{2}\rho v_{top}^2 = P_a + \frac{1}{2}\rho v^2 - \rho gh$. (We find it convenient to measure heights from the water level in the tank.) As in Example 18-8, if the siphon cross-sectional area is much smaller than the tank

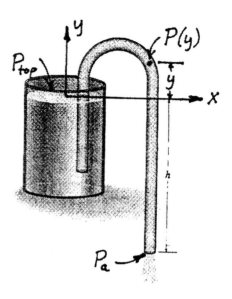

FIGURE 18-52 Problem 59.

area, the continuity equation, $v_{top}A_{tank} = vA$, implies $v_{top}/v = A/A_{tank} \ll 1$ so $v_{top} \approx 0$ can be neglected. Then $v = \sqrt{2gh}$. The volume rate of flow (Equation 18-5) is just $R_V = vA = A\sqrt{2gh}$. (Note: We assume the siphon tube has uniform cross-section and the water in it has constant flow speed, so the pressure at any other point in the siphon tube is $P(y) = P_a - \rho g(h + y)$, where y is the distance above the tank's water level. Since the absolute pressure is always positive, i.e., $P(y) \geq 0$, it follows that $y + h \leq P_a/\rho g = (101.3$ kPa$)/(9800$ N/m$^3) = 10.3$ m ≈ 34 ft. A siphon doesn't work if the highest point of its tube is more than this distance above the water surface. More precisely, h is the distance of the siphon's mouth below the water level, which we've assumed to be positive ($h \geq 0$, otherwise water doesn't flow out of the tank). Then $y < 10.3$ m $- h < 10.3$ m, which gives the previously stated limit for a siphon. On the other hand, when $h + y > 10.3$ m, the flow becomes unsteady. The assumption of steady incompressible flow, Equations 18-5 and 6, is quite restrictive.)

Supplementary Problems
Problem

61. A 1.0-m-diameter tank is filled with water to a depth of 2.0 m and is open to the atmosphere at the top. The water drains through a 1.0-cm-diameter pipe at the bottom; that pipe then joins a 1.5-cm-diameter pipe open to the atmosphere, as shown in Fig. 18-53. Find (a) the flow speed in the narrow section and (b) the water height in the *sealed* vertical tube shown.

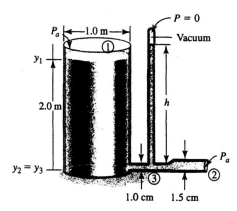

FIGURE 18-53 Problem 61.

Solution

(a) If we assume a steady incompressible flow (Equations 18-5 and 6), an argument similar to Example 18-8, comparing point 1 at the top of the tank with point 2 at the opening of the 1.5 cm pipe, gives $P_a + \rho g y_1 \approx P_a + \rho g y_2 + \frac{1}{2}\rho v_2^2$ or $v_2 = \sqrt{2g(y_1 - y_2)}$. Here, we neglected the flow speed at the top, $v_1 \approx 0$, and $y_1 - y_2 = 2$ m. The continuity equation gives the speed in the narrower section of pipe, $v_3 = v_2(A_2/A_3) = (1.5/1.0)^2 \times \sqrt{2(9.8 \text{ m/s}^2)(2 \text{ m})} = 14.1$ m/s. (b) The pressure at the bottom of the stagnant column of water over the narrow section of pipe is $P_3 = \rho g h$, because there is no pressure exerted by a vacuum, and we assume this pressure is uniform over the cross-section of the narrow pipe. Another application of Bernoulli's equation gives $P_a + \rho g y_1 \approx P_3 + \rho g y_2 + \frac{1}{2}\rho v_3^2 = \rho g h + \rho g y_2 + (1.5)^4 \rho g (y_1 - y_2)$, where we have again neglected the flow speed at the top of the tank, and we used the expression for v_3 from part (a). Therefore, $h = (P_a/\rho g) - (y_1 - y_2)((1.5)^4 - 1) = (101.3 \text{ kPa} \div 9800 \text{ N/m}^3) - (2 \text{ m})(65/16) = 2.21$ m.

Problem

63. Figure 18-54 shows a simplified diagram of a Pitot tube, used for measuring aircraft speeds. The tube is mounted on the underside of the aircraft wing with opening A at right angles to the flow and opening B pointing into the flow. The gauge prevents airflow through the tube. Use Bernoulli's equation to show that the air speed relative to the wing is given by $v = \sqrt{2\Delta P/\rho}$, where ΔP is the pressure difference between the tubes and ρ is the density of air. *Hint:* The flow must be stopped at B, but continues past A with its normal speed.

Solution

Any difference in height between A and B is practically negligible ($y_A \approx y_B$), and $v_B = 0$, so Bernoulli's

equation gives $P_B = P_A + \frac{1}{2}\rho v_A^2$. Thus, $v_A = \sqrt{2(P_B - P_A)/\rho}$. (Note: Even though Equation 18-6 applies strictly to incompressible steady fluid flow, density variations in a gas are generally insignificant when the flow speed is much less than the speed of sound.)

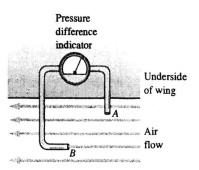

FIGURE 18-54 Problem 63 Solution.

Problem

65. With its throttle valve wide open, an automobile carburetor has a throat diameter of 2.4 cm. With each revolution, the engine draws 0.50 L of air through the carburetor. At an engine speed of 3000 rpm, what are (a) the volume flow rate, (b) the airflow speed, and (c) the difference between atmospheric pressure and air pressure in the carburetor throat? The density of air is 1.2 kg/m^3.

Solution

(a) The volume rate of flow of intake air is $R_V = (3000 \text{ rpm})(1 \text{ min}/60 \text{ s})(0.5 \text{ L/rev}) = 25$ L/s $= 0.025$ m^3/s. (b) This rate of flow, assumed constant over the cross-sectional area of the carburetor throat, implies a flow speed of $v = R_V/A = (0.025 \text{ m}^3/\text{s}) \div \frac{1}{4}\pi(0.024 \text{ m})^2 = 55.3$ m/s. (c) Since the flow speed is much smaller than the speed of sound in air at this density, we can use Equation 18-6 to calculate the pressure difference. We suppose that air enters the carburetor intake at a speed which is negligible compared to v, at essentially the same height as the throat. Then $\Delta P = P_a - P_{\text{throat}} = \frac{1}{2}\rho v^2 = \frac{1}{2} \times (1.2 \text{ kg/m}^3)(55.3 \text{ m/s})^2 = 1.83$ kPa.

Problem

67. A can of height h and cross-sectional area A_0 is initially full of water. A small hole of area $A_1 \ll A_0$ is cut in the bottom of the can. Find an expression for the time it takes all the water to drain from the can. *Hint:* Call the water depth y,

use the continuity equation to relate dy/dt to the outflow speed at the hole, then integrate.

Solution

If y is the height of the water above the bottom of the can, then $-dy/dt$ is the magnitude of the flow speed of the top surface of the water draining out (y decreases as a function of time). The continuity equation gives $-(dy/dt)A_0 = v_1 A_1$, where subscript 1 refers to the small hole in the bottom, so $dt = -(A_0/A_1)dy/v_1$. For most of the time, $v_1 \approx \sqrt{2gy}$ (see Example 18-8 and we assume the top of the can is open), thus

$$t = \int dt \approx -\int_h^0 \left(\frac{A_0}{A_1}\right) \frac{dy}{\sqrt{2gy}}$$

$$= \frac{A_0}{A_1\sqrt{2g}} \left.\frac{y^{1/2}}{(1/2)}\right|_0^h = \frac{A_0}{A_1}\sqrt{\frac{2h}{g}}.$$

This result is approximate since dy/dt cannot be neglected compared to v_1 when y is small. If we use Bernoulli's equation without this approximation, then $\frac{1}{2}\rho(dy/dt)^2 + \rho gy = \frac{1}{2}\rho v_1^2$, since the pressure is atmospheric pressure at both the top of the can and the hole. Combining with the continuity equation gives $v_1 = \sqrt{2gy + (dy/dt)^2} = -(A_0/A_1)\,dy/dt$, or $dy/dt = -\sqrt{2gy/[(A_0/A_1)^2 - 1]}$. Integration of this yields a more exact outflow time of $t = \sqrt{(2h/g)[(A_0/A_1)^2 - 1]}$.

Problem

69. A circular pan of liquid (density ρ) is centered on a horizontal turntable rotating with angular speed ω. Its axis coincides with the rotation axis, as shown in Fig. 18-56. Atmospheric pressure is P_a. Find expressions for (a) the pressure at the bottom of the pan and (b) the height of the liquid surface as functions of the distance r from the axis, given that the height at the center is h_0.

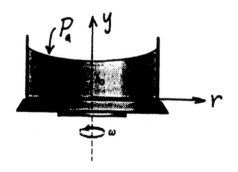

FIGURE 18-56 Problem 69.

Solution

When the water is in equilibrium at constant angular velocity, the vertical change in pressure balances the weight of the water, the radial change in pressure supplies the centripetal acceleration, and there is no change in pressure in the direction tangent to the rotation. Introduce vertical, radial, and tangential coordinates, y, r, and φ respectively, with origin at the bottom center of the pan and y axis positive upward. (These are cylindrical coordinates.) Consider a fluid element $dm = \rho\,dV = \rho\,dr(r\,d\varphi)\,dy$ as shown. (ρ is the density and dV is the volume element.)

The vertical pressure difference balances the gravitational force, as in Equation 18-2, $dF_\text{press} + dF_\text{grav} = 0 = -dP_y A_y - \rho g\,dV$, or $\partial P/\partial y = -\rho g$. Here, $A_y = r\,dr\,d\varphi$ is the area of the faces perpendicular to the y direction, and we wrote a partial derivative because the pressure varies with both y and r. Note that $\partial P/\partial y$ is negative because the pressure increases with depth (decreasing y).

Similarly, the pressure force in the radial direction equals the mass element times the centripetal acceleration, $dF_\text{press} = -dm\,\omega^2 r = -dP_r A_r = -\rho\,dV\,\omega^2 r$. (Recall that $a_r = -v^2/r = -\omega^2 r$.) In this equation, $A_r = r\,d\varphi\,dy$ is the area of the faces perpendicular to the radial direction. Since $dV = A_r\,dr$, after canceling $-A_r$, we find $dP_r = \rho\omega^2 r\,dr$, or $\partial P/\partial r = \rho\omega^2 r$. Here, $\partial P/\partial r$ is positive because the pressure increases with r.

For an incompressible fluid, ρ is a constant (not a function of r and y), thus $\partial P/\partial y = -\rho g$ and $\partial P/\partial r = \rho\omega^2 r$ require the presence of terms equal to $-\rho gy$ and $\frac{1}{2}\rho\omega^2 r^2$ in the expression for the pressure (then the partial derivatives have their specified values). Thus $P(r, y) = -\rho gy + \frac{1}{2}\rho\omega^2 r^2 + \text{constant}$. The constant term can be evaluated, since the pressure is atmospheric pressure at the surface above the center, i.e., $P(0, h_0) = P_a = -\rho gh_0 + \text{constant}$, or the constant $= P_a + \rho gh_0$. Then $P(r, y) = P_a - \rho g \times (y - h_0) + \frac{1}{2}\rho\omega^2 r^2$.

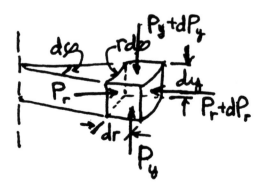

Problem 69 Solution.

(a) Along the bottom of the pan ($y = 0$), $P(r, 0) = P_a + \rho g h_0 + \frac{1}{2}\rho\omega^2 r^2$. (b) The pressure at the water's surface is P_a for all values of r, so the height of the surface, $y = h(r)$, is given by the equation $P(r, h(r)) = P_a$, or $-\rho g[h(r) - h_0] + \frac{1}{2}\rho\omega^2 r^2 = 0$. Thus, $h(r) = h_0 + \omega^2 r^2/2g$, i.e., parabolic. (Such a technique is used to shape large mirrors for astronomical telescopes by a process called spin casting.)

Problem

71. (a) Use the result of the preceding problem to express Earth's atmospheric density as a function of height (this is simple). (b) Use the result of (a) to find the height below which half of Earth's atmospheric mass lies (this will require integration).

Solution

(a) The variation of pressure with height in the Earth's atmosphere follows from Equation 18-2 (with h replaced by $-h$, since height is positive upward whereas depth is positive downward). Thus, $dP = -\rho g\,dh$. If pressure and density are proportional (as given in the previous problem), $dP = -P\,dh/h_0$. This equation can be integrated from the surface values, $h = 0$ and P_0, to yield $\int_{P_0}^{P} dP/P = \ln(P/P_0) = -\int_0^h dh/h_0 = -h/h_0$, or after exponentiation, $P = P_0 e^{-h/h_0}$. (This is called the law of atmospheres; it applies exactly if the temperature is constant.) In

terms of density, $\rho = \rho_0 e^{-h/h_0}$, where $\rho_0 = P_0/h_0 g$. Both P and ρ fall to half their surface values at a height $h_0\ln 2 = (8.2 \text{ km})(0.693) = 5.7 \text{ km}$ (since $e^{-h_0\ln 2/h_0} = \frac{1}{2}$). (b) The mass of atmosphere contained in a thin spherical shell of thickness dh, at height h, is $dm = \rho\,dV = 4\pi\rho_0(R_E + h)^2 e^{-h/h_0}\,dh$, where R_E is the radius of the Earth and $R_E + h$ the radius of the shell. The mass of atmosphere below height h_1 is

$$M(h_1) = \int_0^{h_1} dm$$
$$= 4\pi\rho_0 R_E^2 \int_0^{h_1} \left(1 + 2\frac{h}{R_E} + \frac{h^2}{R_E^2}\right) e^{-h/h_0}\,dh.$$

The integrals can be evaluated easily enough with the use of the table of integrals in Appendix B, however, if $h_1/R_E \ll 1$, only the first term is important. (Even if h_1 is large, the exponential term is negligibly small for $h_1 \gg h_0$ and none of the terms contribute significantly for large h.) To a good approximation, therefore

$$M(h_1) \simeq 4\pi\rho_0 R_E^2 \int_0^{h_1} e^{-h/h_0}\,dh$$
$$= 4\pi\rho_0 R_E^2 h_0(1 - e^{-h_1/h_0}).$$

The total mass of the atmosphere is approximately $M(\infty) = 4\pi\rho_0 R_E^2 h_0$, so the height bounding half the total mass is given by the equation $\frac{1}{2}M = M(1 - e^{-h_1/h_0})$, or $h_1 = h_0\ln 2$ as in part (a).

PART 2   CUMULATIVE PROBLEMS

Problem

1. A cylindrical log of total mass M and uniform diameter d has an uneven mass distribution that causes it to float in a vertical position, as shown in Figure 1. (a) Find an expression for the length ℓ of the submerged portion of the log when it is floating in equilibrium, in terms of M, d, and the water density ρ. (b) If the log is displaced vertically from its equilibrium position and released, it will undergo simple harmonic motion. Find an expression for the period of this motion, neglecting viscosity and other frictional effects.

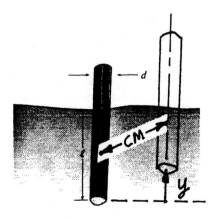

FIGURE 1 Cumulative Problem 1.

Solution

(This problem is similar to Problem 18-68.)
(a) At equilibrium, the weight of the log is balanced by the buoyant force, as in Example 18-6. The former has magnitude Mg, while that of the latter is $F_b = \rho g V_{\text{sub}} = \rho g A \ell$, where $A = \frac{1}{4}\pi d^2$ is the cross-sectional

area and ℓ the equilibrium submerged length. Thus $\ell = M/\rho A = 4M/\rho\pi d^2$. (b) If the log is given a vertical displacement y (positive upwards as shown), the net force (neglecting frictional effects) is $F_b - Mg = \rho g A(\ell - y) - \rho g A \ell = -(Mg/\ell)y$, where we expressed the weight in terms of the equilibrium submerged length from part (a). Since y is also the displacement of the log's center of mass from its equilibrium position, the net force equals $M \, d^2y/dt^2$, or $d^2y/dt^2 = -(g/\ell)y$. This is the equation for simple harmonic motion with frequency $\omega^2 = g/\ell$ and period $T = 2\pi/\omega = 2\pi\sqrt{\ell/g} = 4\sqrt{\pi M/\rho g d^2}$.

Problem

3. Let P_0 and ρ_0 be the atmospheric pressure and density at Earth's surface. Assume that the ratio P/ρ is the same throughout the atmosphere (this implies that the temperature is uniform). Show that the pressure at vertical height z above the surface is given by $P(z) = P_0 e^{-\rho_0 g z/P_0}$, for z much less than Earth's radius (this amounts to neglecting Earth's curvature, and thus taking g to be constant).

Solution

(This problem is similar to Problems 18-70 and 71.) First, rewrite Equation 18-2 in terms of the height z above, instead of the depth h below, the Earth's surface ($z = -h$). Then the pressure variation with height in the atmosphere is given by $dP/dz = -\rho g$. If we assume $P/\rho = P_0/\rho_0$ is a constant (as for an ideal isothermal atmosphere—see Equation 20-1) then $dP/dz = -(\rho_0 g/P_0)P$. For $z \ll R_E$, g is nearly constant, and the pressure equation can be integrated by separating variables:

$$\int_{P_0}^{P} \frac{dP}{P} = -\left(\frac{\rho_0 g}{P_0}\right) \int_0^z dz, \text{ or } \ln(P/P_0) = -(\rho_0 g/P_0)z.$$

Exponentiation gives the desired result, $P = P_0 e^{-z/H_0}$, which is called the barometric law. The constant $H_0 = P_0/\rho_0 g \approx 8.4$ km is known as the scale height.

Problem

5. A U-shaped tube containing liquid is mounted on a table that tilts back and forth through a slight angle, as shown in Fig. 4. The diameter of the tube is much less than either the height of it's arms or their separation. When the table is rocked very

slowly or very rapidly, nothing particularly dramatic happens. But when the rocking takes place at a few times per second, the liquid level in the tube oscillates violently, with maximum amplitude at a rocking frequency of 1.7 Hz. Explain what is going on, and find the total length of the liquid including both vertical and horizontal portions.

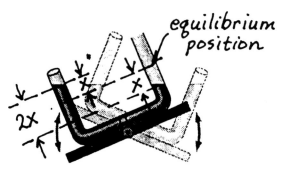

FIGURE 4 Cumulative Problem 5.

Solution

When the tube is rocked back and forth, the liquid in it is dragged along by viscous forces. We suppose that the dimensions of the tube (its small diameter compared to the height of the tube arms or their separation) allow us to treat the column of liquid, of total length ℓ, as a one-dimensional system which undergoes underdamped oscillations with weak damping (as in Section 15-7). The maximum amplitude occurs at a driving frequency very close to the undamped natural frequency, $\omega_d = 2\pi(1.7$ Hz$) \approx \omega_0$. To find ω_0 in terms of ℓ, suppose one end of the liquid column is depressed a distance x from equilibrium, as shown. The net restoring force is the weight of a length $2x$ of liquid, or $F = -(\Delta m)g = -\rho g A \cdot 2x$, where A is the cross-sectional area of the tube and ρ is the density of the liquid. The mass of the entire column is $\rho A \ell$, so Newton's second law gives $-2\rho g A x = \rho A \ell \, d^2x/dt^2$. This is the equation for simple harmonic motion with natural frequency $\omega_0^2 = 2g/\ell$. In this case, $\ell = 2g/\omega_0^2 = 2(9.8$ m/s$^2) \div (2\pi \times 1.7$ Hz$)^2 = 17.2$ cm.

PART 3 THERMODYNAMICS

CHAPTER 19 TEMPERATURE AND HEAT

Section 19-1: Macroscopic and Microscopic Descriptions

Problem

1. The macroscopic state of a carton capable of holding a half-dozen eggs is specified by giving the number of eggs in the carton. The microscopic state is specified by telling where each egg is in the carton. How many microscopic states correspond to the macroscopic state of a full carton?

Solution

If we number the eggs (so that they are distinguishable), we could put the first egg in any one of six places, the second in any one of the remaining five places, etc. The total number of microscopic states is $6\cdot5\cdot4\cdot3\cdot2\cdot1 = 6! = 720$. (If the eggs are indistinguishable, there is only one microscopic state for a full carton.)

Section 19-3: Measuring Temperature

Problem

3. Normal room temperature is 68°F. What is this in Celsius?

Solution

Equation 19-3, solved for the Celsius temperature, gives $T_C = \frac{5}{9}(T_F - 32) = 5(68 - 32)/9 = 20°C$.

Problem

5. At what temperature do the Fahrenheit and Celsius scales coincide?

Solution

In Equation 19-3, T_F and T_C are numerically equal when $T_F = \left(\frac{9}{5}\right)T_C + 32 = T_C$, or $T_C = -\left(\frac{5}{4}\right)(32) = -40 = T_F$.

Problem

7. The normal boiling point of nitrogen is 77.3 K. Express this in Celsius and Fahrenheit.

Solution

Equations 19-2 and 3 give $T_C = 77.3 - 273.15 \simeq -196°C$, and $T_F = \left(\frac{9}{5}\right)(-196) + 32 = -321°F$.

Problem

9. A constant-volume gas thermometer is filled with air whose pressure is 101 kPa at the normal melting point of ice. What would its pressure be at (a) the normal boiling point of water, (b) the normal boiling point of oxygen (90.2 K), and (c) the normal boiling point of mercury (630 K)?

Solution

The thermometric equation for an ideal constant-volume gas thermometer is $P/T = P_{ref}/T_{ref}$. (This is Equation 19-1 written for a reference point not necessarily equal to the triple point of water.) If we use the given values at the normal melting point of ice, $P = T(101 \text{ kPa})/(273.15 \text{ K})$. When the temperatures of the normal boiling points of water (100°C = 373.15 K), oxygen (90.2 K), and mercury (630 K) are substituted, pressures of (a) 138 kPa, (b) 33.4 kPa, and (c) 233 kPa are calculated.

Problem

11. The temperature of a constant-pressure gas thermometer is directly proportional to the gas volume. If the volume is 1.00 L at the triple point of water, what is it at water's normal boiling point?

Solution

The absolute temperature (for a given mass of gas at constant pressure) is proportional to the volume (this is known as the law of Charles and Gay-Lussac), therefore $T/T_3 = V/V_3$, where subscript 3 refers to the triple point values. Then $V = (T/T_3)V_3 = (373.15 \div 273.16)(1.00 \text{ L}) = 1.37 \text{ L}$, when $T = 100°C$.

Problem

13. A constant-volume gas thermometer supports a 72.5-mm-high mercury column when it's immersed

in liquid nitrogen at $-196°C$. What will be the column height when the thermometer is in molten lead at $350°C$?

Solution

For a constant-volume gas thermometer, P/T is constant (see Equation 19-1). Since pressure can be measured in mm of mercury ($P = \rho g h$) it is also true that h/T is constant. Under the conditions specified for liquid nitrogen and molten lead, $h/T = h'/T'$ implies $h' = (T'/T)h = (7.25 \text{ mm})(350 + 273) \div (-196 + 273) = 587$ mm. (Note: the temperature in Equation 19-1 is the absolute Kelvin temperature.)

Sections 19-4 and 19-5: Temperature and Heat, Heat Capacity and Specific Heat

Problem

15. If your mass is 60 kg, what is the minimum number of calories you would "burn off" climbing a 1700-m-high mountain? (The actual metabolic energy used would be much greater.)

Solution

The minimum energy burned-off is the work done against gravity, which equals the potential energy change: $-W_{grav} = \Delta U_{grav} = mg\,\Delta y = (60 \times 9.8 \text{ N})(1700 \text{ m})(1 \text{ kcal}/4184 \text{ J}) = 239$ kcal (recall Equations 8-2 and 3).

Problem

17. Typical fats contain about 9 kcal per gram. If the energy in body fat could be utilized with 100% efficiency, how much mass could a 78-kg person lose running a 26.2-mile marathon? The energy expenditure rate for that mass is 125 kcal/mile.

Solution

The energy expended in running a marathon for a person with the given mass is $(125 \text{ kcal/mi}) \times (26.2 \text{ mi}) = 3.28 \times 10^3$ kcal. This is equivalent to the energy content of $3.28 \times 10^3 \text{ kcal}/(9 \text{ kcal/g}) = 364$ g, or about 13 oz, of fat.

Problem

19. A circular lake 1.0 km in diameter averages 10 m deep. Solar energy is incident on the lake at an average rate of 200 W/m^2. If the lake absorbs all this energy and does not exchange heat with its surroundings, how long will it take to warm from $10°C$ to $20°C$?

Solution

Since the energy absorbed by the lake equals the solar power times the time, $\Delta t = \Delta Q/\mathcal{P} = mc\Delta T \div (200 \text{ W/m}^2)A$, where m/A is the mass per unit area of lake surface. Therefore:

$\Delta t = (10^3 \text{ kg/m}^3)(10 \text{ m})(4184 \text{ J/kg·K})(10 \text{ K})/(200 \text{ W/m}^2)$
$= 2.09 \times 10^6 \text{ s} = 24.2 \text{ d}.$

Problem

21. How much heat is required to raise an 800-g copper pan from $15°C$ to $90°C$ if (a) the pan is empty; (b) the pan contains 1.0 kg of water; (c) the pan contains 4.0 kg of mercury?

Solution

(a) When just the pan is heated, $\Delta Q = m_{Cu}c_{Cu}\,\Delta T = (0.8 \text{ kg})(386 \text{ J/kg·K})(90 - 15)\text{K} = 23.2 \text{ kJ} = 5.54$ kcal. (b) If the pan contains water and both are heated between the same temperatures, $\Delta Q = (m_{Cu}c_{Cu} + m_w c_w)\,\Delta T = 23.2 \text{ kJ} + (1 \text{ kg})(4184 \text{ J/kg·K}) \times (75 \text{ K}) = 337 \text{ kJ} = 80.5$ kcal. (c) With 4 kg of mercury replacing the water, $\Delta Q = 23.2 \text{ kJ} + (4 \text{ kg}) \times (140 \text{ J/kg·K})(75 \text{ K}) = 65.2 \text{ kJ} = 15.6$ kcal. (See Table 19-1 for the specific heats.)

Problem

23. How much power does it take to raise the temperature of a 1.3-kg copper pipe by $15°C/s$?

Solution

Dividing Equation 19-5 by the time, we get $\mathcal{P} = \Delta Q/\Delta t = mc\Delta T/\Delta t = (1.3 \text{ kg})(386 \text{ J/kg·K}) \times (15 \text{ K/s}) = 7.53$ kW.

Problem

25. You insert your microwave oven's temperature probe in a roast and start it cooking. You notice that the temperature goes up $1°C$ every 20 s. If the roast has the same specific heat as water, and if the oven power is 500 W, what is the mass of the roast? Neglect heat loss.

Solution

With no losses, the heat absorbed by the roast per second (power) equals the mass times the specific heat of the roast times the temperature rise per second, or $\mathcal{P} = \Delta Q/\Delta t = mc\Delta T/\Delta t$. Thus $m = (500 \text{ W}) \div (4184 \text{ J/kg·K})(1 \text{ K}/20 \text{ s}) = 2.39$ kg, or about $5\frac{1}{4}$ lb.

Problem

27. A stove burner supplies heat at the rate of 1.0 kW, a microwave oven at 625 W. You can heat water in

the microwave in a paper cup of negligible heat capacity, but the stove requires a pan whose heat capacity is 1.4 kJ/K. (a) How much water do you need before it becomes quicker to heat on the stovetop? (b) What will be the rate at which the temperature of this much water rises?

Solution

The temperature rise per second is equal to the heat supplied per second (i.e., the power supplied if there are no losses) divided by the total heat capacity of the water and its container: $\Delta T/\Delta t = (\Delta Q/\Delta t)/C_{tot} = \mathcal{P}/C_{tot}$ (Equation 19-4 divided by Δt). The total heat capacity is $C_{tot} = C_W + C_{cnt}$, provided the water and container both have the same instantaneous temperature. (This assumes that heat is supplied sufficiently slowly that the water and container share it and stay in instantaneous thermal equilibrium.) For the paper cup used in the microwave oven, $C_{cnt} \approx 0$, whereas for the pan used on the stove burner, $C_{cnt} = 1.4$ kJ/K. Thus, the rate of temperature rise is 625 W/C_W for the microwave and 1.0 kW/(C_W + 1.4 kJ/K) for the stove burner. (a) When $C_W = m_W c_W$ is small, the microwave is faster, whereas when C_W is large, the stove burner is faster. (To see this, plot both rates as a function of C_W.) The rates of temperature rise are equal for $C_W = m_W \times$ (4.184 kJ/kg·K) = (1.4 kJ/K)(0.625)/(1 − 0.625) = 2.33 kJ/K. Therefore, $m_W = (2.33$ kJ/K)÷ (4.184 kJ/kg·K) = 0.558 kg. (b) For m_W in part (a), the rate of temperature rise is $\Delta T/\Delta t = (0.625$ kW)÷ (2.33 kJ/K) = 1.0 kW/(2.33 + 1.4)(kJ/K) = 0.268 K/s.

Problem

29. A 1.2-kg iron tea kettle sits on a 2.0-kW stove burner. If it takes 5.4 min to bring the kettle and the water in it from 20°C to the boiling point, how much water is in the kettle?

Solution

The energy supplied by the stove burner heats the kettle and water in it from 20°C to 100°C. If we neglect any losses of heat and the heat capacity of the burner, this energy is just the burner's power output times the time, so $\Delta Q = \mathcal{P}\,\Delta t = (m_W c_W + m_K c_K) \times \Delta T$ (Equation 19-5 for water and kettle). Since all of these quantities are given except for the mass of the water, we can solve for m_W:

$$\begin{aligned} m_W &= [(\mathcal{P}\,\Delta t/\Delta T) - m_K c_K]/c_W \\ &= \{[(2 \text{ kW})(5.4 \times 60 \text{ s})/80 \text{ K}] - (1.2 \text{ kg}) \\ &\quad \times (447 \text{ J/kg·K})\}/(4184 \text{ J/kg·K}) \\ &= 1.81 \text{ kg}. \end{aligned}$$

Problem

31. Two cars collide head-on at 90 km/h. If all their kinetic energy ended up as heat, what would be the temperature increase of the wrecks? The specific heat of the cars is essentially that of iron.

Solution

$\Delta Q = \Delta K = 2(\frac{1}{2}mv^2) = 2mc\,\Delta T$ (if there are no energy losses), therefore $\Delta T = v^2/2c_{Iron} =$ (90 m/3.6 s)^2/(2×447 J/kg·K) = 0.699 K.

Problem

33. A leaf absorbs sunlight with intensity 600 W/m^2. The leaf has a mass per unit area of 100 g/m^2, and its specific heat is 3800 J/kg·K. In the absence of any heat loss, at what rate would the leaf's temperature rise?

Solution

The derivative of Equation 19-5 with respect to time relates the rate of temperature rise to the rate of heat energy absorbed, $dQ/dt = mc(dT/dt)$. Using the values of dQ/dt and m given for unit areas of leaf, one finds $dT/dt = (600$ W/m^2)/(0.1 kg/m^2)× (3800 J/kg·K) = 1.58 K/s.

Problem

35. A piece of copper at 300°C is dropped into 1.0 kg of water at 20°C. If the equilibrium temperature is 25°C, what is the mass of the copper?

Solution

Let us assume that all the heat lost by the copper is gained by the water, with no heat transfer to the container or its surroundings. Then $-\Delta Q_{Cu} = \Delta Q_W$ (as in Example 19-3) or $-m_{Cu}c_{Cu}(T - T_{Cu}) = m_W c_W(T - T_W)$. Solving for m_{Cu} (in terms of the other quantities given in the problem or in Table 19-1) one finds $m_{Cu} = m_W c_W(T - T_W)/c_{Cu}(T_{Cu} - T) =$ (1 kg)(4184 J/kg·K)(25 − 20) K/(386 J/kg·K)× (300 − 25) K = 0.197 kg.

Problem

37. A thermometer of mass 83.0 g is used to measure the temperature of a 150-g water sample. The thermometer's specific heat is 0.190 cal/g·°C, and it reads 20.0°C before immersion in the water. The water temperature is initially 60.0°C. What does the thermometer read after it comes to equilibrium with the water?

Solution

If we assume that the thermometer and water are thermally insulated from their surroundings, Equation 19-6 (and its solution from Example 19-4) gives:

$$T = \frac{m_t c_t T_t + m_W c_W T_W}{m_t c_t + m_W c_W}$$
$$= \frac{(83.0)(0.190)(20.0°C) + (150)(1)(60.0°C)}{(83.0)(0.190) + (150)(1)}$$
$$= 56.2°C,$$

(we omitted common units in the numerator and denominator).

Sections 19-6 and 19-7: Heat Transfer and Thermal Energy Balance

Problem

39. The top of a steel wood stove measures 90 cm×40 cm, and is 0.45 cm thick. The fire maintains the inside surface of the stove top at 310°C, while the outside surface is at 295°C. Find the rate of heat conduction through the stove top.

Solution

Assuming a steady flow of heat through the 90×40 cm^2 = 0.36 m^2 area face, with no flow through the edges, we can use Equation 19-7 and Table 19-2: $H = -kA \Delta T/\Delta x = -(46 \text{ W/m·K})(0.36 \text{ m}^2)(295°C - 310°C)/(0.45 \text{ cm}) = 55.2$ kW. (The heat flow is positive, for x going from the inside of the stove to the outside, because the temperature gradient, $\Delta T/\Delta x$, is negative.)

Problem

41. Building heat loss in the United States is usually expressed in Btu/h. What is 1 Btu/h in SI?

Solution

The conversion to SI units is (1 Btu/h)(1055 J/Btu)× (1 h/3600 s) = 0.293 W.

Problem

43. What is the R-factor of a wall that loses 0.040 Btu each hour through each square foot for each °F temperature difference?

Solution

Equation 19-7 for the rate of heat-flow through a slab, written in terms of the thermal resistance of the slab (Equation 19-9), is $H = -\Delta T/R$. Therefore, a heat loss of 0.040 Btu/h per Fahrenheit degree of temperature difference, corresponds to a thermal

resistance of $R = 1$ F°/(0.040 Btu/h) = 25 F°·h/Btu (the heat-flow is in the direction of decreasing temperature, so the thermal resistance is positive). Equation 19-11 gives the R-factor of $A = 1$ ft^2 of slab as $\mathcal{R} = 25$. (The units of the R-factor are such that the numerical value of $\mathcal{R}$ divided by the area in ft^2 is the thermal resistance in F°·h/Btu.)

Problem

45. A biology lab's walk-in cooler measures 3.0m× 2.0 m ×2.3 m and is insulated with 8.0-cm-thick styrofoam. If the surrounding building is at 20°C, at what average rate must the cooler's refrigeration unit remove heat in order to maintain 4.0°C in the cooler?

Solution

The total surface area (sides, top, and bottom) of the cooler is $A = 2(3×2 + 3×2.3 + 2×2.3)$ m^2 = 35 m^2. A thickness of 8 cm of styrofoam of this area has a thermal resistance of $R = \Delta x/kA = (0.08 \text{ m}) \div$ (0.029 W/m·K)(35 m^2) = $7.88×10^{-2}$ K/W (see Equation 19-9). Therefore, a heat-flow of magnitude $|\Delta T|/R = (20°C - 4°C)/(7.88×10^{-2}$ K/W) = 203 W (see Equation 19-7) must be balanced by the refrigeration unit to maintain the desired steady state temperatures.

Problem

47. (a) What is the R-factor for a wall consisting of $\frac{1}{4}$-in. pine paneling, $\mathcal{R}$-11 fiberglass insulation, $\frac{3}{4}$-in. pine sheathing, and 2.0-mm aluminum siding? (b) What is the heat-loss rate through a 20 ft×8 ft section of wall when the temperature difference across the wall is 55°F?

Solution

(a) The wall consists of conducting slabs of different materials and thickness, of the same area (connected in "series"), so the discussion following Equation 19-10 shows that the R-factor of the combination is the sum of the individual R-factors, $\mathcal{R} = \mathcal{R}_{\text{pine}} + \mathcal{R}_{\text{fiberglass}} + \mathcal{R}_{\text{Al}}$. The first and last terms we calculate from Equation 19-11; the middle term is given:

$$\mathcal{R} = (\tfrac{1}{4} + \tfrac{3}{4})/(0.78) + 11 + (0.2/2.54)/(1644) = 12.3.$$

(We remembered to express Δx in inches and k in Btu·in·/h·ft^2·F°. The contribution of the aluminum siding is negligible.) (b) The thermal resistance of a 20×8 ft^2 area of such a wall is $R = (12.3/20 \times 8)×$ (h·F°/Btu) (see solution to Problem 43), so the heat-flow through the wall, for a steady temperature difference of −55 F° (i.e., $T_{\text{outside}} - T_{\text{inside}} = \Delta T$), is

$H = -\Delta T/R = (55 \text{ F}°)(20 \times 8/12.3)(\text{Btu/h·F}°) =$
715 Btu/h.

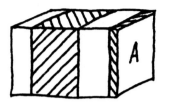

Problem 47 Solution.

Problem

49. Repeat the preceding problem for a south-facing window where the average sunlight intensity is 180 W/m².

Solution

The difference in heat loss between R-factors of 19 and 2.1, for a window area of 40 ft² and given temperature difference, is $\Delta H = -A \, \Delta T (\mathcal{R}_2^{-1} - \mathcal{R}_1^{-1}) = -(40 \text{ ft}^2) \times$ $(15°\text{F} - 68°\text{F})(2.1^{-1} - 19^{-1})(\text{ft}^2 \cdot \text{F}° \cdot \text{h/Btu})^{-1} =$ 898 Btu/h. (A positive ΔH represents a greater heat-flow from inside the house to outside, or a loss of energy.) Over a winter month, (898 Btu/h) (30 d)(24 h/d)(1 gal/10^5 Btu) = 6.47 gal of oil would have to be consumed to compensate for this loss.

On the other hand, if a southern window location resulted in a net gain from solar power of $(180 \text{ W/m}^2)(1 \text{ Btu/1055 J})(3600 \text{ s/h})(40 \text{ ft}^2) \times$ $(0.3048 \text{ m/ft})^2 = 2284$ Btu/h, this would be equivalent to a savings of (2284 Btu/h)(30 d)(24 h/d) × (1 gal/10^5 Btu) = 16.4 gal of oil over a month. The resulting net savings is $16.4 - 6.47 = 9.97$ gal of oil for one winter month.

Problem

51. A house is insulated so its total heat loss is 370 W/°C. On a night when the outdoor temperature is 12°C the owner throws a party, and 40 people come. The average power output of the human body is 100 W. If there are no other heat sources in the house, what will be the house temperature during the party?

Solution

The average thermal resistance of the house is given, since $1/R = 370$ W/C°. (The thermal resistance is defined as the reciprocal of the rate of heat-flow per degree temperature difference, i.e., $-H/\Delta T = 1/R$; see Equations 19-7 and 9.) In thermal energy balance, the power released by the people (owner plus guests) is equal to the rate of heat loss from the house (otherwise

the house would heat up or cool down). Therefore, $\mathcal{P} = 41 \times 100$ W $= |H| = |\Delta T|/R = |\Delta T|$ (370 W/C°), or $|\Delta T| = 11.1$ C°. Since the outside temperature is 12°C, the temperature inside the house is $12°\text{C} + |\Delta T| = 23.1°\text{C}$.

Problem

53. An electric stove burner has surface area 325 cm² and emissivity $e = 1.0$. The burner is at 900 K and the electric power input to the burner is 1500 W. If room temperature is 300 K, what fraction of the burner's heat loss is by radiation?

Solution

The net power radiated (emitted at T_1, absorbed at T_2) is $\mathcal{P} = e\sigma A(T_1^4 - T_2^4) = (1)(5.67 \times 10^{-8} \text{ W/m}^2 \cdot \text{K}^4) \times$ $(3.25 \times 10^{-2} \text{ m}^2)(300 \text{ K})^4(3^4 - 1) = 1194$ W. This is 79.6% of the input power (1500 W).

Problem

55. The average human body produces heat at the rate of 100 W and has total surface area of about 1.5 m². What is the coldest outdoor temperature in which a down sleeping bag with 4.0-cm loft (thickness) can be used without the body temperature dropping below 37°C? Consider only conductive heat loss.

Solution

Assume that in thermal energy balance, the rate of heat generation by a human body equals the rate of heat-flow lost by conduction through the sleeping bag, i.e., 100 W $= -kA \, \Delta T/\Delta x$. The sleeping bag may be considered to be closefitting (same surface area as the body), consisting of goose down insulation (see Table 19-2) and a negligible fabric shell. Then 100 W $= -(0.043 \text{ W/m·K})(1.5 \text{ m}^2) \times (T - 37°\text{C}) \div$ (0.04 m), or $T = 37°\text{C} - 62.0°\text{C} = -25°\text{C} = -13°\text{F}$.

Problem

57. Scientists worry that a nuclear war could inject enough dust into the upper atmosphere to reduce significantly the amount of solar energy reaching Earth's surface. If an 8% reduction in solar input occurred, what would happen to Earth's 287-K average temperature?

Solution

If we assume that the Earth's average temperature is proportional to the one-fourth power of the effective solar intensity ($T_{\text{av}} \sim S^{1/4}$), as explained in the text's application to the greenhouse effect and global warming, then reducing the intensity to $0.92S$ alters the average temperature according to $T'_{av} = T_{av} \times (0.92)^{1/4}$. This would result in a decrease in the present $T_{av} = 287$ K of $\Delta T_{av} = T_{av} - T'_{av} = [1 - (0.92)^{1/4}](287 \text{ K}) = 5.92$ K.

Paired Problems

Problem

59. A blacksmith heats a 1.1-kg iron horseshoe to 550°C, then plunges it into a bucket containing 15 kg of water at 20°C. What is the final temperature?

Solution

If we assume that all of the heat lost by the horseshoe is transferred to the water (in reality, some heat is lost to the surroundings and bucket), then the analysis of Example 19-3 applies and the equilibrium temperature is

$$T = \frac{(1.1)(0.107)(550°C) + (15)(1)(20°C)}{(1.1)(0.107) + (15)(1)} = 24.1°C.$$

(Note: We used specific heats from Table 19-1 in cal/g·C°, since in those units, the numerical value for water is unity, and we canceled the common units from the numerator and denominator in the expression for T.)

Problem

61. What is the power output of a microwave oven that can heat 430 g of water from 20°C to the boiling point in 5.0 minutes? Neglect the heat capacity of the container.

Solution

The average power supplied to the water is $\mathcal{P} = \Delta Q/\Delta t = mc \, \Delta T/\Delta t = (430 \text{ g})(1 \text{ cal/g·C}°)(100°C - 20°C) \times (4.184 \text{ J/cal})/(5 \times 60 \text{ s}) = 480$ W. This is also the output of the microwave, if we neglect the power absorbed by the container and any leakage in the unit.

Problem

63. A cylindrical log 15 cm in diameter and 65 cm long is glowing red hot in a fireplace. If it's emitting radiation at the rate of 34 kW, what is its temperature? The log's emissivity is essentially 1.

Solution

If we neglect the radiation absorbed by the log from its environment (the fireplace brick, for example, does radiate heat to the room, but is probably at a temperature far less than red hot), then the net power radiated by the log is just $\mathcal{P} = e\sigma AT^4$. The surface

area of the log is $\pi dL + 2\pi R^2 = \pi d(L + R) = \pi(0.15 \text{ m})(0.65 \text{ m} + 0.075 \text{ m}) = 0.342 \text{ m}^2$, so solving for T, we find $T = [(34 \times 10^3 \text{ W})/(5.67 \times 10^{-8} \text{ W/m}^2 \cdot \text{K}^4) \times (0.342 \text{ m}^2)]^{1/4} = 1.15$ kK.

Problem

65. An enclosed rabbit hutch has a thermal resistance of 0.25 K/W. If you put a 50-W heat lamp in the hutch on a day when the outside temperature is −15°C, what will be the hutch temperature? Neglect the rabbit's metabolism.

Solution

The rate of heat loss of the hutch by conduction is $H = -\Delta T/R = -[(-15°C) - T]/(0.25 \text{ K/W}) = (4 \text{ W/K})(T + 15°C)$ (see Equations 19-7 and 9). If we neglect any heat loss by radiation and convection, and any heat generated by the rabbit, this is equal to the power supplied by the 50 W lamp at the equilibrium temperature of the hutch. Thus, $T = [50 \text{ W} \div (4 \text{ W/K})] - 15°C = -2.5°C$. (Perhaps the rabbit would be more comfortable with a 100 W lamp.)

Supplementary Problems

Problem

67. Rework Example 19-5, now assuming that the house has 10 single-glazed windows, each measuring 2.5 ft × 5.0 ft. Four of the windows are on the south, and admit solar energy at the average rate of 30 Btu/h·ft². *All* the windows lose heat; their R-factor is 0.90. (a) What is the total heating cost for the month? (b) How much is the solar gain worth?

Solution

The window area is 10(2.5 ft × 5.0 ft) = 125 ft². The wall area is 125 ft² less than in Example 19-5, or $A_{walls} = 1506 \text{ ft}^2 - 125 \text{ ft}^2 = 1381 \text{ ft}^2$. The heat losses through the various structural parts are:

$$|H|_{walls} = \left(\frac{1}{12.37} \frac{\text{Btu}}{\text{h·ft}^2 \cdot °\text{F}}\right)(1381 \text{ ft}^2)(50°\text{F})$$
$$= 5583 \text{ Btu/h},$$

$$|H|_{roof} = \left(\frac{1}{31.37} \frac{\text{Btu}}{\text{h·ft}^2 \cdot °\text{F}}\right)(1164 \text{ ft}^2)(50°\text{F})$$
$$= 1855 \text{ Btu/h},$$

$$|H|_{windows} = \left(\frac{1}{0.90} \frac{\text{Btu}}{\text{h·ft}^2 \cdot °\text{F}}\right)(125 \text{ ft}^3)(50°\text{F})$$
$$= 6944 \text{ Btu/h}.$$

If we include the gain from the south windows, 4(12.5 ft²)(30 Btu/h·ft²) = 1500 Btu/h, the net rate of loss of energy from the entire house is $(5583 + 1855 + 6944 - 1500)$ Btu/h $= 12.88 \times 10^3$ Btu/h. The monthly fuel bill is $(12.88 \times 10^3$ Btu/h$)(24 \times 30$ h/mo$)(1$ gal $\div 10^5$ Btu$)(\$0.94$/gal$) = \$87.19$/mo. The solar gain from the south windows is worth $(1500)(24 \times 30) \times (\$0.94$/mo$)/10^5 = \$10.11$/mo.

Problem

69. My house currently burns 160 gallons of oil in a typical winter month when the outdoor temperature averages 15°F and the indoor temperature averages 66°F. Roof insulation consists of $\mathcal{R} = 19$ fiberglass, and the roof area is 770 ft². If I double the thickness of the roof insulation, by what percentage will my heating bills drop? A gallon of oil yields about 100,000 Btu of heat.

Solution

The rate of heat loss by conduction from the currently insulated house can be written as $H_0 = -\Delta T \times [(A/\mathcal{R})_{\text{roof}} + (A/\mathcal{R})_{\text{rest}}]$, where $\Delta T = 15°\text{F} - 66°\text{F} = -51$ F°, $A_{\text{roof}} = 770$ ft², $\mathcal{R}_{\text{roof}} = 19$ (ft²·F°·h/Btu), and A_{rest} and $\mathcal{R}_{\text{rest}}$ are the effective area and R-factor for the rest of the house (i.e., walls, windows, floor, etc.). If the R-factor for the roof is doubled, the rate of heat loss will be changed by $\Delta H = \Delta T A_{\text{roof}}/2 \mathcal{R}_{\text{roof}}$, which can be calculated from the given data: $\Delta H = (-51$ F°$)(770$ ft²$)/2(19$ ft²·F°·h/Btu$) = -1.03 \times 10^3$ Btu/h. (A negative change represents a reduction in heat loss; or a drop in heating costs.) The original rate of heat loss can be calculated from the given oil consumption: $H_0 = (160$ gal/mo$)(10^5$ Btu/gal$) \times (1$ mo/30×24 h$) = 2.22 \times 10^4$ Btu/h. Thus, the extra insulation would result in a savings of $|\Delta H/H_0| = 1.03/22.2 = 4.65\%$.

Problem

71. A copper pan 1.5 mm thick and a cast iron pan 4.0 mm thick are sitting on electric stove burners; the bottom area of each pan is 300 cm². Each contains 2.0 kg of water whose temperature is rising at the rate of 0.15 K/s. Find the temperature difference between the inside and outside bottom of each pan.

Solution

We assume that the heat-flow through the bottom of each pan by conduction, $H = -kA \, \Delta T_{\text{pan}}/\Delta x$ from Equation 19-7, raises the temperature of the water at the given rate, $H = \Delta Q/\Delta t = m_W c_W(\Delta T_W/\Delta t)$ from energy balance and Equation 19-5 divided by Δt. (Note that the heat-flow through the pan is from its

outside to its inside, so $\Delta T_{\text{pan}} = T_{\text{in}} - T_{\text{out}}$ is negative. We are also ignoring any heat transfer by convection and radiation.) Then, $T_{\text{out}} - T_{\text{in}} = -\Delta T_{\text{pan}} = m_W c_W(0.15$ K/s$) \, \Delta x/kA$. Using the given values for each pan and Tables 19-1 and 2, we find (a) $-\Delta T_{cu} = (2.0$ kg$)(4184$ J/kg·K$)(0.15$ K/s$)(1.5 \times 10^{-3}$ m$) \div (401$ W/m·K$)(0.03$ m²$) = 0.157$ K, and (b) $-\Delta T_{Fe} = (4/1.5)/(80.4/401)(-\Delta T_{cu}) = 2.08$ K.

Problem

73. At low temperatures the specific heat of a solid is approximately proportional to the cube of the temperature; for copper the specific heat is given by $c = 31(T/343$ K$)^3$ J/g·K. When heat capacity is not constant, Equations 19-4 and 19-5 must be written in terms of the derivative dQ/dT and integrated to get the total heat involved in a temperature change. Find the heat required to bring a 40-g sample of copper from 10 K to 25 K.

Solution

If we write Equation 19-5 in the form $dQ = mc(T) \, dT$ and integrate, as suggested in the problem, we obtain

$$
\begin{aligned}
Q &= m \int_{T_1}^{T_2} c(T) \, dT \\
&= m \int_{10 \text{ K}}^{25 \text{ K}} (31 \text{ J/g·K})(T/343 \text{ K})^3 \, dT \\
&= (40 \text{ g})(31 \text{ J/g·K}) \frac{(25 \text{ K})^4 - (10 \text{ K})^4}{4(343 \text{ K})^3} \\
&= 2.92 \text{ J} = 0.699 \text{ cal.}
\end{aligned}
$$

Problem

75. A pipe of length ℓ and radius R_1 is surrounded by insulation of outer radius R_2 and thermal conductivity k. Use the methods of the preceding problem to show that the heat loss rate through the insulation is

$$
H = \frac{2\pi k\ell(T_1 - T_2)}{\ln(R_2/R_1)}.
$$

Hint: Consider the heat flow through a thin layer of thickness dr and temperature difference dT as shown in Fig. 19-28.

Solution

Although heat-flow is essentially a 3-dimensional process, the one-dimensional Equation 19-14 from the previous problem can be used if we assume a steady heat-flow, H, in the radial direction, through each thin cylindrical layer of insulating material of thickness dr and area $A = 2\pi r\ell$, so that $H = -kA \times dT/dr$. For steady flow, the temperature difference across any cylindrical layer is constant in time, so H is constant and the temperature must vary with radial distance, from T_1 at $r = R_1$ to T_2 at $r = R_2$, such that $dT = -(H/k)dr/2\pi r\ell$. Thus,

$$\int_{T_1}^{T_2} dT = T_2 - T_1 = -\frac{H}{2\pi k\ell} \int_{R_1}^{R_2} \frac{dr}{r}$$

$$= -\frac{H}{2\pi k\ell} \ln\left(\frac{R_2}{R_1}\right),$$

or $H = 2\pi k\ell(T_1 - T_2)/\ln(R_2/R_1)$. (Note that H is in the positive radial direction for $T_1 > T_2$ and we assumed no heat-flow along the length of the pipe.)

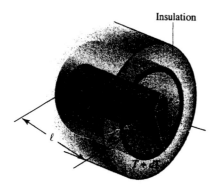

Insulation

FIGURE 19-28 Problem 75 Solution.

Problem

77. A house is at 20°C on a winter day when the outdoor temperature is −15°C. Suddenly the furnace fails. Use the result of the previous problem to determine how long it will take the house temperature to reach the freezing point. The heat capacity of the house is 6.5 MJ/K, and its thermal resistance is 6.67 mK/W.

Solution

In the previous problem, the heat flow from the object is proportional to the temperature difference between it and the surroundings, $H = dQ/dt = -(T - T_0)/R$. This can be transformed into the desired equation by using the chain rule and the definition of heat capacity: $dQ/dt = (dQ/dT)(dT/dt) = C(dT/dt) = -(T - T_0)/R$. If we separate variables and integrate from initial values $t = 0$ and T_1, to arbitrary final values t and T, we obtain:

$$\int_{T_1}^{T} \frac{dT'}{T' - T_0} = \ln\left(\frac{T - T_0}{T_1 - T_0}\right)$$

$$= -\int_0^t \frac{1}{RC} dt' = -\frac{t}{RC},$$

or $T - T_0 = (T_1 - T_0)\exp(-t/RC)$. The temperature at $t = 0$ was chosen to be T_1; as $t \to \infty$, $T - T_0 \to 0$, i.e., the body cools to the temperature of its surroundings.

This result can be applied to the house described in this problem: $(T - T_0)/(T_1 - T_0) = [0°C - (-15°C)]/[20°C - (-15°C)] = 3/7 = \exp(-t/RC)$ or $t = RC \ln(7/3) = (6.67 \text{ mK/W})(6.5 \text{ MJ/K}) \ln(7/3) = 3.67 \times 10^4 \text{ s} = 10.2 \text{ h}$ (enough time for the emergency service to arrive?).

CHAPTER 20   THE THERMAL BEHAVIOR OF MATTER

ActivPhysics can help with these problems:
Activities 8.1–8.4

Section 20-1:   Gases

Problem

1. At Mars's surface, the planet's atmosphere has a pressure only 0.0070 times that of Earth, and an average temperature of 218 K. What is the volume of 1 mole of the Martian atmosphere?

Solution

The molar volume of an ideal gas at STP for the surface of Mars can be calculated as in Example 20-1. However, expressing the ideal gas law for 1 mole of gas at the surfaces of Mars and Earth as a ratio, $P_M V_M / T_M = P_E V_E / T_E$, and using the previous numerical result, we find $V_M = (P_E / P_M)(T_M / T_E) \times V_E = (1/0.0070)(218/273)(22.4 \times 10^{-3} \text{ m}^3) = 2.56 \text{ m}^3$.

Problem

3. What is the pressure of an ideal gas if 3.5 moles occupy 2.0 L at a temperature of $-150°C$?

Solution

The ideal gas law in terms of the gas constant per mole, Equation 20-2, gives $P = nRT/V = (3.5 \text{ mol})(8.314 \text{ J/K·mol})(123 \text{ K})/(0.002 \text{ m}^3) = 1.79 \times 10^6$ Pa. (The absolute temperature must be used, but any convenient units for the gas constant can be used, e.g., $R \simeq 0.0821$ L·atm/K·mol. Then $P = (3.5 \text{ mol})(0.0821 \text{ L·atm/K·mol})(123 \text{ K})/(2 \text{ L}) = 17.7$ atm.)

Problem

5. If 2.0 mol of an ideal gas are at an initial temperature of 250 K and pressure of 1.5 atm, (a) what is the gas volume? (b) The pressure is now increased to 4.0 atm, and the gas volume drops to half its initial value. What is the new temperature?

Solution

(a) From Equation 20-2:

$$V = \frac{nRT}{P} = \frac{(2 \text{ mol})(8.314 \text{ J/mol·K})(250 \text{ K})}{(1.5 \text{ atm})(1.013 \times 10^5 \text{ Pa/atm})}$$

$= 2.74 \times 10^{-2} \text{ m}^3 = 27.4$ L.

(b) The ideal gas law in ratio form (for a fixed quantity of gas, $N_1 = N_2$) gives:

$$\frac{T_2}{T_1} = \frac{P_2 V_2}{P_1 V_1}, \quad \text{or}$$

$$T_2 = \left(\frac{4.0 \text{ atm}}{1.5 \text{ atm}} \right) \left(\frac{0.5 V_1}{V_1} \right) (250 \text{ K}) = 333 \text{ K}.$$

Problem

7. A pressure of 1.0×10^{-10} Pa is readily achievable with laboratory vacuum apparatus. If the residual air in this "vacuum" is at $0°C$, how many air molecules are in one liter?

Solution

$$N = PV/kT$$
$$= (10^{-10} \text{ Pa})(10^{-3} \text{ m}^3)/(1.38 \times 10^{-23} \text{ J/K})(273 \text{ K})$$
$$= 2.65 \times 10^7 \text{ (see Equation 20-1)}.$$

Problem

9. A helium balloon occupies 8.0 L at 20°C and 1.0 atm pressure. The balloon rises to an altitude where air pressure is 0.65 atm and the temperature is $-10°C$. What is its volume when it reaches equilibrium at the new altitude? (Neglect tension forces in the material of the balloon.)

Solution

Use the ideal gas law (Equation 20-1) in ratio form, to compare two different states: $P_1 V_1 / P_2 V_2 = N_1 T_1 / N_2 T_2$. Since the balloon contains the same number of molecules of gas (if none escape), $N_1 = N_2$, and $V_2 = (P_1/P_2)(T_2/T_1)V_1 = (1/0.65)(263/293) \times (8.0 \text{ L}) = 11.0$ L. (Note that absolute temperatures must be used, and that any consistent units for the ratio of the other quantities conveniently cancel.)

Problem

11. An aerosol can of whipped cream is pressurized at 440 kPa when it's refrigerated at 3°C. The can warns against temperatures in excess of 50°C. What is the maximum safe pressure for the can?

Solution

For a fixed amount of ideal gas at constant volume, the pressure is proportional to the absolute temperature, $P_1/T_1 = P_2/T_2 = $ constant. (See the solution to Problem 9.) Thus, the maximum safe aerosol pressure is $P_2 = (T_2/T_1)P_1 = (323/276)(440 \text{ kPa}) = 515 \text{ kPa}$, or about 5.1 atm.

Problem

13. A 3000-ml flask is initially open while in a room containing air at 1.00 atm and 20°C. The flask is then closed, and immersed in a bath of boiling water. When the air in the flask has reached thermodynamic equilibrium, the flask is opened and air allowed to escape. The flask is then closed and cooled back to 20°C. (a) What is the maximum pressure reached in the flask? (b) How many moles escape when air is released from the flask? (c) What is the final pressure in the flask?

Solution

The initial conditions of the gas are $P_1 = 1$ atm, $V_1 = 3$ L, $T_1 = 293$ K, and $n_1 = P_1V_1/RT_1 = (1 \text{ atm})(3 \text{ L})/(8.206 \times 10^{-2} \text{ L·atm/mol·K})(293 \text{ K}) = 0.125$ mol. (a) T_2 is the temperature of boiling water at 1 atm of pressure, or 373 K. Since the original quantity of gas was heated at constant volume, $P_2 = (T_2/T_1)P_1 = (373/293)(1 \text{ atm}) = 1.27$ atm, which is the maximum. (b) When the flask is opened at 373 K, the pressure decreases to 1 atm, so the quantity of gas remaining is $n_2 = P_1V_1/RT_2 = n_1(T_1/T_2) = (0.125 \text{ mol})(293/373) = 0.0980$ mol. Therefore, the amount which escaped was $n_1 - n_2 = 0.0268$ mol. (c) The pressure of the remaining gas is $P_3 = n_2RT_1/V_1 = (n_2/n_1)P_1 = (0.098/0.125)(1 \text{ atm}) = 0.786$ atm.

Problem

15. In which gas are the molecules moving faster: hydrogen (H_2) at 75 K or sulfur dioxide (SO_2) at 350 K?

Solution

Comparing the thermal speeds, $v_{th} = \sqrt{3kT/m}$, for H_2 (mass $\simeq 2$ u) and SO_2 (mass $\simeq 64$ u) at the given temperatures, we find $v_{th}(H_2)/v_{th}(SO_2) = \sqrt{(T_{H_2}/T_{SO_2})(m_{SO_2}/m_{H_2})} = \sqrt{(75/350)(64/2)} = 2.62$; the hydrogen is faster.

Problem

17. The van der Waals constants for helium gas (He) are $a = 0.0341$ L^2·atm/mol^2 and $b = 0.0237$ L/mol. What is the temperature of 3.00 mol of helium at 90.0 atm pressure if the gas volume is 0.800 L? How does this result differ from the ideal gas prediction?

Solution

From Equation 20-7,

$$T = \left(90 \text{ atm} + \frac{(3 \text{ mol})^2(0.0341 \text{ L}^2\text{·atm/mol}^2)}{(0.8 \text{ L})^2}\right)$$
$$\times \frac{[0.8 \text{ L} - (3 \text{ mol})(0.0237 \text{ L/mol})]}{(3 \text{ mol})(8.206 \times 10^{-2} \text{ L·atm/mol·K})} = 268 \text{ K}.$$

This differs from $(90 \text{ atm})(0.8 \text{ L})/(3 \text{ mol}) \times (8.206 \times 10^{-2} \text{ L·atm/mol·K}) = 292$ K, the ideal gas temperature, by about 8.4%.

Problem

19. Because the correction terms (n^2a/V^2 and $-nb$) in the van der Waals equation have opposite signs, there is a point at which the van der Waals and ideal gas equations predict the same temperature. For the gas of Example 20-3, at what pressure does that occur?

Solution

The van der Waals and ideal gas temperatures are the same when $(P + n^2a/V^2)(V - nb) = PV$, or $P = na(V - nb)/bV^2$. If $n = 1, V = 2$ L and the values of a and b from Example 20-3 are substituted, one finds $P = 1.76$ MPa.

Problem

21. In a sample of 10^{24} hydrogen (H_2) molecules, how many molecules have speeds between 900 and 901 m/s (a) at a temperature of 100 K and (b) at 450 K?

Solution

The right-hand side of Equation 20-6 is the number of molecules with speeds in the given range. If we substitute $N = 10^{24}$, $v = 900$ m/s, $\Delta v = 1$ m/s, $m = 2 \times 1.66 \times 10^{-27}$ kg (for H_2 molecules), and $k = 1.38 \times 10^{-23}$ J/K, we get $\Delta N = N(v) \Delta v = (2.41 \times 10^{27} \text{ K}^{3/2})T^{-3/2} \exp\{-97.4 \text{ K}/T\}$. (a) For $T = 100$ K, $\Delta N = 9.10 \times 10^{20}$, and (b) for $T = 450$ K, $\Delta N = 2.03 \times 10^{20}$.

Section 20-2: Phase Changes

Problem

23. How much energy does it take to melt a 65-g ice cube?

Solution

The energy required for a solid-liquid phase transition at the normal melting point of water (0°C) is (Equation 20-8) $Q = mL_f = (0.065 \text{ kg})(334 \text{ kJ/kg}) = 21.7$ kJ, or 5.19 kcal. (See Table 20-1 for the heats of transformation.)

Problem

25. If it takes 840 kJ to vaporize a sample of liquid oxygen, how large is the sample?

Solution

Assuming the vaporization takes place at the normal boiling point for oxygen at atmospheric pressure, we may use Equation 20-8 and Table 20-1 to obtain $m = Q/L_v = 840 \text{ kJ}/(213 \text{ kJ/kg}) = 3.94$ kg.

Problem

27. Find the energy needed to convert 28 kg of liquid oxygen at its boiling point into gas.

Solution

From Equation 20-8 and Table 20-1, $Q = mL_v = (28 \text{ kg})(213 \text{ kJ/kg}) = 5.96$ MJ.

Problem

29. If a 1-megaton nuclear bomb were exploded deep in the Greenland ice cap, how much ice would it melt? Assume the ice is initially at about its freezing point, and consult Appendix C for the appropriate energy conversion.

Solution

A 1-megaton nuclear device releases about 4.16×10^{15} J. This amount of energy is capable of melting $m = Q/L_f = 4.16 \times 10^{15} \text{ J}/(334 \text{ kJ/kg}) = 1.25 \times 10^{10}$ kg of ice at the normal melting point of 0°C.

Problem

31. What is the power of a microwave oven that takes 20 min to boil dry a 300-g cup of water initially at its boiling point?

Solution

The energy required to vaporize the water at 100°C in 20 min is $Q = mL_v$ (see Equation 20-8 and Table 20-1), so the average power supplied by the microwave oven was $\mathcal{P} = Q/t = (0.3 \text{ kg}) \times (2257 \text{ kJ/kg})/(20 \times 60 \text{ s}) = 564$ W.

Problem

33. A refrigerator extracts energy from its contents at the rate of 95 W. How long will it take to freeze

750 g of water already at 0°C?

Solution

The refrigerator must extract $Q = mL_f = (0.75 \text{ kg}) \times (334 \text{ kJ/kg}) = 251$ kJ of heat energy in order to freeze the given quantity of water at 0°C. Since the rate of energy extraction is $\mathcal{P} = Q/t = 95$ W, this requires a time $t = (251 \text{ kJ})/(95 \text{ W}) = 2.64 \times 10^3$ s $= 43.9$ min.

Problem

35. At its "thaw" setting a microwave oven delivers 210 W. How long will it take to thaw a frozen 1.8-kg roast, assuming the roast is essentially water and is initially at 0°C?

Solution

Using the same reasoning as in the solution to Problem 33, we find $t = mL_f/\mathcal{P} = (1.8 \text{ kg}) \times (334 \text{ kJ/kg})/(210 \text{ W}) = 2.86 \times 10^3$ s $= 47.7$ min.

Problem

37. A 100-g block of ice, initially at −20°C, is placed in a 500-W microwave oven. (a) How long must the oven be on to produce water at 50°C? (b) Make a graph showing temperature versus time during this entire interval.

Solution

(a) To bring the ice to 0°C requires heat: $Q_1 = mc_{\text{ice}}\Delta T = (0.1 \text{ kg})(2.05 \text{ kJ/kg·K})[0°\text{C} - (-20°\text{C})] = 4.10$ kJ. To melt the ice requires $Q_2 = mL_f = (0.1 \text{ kg})(334 \text{ kJ/kg}) = 33.4$ kJ. Finally, to bring the meltwater from 0°C to 50°C requires heat $Q_3 = mc_{\text{water}}\Delta T = (0.1 \text{ kg})(4.184 \text{ kJ/kg·K})(50°\text{C} - 0°\text{C}) = 20.9$ kJ. Power must be supplied for a time $t = Q_{\text{tot}}/\mathcal{P}$, or $t = (4.10 + 33.4 + 20.9) \text{ kJ}/0.5 \text{ kW} = 117$ s. (b) It takes times $t_1 = Q_1/0.5 \text{ kW} = 8.2$ s, $t_2 = 66.8$ s, and $t_3 = 41.8$ s for the preceding steps, respectively. Since the power input is constant, the temperature is

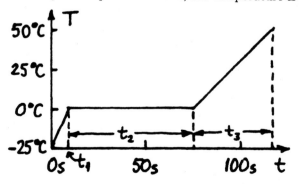

Problem 37 Solution.

linear for steps 1 and 3, and, of course, constant during melting, as shown.

Problem

39. How much energy does it take to melt 10 kg of ice initially at $-10°C$? Consult Table 19-1.

Solution

Energy must be supplied to first raise the ice temperature to the melting point, and then change its phase. Thus, $Q = mc_{ice}\Delta T + mL_f = (10 \text{ kg}) \times [(2.05 \text{ kJ/kg·K})(10 \text{ K}) + 334 \text{ kJ/kg}] = 3.55 \text{ MJ}$. (Combine Equations 19-5 and 20-8.)

Problem

41. A 250-g piece of ice at $0°C$ is placed in a 500-W microwave oven and the oven run for 5.0 min. What is the temperature at the end of this time?

Solution

The total energy supplied by the microwave oven is $500 \text{ W} \times 300 \text{ s} = 150 \text{ kJ}$. The 0.25 kg piece of ice at $0°C$ absorbs $mL_f = 0.25 \text{ kg}(334 \text{ kJ/kg}) = 83.5 \text{ kJ}$ while melting completely. Thus, there is $(150 - 83.5) \text{ kJ} = 66.5 \text{ kJ}$ of energy available to raise the temperature of 0.25 kg of water. The temperature rise is $\Delta T = \Delta Q/mc = 66.5 \text{ kJ}/(0.25 \text{ kg})(4.184 \text{ kJ/kg·K}) = 63.6 \text{ K}$, which is also the numerical final Celsius temperature $T_f = T_i + \Delta T = 63.6°C$, since the initial temperature was $0°C$.

Problem

43. What is the minimum amount of ice in Example 20-6 that will ensure a final temperature of $0°C$?

Solution

In order for the final equilibrium temperature in Example 20-6 to be $0°C$, the original 1 kg of water must lose at least $Q_2 = 62.8 \text{ kJ}$ of heat energy. (It could lose more, if some or all of it froze, but this would clearly require a greater amount of original ice.) The minimum amount of original ice that could gain Q_2, without exceeding $0°C$, would be just completely melted, so $Q_2 = m_{ice}(c_{ice}\Delta T + L_f) = m_{ice}[(2.05 \text{ kJ} \div \text{kg·K})(0°C - (-10°C)) + 334 \text{ kJ/kg}]$. Therefore $m_{ice} = 62.8 \text{ kJ}/(354.5 \text{ kJ/kg}) = 177 \text{ g}$. (Note: The maximum amount of original ice, which could produce a final temperature of $0°C$, while freezing all the original water, is $m_W(c_W\Delta T_W + L_f)/c_{ice}\Delta T_{ice} = (62.8 + 334) \text{ kJ}/(20.5 \text{ kJ/kg}) = 19.4 \text{ kg}$. Between these limits, $m_{ice} = m_W c_W \Delta T_W/c_{ice}\Delta T_{ice} = (1 \text{ kg}) \times (4.184/2.05)(15/10) = 3.06 \text{ kg}$ gives a final mixture

with the original amounts of water and ice at $0°C$. For $177 \text{ g} < m_{ice} < 3.06 \text{ kg}$, some of the original ice melts, and for $3.06 \text{ kg} < m_{ice} < 19.4 \text{ kg}$, some of the original water freezes.)

Problem

45. A 500-g chunk of solid mercury at its 234 K melting point is added to 500 g of liquid mercury at room temperature (293 K). Determine the equilibrium mix and temperature.

Solution

Since the liquid mercury (Hg) is at a higher initial temperature than the solid chunk, it will lose heat energy (all of which is assumed to be absorbed by the solid chunk) and cool. The solid Hg will gain heat energy and start to melt. The heat energy that the liquid Hg could lose if it were to cool to the melting point is $m_{liq}c_{liq}\Delta T_{liq} = (0.5 \text{ kg})(0.140 \text{ kJ/kg·K}) \times (293 - 234) \text{ K} = 4.13 \text{ kJ}$. The heat energy that the solid Hg would gain if it were to melt completely at 234 K is $m_{solid}L_f = 0.5 \text{ kg} \times 11.3 \text{ kJ/kg} = 5.65 \text{ kJ}$. Since the latter is greater than the former, we conclude that not all of the solid Hg melts, and that the final equilibrium temperature of the mixture is 234 K. The amount of solid Hg that does melt is determined by the heat energy lost by the liquid, $\Delta m = 4.13 \text{ kJ}/L_f = 365 \text{ g}$. Therefore, there is $500 - 365 = 135 \text{ g}$ of solid Hg and $500 + 365 = 865 \text{ g}$ of liquid Hg in the final mixture.

Problem

47. A bowl contains 16 kg of punch (essentially water) at a warm $25°C$. What is the minimum amount of ice at $0°C$ that will cool the punch to $0°C$?

Solution

Assume that the only heat transfer is between the punch and the ice. To cool to $0°C$, $\Delta Q = (16 \text{ kg})(4.184 \text{ kJ/kg·K})(25°C - 0°C) = 1.67 \text{ MJ}$ of heat must be extracted from the punch. A minimum mass $m = \Delta Q/L_f = 1.67 \text{ MJ}/(334 \text{ kJ/kg}) = 5.01 \text{ kg}$ of ice at $0°C$ could do this, but the punch would be diluted with 5.01 kg of melt-water. (To reduce the dilution, sufficient ice at a temperature below $0°C$ is needed.)

Problem

49. A 50-g ice cube at $-10°C$ is placed in an equal mass of water. What must be the initial water temperature if the final mixture still contains equal amounts of ice and water?

Solution

Let us assume that all the heat gained by the ice was lost by the water, with no heat transfer to a container or the surroundings. An equilibrium mixture of ice and water (at atmospheric pressure) must be at 0°C, and if the masses of ice and water start out and remain equal, there is no net melting or freezing. Then $\Delta Q_{ice} = m_{ice}c_{ice}(0°C - T_{ice}) = -\Delta Q_W = m_W c_W \times (T_W - 0°C)$, or $T_W = m_{ice}c_{ice}(-T_{ice})/m_W c_W = (2.05 \div 4.184)(10°C) = 4.90°C$, where we canceled equal quantities and units.

Section 20-3: Thermal Expansion

Problem

51. A Pyrex glass marble is 1.00000 cm in diameter at 20°C. What will be its diameter at 85°C?

Solution

The linear expansion coefficient for Pyrex glass is given in Table 20-2, so we can calculate the diameter of the marble from Equation 20-10. $\Delta L = \alpha L \Delta T = (3.2 \times 10^{-6} \text{ K}^{-1})(1 \text{ cm})(85°C - 20°C) = 2.08 \times 10^{-4}$ cm, thus $L' = L + \Delta L = 1.00021$. (Note: We expressed the diameter at 85°C to the same accuracy as that given for 20°C.)

Problem

53. Suppose a single piece of welded steel railroad track stretched 5000 km across the continental United States. If the track were free to expand, by how much would its length change if the entire track went from a cold winter temperature of −25°C to a hot summer day of 40°C?

Solution

A naive application of Equation 20-10, with α for steel from Table 20-2 to two significant figures, gives $\Delta L = \alpha L \Delta T = (12 \times 10^{-6} \text{ K}^{-1})(5000 \text{ km})(40°C - (-25°C)) = 3.9$ km.

Problem

55. The tube in a mercury thermometer is 0.10 mm in diameter. What should be the volume of the thermometer bulb if a 1.0-mm rise is to correspond to a temperature change of 1.0°C? Neglect the expansion of the glass.

Solution

There should be a volume of mercury (V) in the reservoir bulb of the thermometer, such that the change in its volume ($\Delta V = \beta V \Delta T$) over the full range of temperature equals the volume of the tube

into which it expands ($\frac{1}{4}\pi d^2 L$). Here, we have neglected the expansion of the glass, as suggested, since $3\alpha_{glass} \ll \beta_{mercury}$ in Table 20-2. Thus $\frac{1}{4}\pi d^2 L = \beta V \Delta T$, or $V = (\frac{1}{4}\pi d^2/\beta)(L/\Delta T)$. Since the gradation of the thermometer, $L/\Delta T = 1$ mm/C°, is given, we find $V = \frac{1}{4}\pi(0.1 \text{ mm})^2(1 \text{ mm/K}) \div (18 \times 10^{-5} \text{ K}^{-1}) = 43.6 \text{ mm}^3$.

Problem

57. A steel ball bearing is encased in a Pyrex glass cube 1.0 cm on a side. At 330 K, the ball bearing fits tightly in the cube. At what temperature will it have a clearance of 1.0 μm all around?

Solution

Since the coefficient of linear expansion of steel is greater than that of Pyrex glass, the unit must be cooled to provide clearance. The difference in the contraction of steel and pyrex equals twice the given clearance on one side, so $|\Delta L_{steel}| - |\Delta L_{pyrex}| = 2 \mu m = (\alpha_{steel} - \alpha_{pyrex})L|\Delta T| = (12 - 3.2) \times 10^{-6} \text{ K}^{-1}(1 \text{ cm})(330 \text{ K} - T)$. Thus, $T = (330 - 2/0.088) \text{ K} = 307 \text{ K}$.

Problem

59. A rod of length L_0 is clamped rigidly at both ends. Its temperature increases by an amount ΔT, and in the ensuing expansion it cracks to form two straight pieces, as shown in Fig. 20-21. Find an expression for the distance d shown in the figure, in terms of L_0, ΔT, and the coefficient of linear expansion, α.

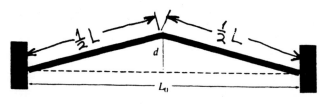

FIGURE 20-21 Problem 59.

Solution

If the two straight pieces in Fig. 20-21 are of equal length, the Pythagorean Theorem gives $d = \sqrt{(\frac{1}{2}L)^2 - (\frac{1}{2}L_0)^2}$, where $L = L_0(1 + \alpha\Delta T)$ is the total expanded length of the rod. Substitution gives $d = (\frac{1}{2}L_0)\sqrt{2\alpha\Delta T + \alpha^2\Delta T^2}$.

Paired Problems

Problem

61. What is the density, in moles per m³, of air in a tire whose absolute pressure is 300 kPa at 34°C?

Solution

The molar density implied by the ideal gas law (which is a good approximation for air under the conditions stated in the problem) is $n/V = P/RT =$ (300 kPa)/(8.314 J/K·mol)(273 + 34) K = 118 mol/m³.

Problem

63. What power is needed to melt 20 kg of ice in 6.0 min?

Solution

If the melting occurs at atmospheric pressure and the normal melting point, the heat of transformation from Table 20-1 requires $\mathcal{P} = Q/t = mL_f/t =$ (20 kg)(334 kJ/kg)/(6×60 s) = 18.6 kW.

Problem

65. You put 300 g of water into a 500-W microwave oven and accidentally set the time for 20 min instead of 2.0 min. If the water is initially at 20°C, how much is left at the end of 20 min?

Solution

In 20 min, $Q = $ (0.5 kW)(20×60 s) = 600 kJ of heat energy is transferred to the water (if we ignore energy absorbed by a container or lost to the surroundings). The energy consumed in raising the water's temperature to the normal boiling point is $mc\Delta T =$ (0.3 kg)(4.184 kJ/kg·K)(100°C − 20°C) = 100 kJ, so 500 kJ is left to vaporize some of the water. Equation 20-6 gives the amount vaporized as 500 kJ/(2257 kJ/kg) = 221 g, therefore $300 - 221 = 78.7$ g of boiling water (or less than 3 oz) is all that remains.

Problem

67. Describe the composition and temperature of the equilibrium mixture after 1.0 kg of ice at −40°C is added to 1.0 kg of water at 5.0°C.

Solution

Assume that all the heat lost by the water is gained by the ice. The temperature of the water drops and that of the ice rises. If either reaches 0°C, a change of phase occurs, freezing or melting, depending on which reaches 0°C first. The water would lose $mc\Delta T =$ (1 kg)(4.184 kJ/kg·K)(5 K) = 20.9 kJ of heat cooling to 0°C, while the ice would gain (1 kg)(2.05 kJ÷ kg·K)(40 K) = 82.0 kJ of heat warming to 0°C. Evidently, the water reaches 0°C first, and can still lose 334 kJ of heat, more than enough to bring the ice to 0°C, if all of it were to freeze. In fact, only $82.0 - 20.9 = 61.1$ kJ of heat is transferred during the change of phase, therefore only 61.1 kJ/(334 kJ/kg) = 0.183 kg of water freezes. The final mixture is at 0°C and contains 1.183 kg of ice and $1 - 0.183 = 0.818$ kg of water.

Supplementary Problems

Problem

69. How long will it take a 500-W microwave oven to vaporize completely a 500-g block of ice initially at 0°C?

Solution

The reasoning required here is similar to that in the Solutions to Problems 41 or 65: $Q = \mathcal{P}t = m(L_f + c_w(100\ \text{C}°) + L_v)$, or $t = $ 0.5 kg [334 kJ/kg + (4.184 kJ/kg·K)(100 K) + 2257 kJ/kg]/(500 W) = 3.01×10^3 s = 50.2 min.

Problem

71. A solar-heated house (Fig. 20-22) stores energy in 5.0 tons of Glauber salt ($Na_2SO_4\cdot10H_2O$), a substance that melts at 90°F. The heat of fusion of Glauber salt is 104 Btu/lb, and the specific heats of the solid and liquid are, respectively, 0.46 Btu/lb·°F and 0.68 Btu/lb·°F. After a week of sunny weather, the storage medium is all liquid at 95°F. Then a cool, cloudy period sets in during which the house loses heat at an average rate of 20,000 Btu/h. (a) How long is it before the temperature of the storage medium drops below 60°F? (b) How much of this time is spent at 90°F?

Solution

(a) In cooling from 95°F to 60°F (including the solidification at 90°F), the medium exhausts heat $Q = m[c_{\text{liquid}}(95°F − 90°F) + L_f + c_{\text{solid}}(90°F − 60°F)] = 1.21\times10^6$ Btu, where given values of m, the specific heats, and the heat of transformation were substituted. If all this heat were supplied to the house, which loses energy at the average rate of 2×10^4 Btu/h, it would take $(1.21\times10^6/2\times10^4)$ h = 60.6 h for this to occur. (b) The time spent during just the solidification at 90°F is $mL_f/H =$ $(5\times2000$ lb)(104 Btu/lb)/(2×10^4 Btu/h) = 52.0 h.

Problem

73. Show that the coefficient of volume expansion of an ideal gas at constant pressure is just the reciprocal of its kelvin temperature.

Solution

As mentioned in the text following Equation 20-9, β is defined in general as $(dV/V)/dT = (dV/dT)/V$. For an ideal gas at constant pressure, $V = (nR/P)T$, so $dV/dT = nR/P$. Thus, $\beta = nR/PV = 1/T$.

Problem

75. Water's coefficient of volume expansion in the temperature range from 0°C to about 20°C is given approximately by $\beta = a + bT + cT^2$, where T is in Celsius and $a = -6.43 \times 10^{-5}$ °C^{-1}, $b = 1.70 \times 10^{-5}$ °C^{-2}, and $c = -2.02 \times 10^{-7}$ °C^{-3}. Show that water has its greatest density at approximately 4.0°C.

Solution

We do not actually need to differentiate the density or the volume [$\rho(T) = $ const. mass$/V(T)$], since Equation 20-9 shows that $dV/dT = \beta V = 0$ when $\beta(T) = 0$. Thus, the maximum density (or minimum volume) occurs for a temperature satisfying $a + bT + cT^2 = 0$. The quadratic formula gives $T = (-b \pm \sqrt{b^2 - 4ac})/2c$, or since both a and c are negative, $T = (b \mp \sqrt{b^2 - 4|a||c|})/2|c|$. Canceling a factor of 10^{-5} from the given coefficients, we find $T = (1.70 \mp \sqrt{(1.70)^2 - 4(6.43)(0.0202)})$°C$/0.0404 = 3.97$°C. (The other root, 80.2°C, can be discarded because it is outside the range of validity, $0 \le T \le 20$°C, of the original $\beta(T)$.) Thus, the maximum density of water occurs at a temperature close to 4°C. (That this represents a minimum volume can be verified by plotting $V(T)$, or from the second derivative, $d^2V/dT^2 = V(d\beta/dT) + \beta(dV/dT) = V(\beta^2 + d\beta/dT) = V(\beta^2 + b + 2cT) > 0$ for $T = 3.97$°C.)

Problem

77. Ignoring air resistance, find the height from which you must drop an ice cube at 0°C so it melts completely on impact. Assume no heat exchange with the environment.

Solution

The assumptions stated in the problem (no air resistance or heat exchange with the environment) imply that the change in the gravitational potential energy of the ice cube, per unit mass, is equal to the heat of transformation, $mgy = mL_f$, or $y = L_f/g = (334 \text{ kJ/kg})/(9.8 \text{ m/s}^2) = 34.1$ km! (This follows from the conservation of energy, since all of the initial mechanical energy of the ice cube goes into melting it on impact. Of course, the expression for potential energy difference, mgy, is not valid over such a large range, but $mgy \, R_E/(R_E + y)$ only changes this result to 34.3 km.) The thermal energies of ordinary macroscopic objects are very large compared to their mechanical energies.

Problem

79. Prove the relation $\beta = 3\alpha$ by considering a cube of side s and therefore volume $V = s^3$ that undergoes a small temperature change dT and corresponding length and volume changes ds and dV.

Solution

For a cubical volume $V = L^3$, the expansion coefficients are related by:

$$\beta = \frac{1}{V}\frac{dV}{dT} = \frac{1}{V}\frac{dV}{dL}\frac{dL}{dT} = \frac{1}{L^3}(3L^2)\frac{dL}{dT} = 3\frac{1}{L}\frac{dL}{dT} = 3\alpha.$$

(We used Equations 20-9 and 10 in differential form, with L in place of s, and the chain rule for differentiation.) Alternatively, use the binomial approximation for $\Delta V = (L + \Delta L)^3 - L^3 = 3L^2 \Delta L$, keeping only the lowest order term in ΔL. Since $\Delta V = \beta V \Delta T$ and $\Delta L = \alpha L \Delta T$, one finds $3L^2(\alpha L \Delta T) = \beta L^3 \Delta T$, or $\beta = 3\alpha$.

CHAPTER 21   HEAT, WORK, AND THE FIRST LAW OF THERMODYNAMICS

ActivPhysics can help with these problems: Activities 8.5–8.13

Section 21-1:   The First Law of Thermodynamics

Problem

1. In a perfectly insulated container, 1.0 kg of water is stirred vigorously until its temperature rises by 7.0°C. How much work was done on the water?

Solution

Since the container is perfectly insulated thermally, no heat enters or leaves the water in it. Thus, $Q = 0$ in Equation 21-1. The change in the internal energy of the water is determined from its temperature rise, $\Delta U = mc\,\Delta T$ (see comments in Section 19-4 on internal energy), so $W = -\Delta U = -(1\text{ kg})\times$ (4.184 kJ/kg·K)(7 K) = −29.3 kJ. (The negative sign signifies that work was done on the water.)

Problem

3. A 40-W heat source is applied to a gas sample for 25 s, during which time the gas expands and does 750 J of work on its surroundings. By how much does the internal energy of the gas change?

Solution

$Q = 40$ W × 25 s = 1000 J of heat is added to the gas, which does $W = 750$ J of work on its surroundings. Thus, the first law of thermodynamics requires that $\Delta U = Q - W = 1000$ J − 750 J = 250 J (an increase in internal energy).

Problem

5. The most efficient large-scale electric power generating systems use high-temperature gas turbines and a so-called combined cycle system that maximizes the conversion of thermal energy into useful work. One such plant produces electrical energy at the rate of 360 MW, while extracting energy from its natural gas fuel at the rate of 670 MW. (a) At what rate does it reject waste heat to the environment? (b) Find its efficiency, defined as the percent of the total energy extracted from the fuel that ends up as work.

Solution

(a) If we assume that the generating system operates in a cycle and choose it as "the system," then $dU/dt = 0$ and Equation 21-2 implies $dQ/dt = dW/dt$. Here, dW/dt is the rate that the generator supplies energy to its surroundings (360 MW in this problem) and dQ/dt is the net rate of heat flow into the generator from the surroundings. Since the system is just the generator, the net heat flow is the difference between the heat extracted from its fuel and the heat exhausted to the environment, i.e., $dQ/dt = (dQ/dt)_{in} - (dQ/dt)_{out} =$ 670 MW − $(dQ/dt)_{out}$. Therefore, $(dQ/dt)_{out} =$ 670 MW − 360 MW = 310 MW. (Note: If the system is assumed to be the generator and its fuel, as in Example 21-1, then dW/dt is still 360 MW, but the system's internal energy decreases because energy is extracted from the fuel, $dU/dt = -670$ MW, and there is no heat input. Then $dQ/dt = -670$ MW + 360 MW = −310 MW, representing the rate of heat rejected to the environment.) (b) The efficiency is $(dW/dt)/(dQ/dt)_{in} = 360$ MW/670 MW = 53.7% (see Section 22-2).

Problem

7. Water flows over Niagara Falls (height 50 m) at the rate of about 10^6 kg/s. Suppose that all the water passes through a turbine connected to an electric generator producing 400 MW of electric power. If the water has negligible kinetic energy after leaving the turbine, by how much has its temperature increased between the top of the falls and the outlet of the turbine?

Solution

Consider the electric generator to be the system. It operates in a cycle, so its internal energy doesn't change $dU/dt = 0$ (otherwise the generator would store energy). The rate of mechanical energy input to the generator from the gravitational potential energy of falling water is $-(dm/dt)gy = -(10^6\text{ kg/s})\times$ (9.8 m/s²)(50 m) = −490 MW (work done on the generator is negative), while the rate of work produced by the generator is 400 MW. Therefore, the first law of thermodynamics requires a heat flow of $dQ/dt = dW \div dt = -490$ MW $+ 400$ MW $= -90$ MW (negative for heat leaving the generator). This heat is absorbed by the water, causing a temperature rise satisfied by $(dm/dt)c\,\Delta T = 90$ MW. Thus $\Delta T = 90$ MW$\div (10^6$ kg/s)$(4.184$ kJ/kg·k$) = 2.15 \times 10^{-2}$ K ≈ 0.02 C°.

Section 21-2:   Thermodynamic Processes

Problem

9. Repeat the preceding problem for a process that follows the path ACB in Fig. 21-26.

Solution

AC is an isovolumic process, so $W_{AC} = 0$. CB is an isobaric process, so $W_{CB} = P_2(V_2 - V_1) = 2P_1 \times (2V_1 - V_1) = 2P_1V_1$. Of course, $W_{ACB} = W_{AC} + W_{CB}$. (In the PV diagram, Fig. 21-26, the area under AC is zero, and that under CB, a rectangle, is $2P_1V_1$. Equation 21-3 could also be used.)

Problem

11. A balloon contains 0.30 mol of helium. It rises, while maintaining a constant 300 K temperature, to an altitude where its volume has expanded 5 times. How much work is done by the gas in the balloon during this isothermal expansion? Neglect tension forces in the balloon.

Solution

During an isothermal expansion, the work done by a given amount of ideal gas is $W = nRT\ln(V_2/V_1) = (0.3$ mol$)(8.314$ J/mol·K$)(300$ K$)\ln(5) = 1.20$ kJ (see Equation 21-4).

Problem

13. How much work does it take to compress 2.5 mol of an ideal gas to half its original volume while maintaining a constant 300 K temperature?

Solution

In an isothermal compression of a fixed quantity of ideal gas, work is done on the gas so W is negative in Equation 21-4. For the values given, $W = nRT\ln(V_2/V_1) = (25$ mol$)(8.314$ J/mol·K$)(300$ K$)\times \ln(\frac{1}{2}) = -4.32$ kJ.

Problem

15. A 0.25 mol sample of an ideal gas initially occupies 3.5 L. If it takes 61 J of work to compress the gas isothermally to 3.0 L, what is the temperature?

Solution

In an isothermal compression, work is done on the gas, so W in Equation 21-4 is negative. Thus $W = -61$ J $= nRT\ln(V_2/V_1)$, or $T = -61$ J/$(0.25$ mol$)\times (8.314$ J/mol·K$)\ln(3.0/3.5) = 190$ K.

Problem

17. It takes 600 J to compress a gas isothermally to half its original volume. How much work would it take to compress it by a factor of 10 starting from its original volume?

Solution

For isothermal compressions starting from the same volume (and temperature), $W_{13}/W_{12} = \ln(V_3/V_1)\div \ln(V_2/V_1)$ (see Equation 20-4). If $V_2 = V_1/2$, $V_3 = V_1/10$, and $W_{12} = -600$ J, then $W_{13} = (-600$ J$)\times (\ln 10)/(\ln 2) = -1.99$ kJ. [Note: $\ln x = -\ln(1/x)$.]

Problem

19. A gas with $\gamma = 1.4$ is at 100 kPa pressure and occupies 5.00 L. (a) How much work does it take to compress the gas adiabatically to 2.50 L? (b) What is its final pressure?

Solution

The work done by an ideal gas undergoing an adiabatic process is $W_{12} = (P_1V_1 - P_2V_2)/(\gamma - 1)$ (see Equation 21-14). Since the compression is specified by given values of P_1, V_1, and V_2, we first find the final pressure from the adiabatic gas law. (b) $P_2 = P_1(V_1 \div V_2)^\gamma = (100$ kPa$)(5$ L/2.5 L$)^{1.4} = 264$ kPa. (a) Then the work done on the gas (which is $-W_{12}$) is $-W_{12} = (P_2V_2 - P_1V_1)/(\gamma - 1) = [(264$ kPa$)(2.5$ L$) - (100$ kPa$)\times (5$ L$)]/0.4 = 399$ J.

Problem

21. Repeat the preceding problem taking AB to be on an adiabat and using a specific heat ratio of $\gamma = 1.4$.

Solution

(a) If AB represents an adiabatic process for an ideal gas, then the adiabatic law and the given values yield $P_B = P_A(V_A/V_B)^\gamma = (60$ kPa$)(5)^{1.4} = 571$ kPa. (b) The work done by the gas over the adiabat AB is $W_{AB} = (P_AV_A - P_BV_B)/(\gamma - 1) = [(60$ kPa$)(5$ L$) - (571$ kPa$)(1$ L$)]/0.4 = -678$ J (see Equation 21-14). The process BC is isovolumic so $W_{BC} = 0$, and the process CA is isobaric so $W_{CA} = P_A(V_A - V_C) = (60$ kPa$)(5 - 1$ L$) = 240$ J. The total work done by the gas is $W_{ABCA} = W_{AB} + W_{BC} + W_{CA} = -678$ J $+$

$0 + 240$ J $= -438$ J. The work done *on* the gas is the negative of this.

Problem

23. A gasoline engine has a compression ratio of 8.5. If the fuel-air mixture enters the engine at 30°C, what will be its temperature at maximum compression? Assume the compression is adiabatic and that the mixture has $\gamma = 1.4$.

Solution

Equation 21-13b gives $T = T_0(V_0/V)^{\gamma-1}$, where V_0/V is the compression ratio (for T and V at maximum compression.) Thus, $T = (303$ K$)(8.5)^{0.4} = 713$ K $= 440$°C. (Note: T appearing in the gas laws is the absolute temperature.)

Problem

25. By how much must the volume of a gas with $\gamma = 1.4$ be changed in an adiabatic process if the kelvin temperature is to double?

Solution

$V/V_0 = (T_0/T)^{1/(\gamma-1)} = (0.5)^{1/0.4} = 0.177$ (Equation 21-13b).

Problem

27. A gas expands isothermally from state A to state B, in the process absorbing 35 J of heat. It is then compressed isobarically to state C, where its volume equals that of state A. During the compression, 22 J of work are done on the gas. The gas is then heated at constant volume until it returns to state A. (a) Draw a PV diagram for this process. (b) How much work is done on or by the gas during the complete cycle? (c) How much heat is transferred to or from the gas as it goes from B to C to A?

Solution

(a) In the PV diagram shown, AB is an isotherm (given by $PV = $ constant $= P_A V_A = P_B V_B$, with $V_B > V_A$ for an expansion), BC is a straight horizontal line ($P = $ constant $= P_B = P_C$), and CA is a vertical line ($V = $ constant $= V_C = V_A$). (b) $W_{tot} = W_{AB} + W_{BC} + W_{CA}$. The first two terms are given, since for the isotherm, $Q_{AB} = W_{AB} = 35$ J, and $W_{BC} = -22$ J is the work done *by* the gas, while $W_{CA} = 0$ for an isovolumic process. Thus $W_{tot} = 35$ J $- 22$ J $+ 0 = 13$ J, positive for work done by the gas. (c) For the whole cycle, $\Delta U_{tot} = 0$, so $Q_{tot} = W_{tot}$. Since $Q_{tot} = Q_{AB} + Q_{BCA}$, we find that $Q_{BCA} = Q_{tot} - Q_{AB} = $

$W_{tot} - Q_{AB} = 13$ J $- 35$ J $= -22$ J. Negative Q_{BCA} means heat leaves the gas during the process BCA.

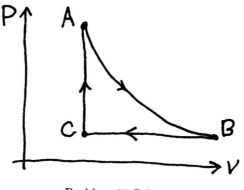

Problem 27 Solution.

Problem

29. A 2.0 mol sample of ideal gas with molar specific heat $C_V = \frac{5}{2}R$ is initially at 300 K and 100 kPa pressure. Determine the final temperature and the work done by the gas when 1.5 kJ of heat is added to the gas (a) isothermally, (b) at constant volume, and (c) isobarically.

Solution

(a) In an isothermal process, T is, of course, constant, so the final temperature is $T_2 = 300$ K. Since $\Delta U = 0$, $W = Q = 1.5$ kJ. (b) In an isovolumic process, $W = 0$ and $Q = nC_V \Delta T$. Therefore, $\Delta T = 1.5$ kJ$/(2$ mol$) \times \frac{5}{2}R = 1.5$ kJ$/(5 \times 8.314$ J/K$) = 36.1$ K, and $T_2 = 300$ K $+ \Delta T = 336$ K. (c) In an isobaric process, $Q = nC_P \Delta T = n(C_V + R) \Delta T = n(\frac{7}{2}R) \Delta T$, so $\Delta T = 2Q/7nR = 2(1.5$ kJ$)/7(2 \times 8.314$ J/K$) = 25.8$ K, and $T_2 = 326$ K. The work done is $W = P \Delta V = nR \Delta T = (R/C_P)Q = (\frac{2}{7})Q = 429$ J. (Refer to the relevant parts of Section 21-2 if necessary.)

Problem

31. An ideal gas with $\gamma = 1.67$ starts at point A in Fig. 21-29, where its volume and pressure are 1.00 m^3 and 250 kPa, respectively. It then undergoes an adiabatic expansion that triples its volume, ending at point B. It's then heated at constant volume to point C, then compressed isothermally back to A. Find (a) the pressure at B, (b) the pressure at C, and (c) the net work done on the gas.

Solution

(a) From the adiabatic law for an ideal gas (Equation 21-13a), $P_B = P_A(V_A/V_B)^\gamma = (250$ kPa$) \times$

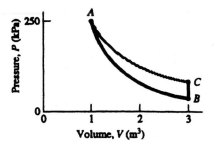

FIGURE 21-29 Problem 31.

$(\frac{1}{3})^{1.67} = 39.9$ kPa. (b) Point C lies on an isotherm with A, so the ideal gas law (Equation 20-2) yields $P_C = P_A V_A / V_C = (250$ kPa$)(\frac{1}{3}) = 83.3$ kPa. (c) $W_{net} = W_{AB} + W_{BC} + W_{CA}$. W_{AB} is for an adiabatic process (Equation 21-14) and equals $(P_A V_A - P_B V_B)/(\gamma - 1) = [(250$ kPa$)(1$ m$^3) - (39.9$ kPa$)(3$ m$^3)]/0.67 = 194$ kJ; W_{BC} is for an isovolumic process and equals zero; W_{CA} is for an isothermal process (Equation 21-4) and equals $nRT_A \ln(V_A/V_C) = P_A V_A \ln(V_A/V_C) = 250$ kJ $\ln(\frac{1}{3}) = -275$ kJ. Thus, $W_{net} = -80.2$ kJ. The work done *on* the gas is the negative of this.

Problem

33. The gas of Example 21-5 starts at state A in Fig. 21-20 and is heated at constant volume until its pressure has doubled. It's then compressed adiabatically until its volume is one-fourth its original value, then cooled at constant volume to 300 K, and finally allowed to expand isothermally to its original state. Find the net work done on the gas.

Solution

The PV diagram for the cyclic process is shown. The work done *on* the gas, $-W_{ABCDA} = W_{ADCBA}$, can be

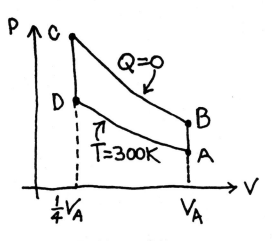

Problem 33 Solution.

calculated from the reversed cycle. AD is isothermal, so $W_{AD} = P_A V_A \ln(V_D/V_A) = (400$ J$)\ln(\frac{1}{4}) = -555$ J. DC and BA are isovolumic, so $W_{DC} = W_{BA} = 0$. CB is adiabatic, so $W_{CB} = (P_C V_C - P_B V_B)/(\gamma - 1)$. Since $V_B = V_A$, $P_B = 2P_A$, and $P_C = P_B(V_B/V_C)^\gamma$, $W_{CB} = P_B V_B[(V_B/V_C)^{\gamma-1} - 1]/(\gamma - 1) = 2P_A V_A \times [(V_A/V_C)^{\gamma-1} - 1]/(\gamma - 1) = 2(400$ J$)(4^{0.4} - 1)/0.4 = 1482$ J. Finally, $W_{ADCBA} = -555$ J $+ 0 + 1482$ J $+ 0 = 928$ J.

Problem

35. A 25 L sample of an ideal gas with $\gamma = 1.67$ is at 250 K and 50 kPa. The gas is compressed adiabatically until its pressure triples, then cooled at constant volume back to 250 K, and finally allowed to expand isothermally to its original state. (a) How much work is done on the gas? (b) What is the minimum volume reached? (c) Sketch this cyclic process in a PV diagram.

Solution

(c) The same individual processes are applied in the same order as in Example 21-5, so the PV diagram looks just like Fig. 21-20, except that $V_A = 25$ L and $P_B = 3P_A = 3(50$ kPa$)$. (b) The minimum volume attained can be found from the adiabatic law (Equation 21-13a): $V_C = V_B = V_A(P_A/P_B)^{1/\gamma} = (25$ L$)(\frac{1}{3})^{1/1.67} = 12.9$ L. (a) The work done *on* the gas is the negative of the work done *by* the gas: $-W_{AB} - W_{BC} - W_{CA} = (P_B V_B - P_A V_A)/(\gamma - 1) - 0 + P_A V_A \ln(V_C/V_A)$, since AB is adiabatic, BC is isovolumic, and CA is isothermal. Numerically, this is $[(150$ kPa$)(12.9$ L$) - (50$ kPa$)(25$ L$)]/0.67 + (50$ kPa$) \times (25$ L$)\ln(12.9/25) = 211$ J. (See Table 21-1 for the individual processes.)

Problem

37. A bicycle pump consists of a cylinder 30 cm long when the pump handle is all the way out. The pump contains air $(\gamma = 1.4)$ at 20°C. If the pump outlet is blocked and the handle pushed until the internal length of the pump cylinder is 17 cm, by how much does the air temperature rise? Assume that no heat is lost.

Solution

If no heat is lost (or gained) by the gas, the compression is adiabatic and Equation 21-13b gives $TV^{\gamma-1} = T_0 V_0^{\gamma-1}$. Therefore, the temperature rise is $T - T_0 = \Delta T = T_0[(V_0/V)^{\gamma-1} - 1]$. Since $V_0/V = (30$ cm$/17$ cm$)$, $\Delta T = [(30/17)^{0.4} - 1](293$ K$) = 74.7$ C°.

Problem

39. A balloon contains 5.0 L of air at 0°C and 100 kPa pressure. How much heat is required to raise the air temperature to 20°C, assuming the gas stays in pressure equilibrium with its surroundings? Neglect tension forces in the balloon. The molar specific heat of air at constant volume is $2.5R$.

Solution

The heat required, at constant pressure, is $Q = nC_P \Delta T$, where $C_P = C_V + R = 3.5R$ is the molar specific heat of air at constant pressure. The number of moles can be found from the ideal gas law and the initial conditions, $n = P_1 V_1 / RT_1$. Therefore: $Q = nC_P \Delta T = (P_1 V_1 / RT_1)(3.5R)(T_2 - T_1) = 3.5 P_1 V_1 (T_2 - T_1)/T_1 = 3.5(100 \text{ kPa})(5 \text{ L})(20 \text{ C}°)/(273 \text{ K}) = 128 \text{ J}$. (The difference in Q between this isobaric process and the isovolumic process described in Problem 21-38 is just a factor of $C_P/C_V = \frac{7}{5}$.)

Problem

41. Problem 70 in Chapter 18 shows that pressure as a function of height in Earth's atmosphere is given approximately by $P = P_0 e^{-h/h_0}$, where P_0 is the surface pressure and $h_0 = 8.2$ km. A parcel of air, initially at the surface and at a temperature of 10°C, rises as described in Application: Smog Alert on page 529. (a) What will be its temperature when it reaches 2.0 km altitude? (b) If the temperature of the surrounding air decreases at the normal lapse rate of 6.5°C/km, is the atmosphere stable or unstable under the conditions of this problem?

Solution

(a) For an adiabatic expansion of the air parcel, the pressure and temperature are related to their surface values by $PT^{\gamma/(1-\gamma)} = P_0 T_0^{\gamma/(1-\gamma)}$ (see Problem 28). At a height of 2 km, where $P = P_0 e^{-2.0/8.2}$, and with $\gamma = \frac{7}{5}$ for air, $T = T_0 (P/P_0)^{(\gamma-1)/\gamma} = (283 \text{ K}) \times (e^{-2.0/8.2})^{2/7} = 264 \text{ K} = -9.05°C$. (b) The temperature of the parcel of air drops about 19°C in 2 km, faster than the environmental lapse rate (13°C in 2 km), indicating stable atmospheric conditions.

Section 21-3: Specific Heats of an Ideal Gas

Problem

43. A mixture of monatomic and diatomic gases has specific heat ratio $\gamma = 1.52$. What fraction of the molecules are monatomic?

Solution

The internal energy of a mixture of two ideal gases is $U = f_1 N \bar{E}_1 + f_2 N \bar{E}_2$, where f_1 is the fraction of the total number of molecules, N, of type 1, and $\bar{E}_1$ is the average energy of a molecule of type 1, etc. Classically, $\bar{E} = g(\frac{1}{2}kT)$, where g is the number of degrees of freedom. The molar specific heat at constant volume is $C_V = (\frac{1}{n})(dU/dT) = (N_A/N)d/dT \times (f_1 N g_1 \frac{1}{2}kT + f_2 N g_2 \frac{1}{2}kT) = \frac{1}{2}R(f_1 g_1 + f_2 g_2)$. Suppose that the temperature range is such that $g_1 = 3$ for the monatomic gas, and $g_2 = 5$ for the diatomic gas, as discussed in Section 21-3. Then $C_V = R(1.5f_1 + 2.5f_2) = R(2.5 - f_1)$, where $f_2 = 1 - f_1$ since the sum of the fractions of the mixture is one. Now, C_V can also be specified by the ratio $\gamma = C_P/C_V = 1 + R/C_V$, or $C_V = R/(\gamma - 1)$, so in this problem, $2.5 - f_1 = 1/0.52$, or $f_1 = 57.7\%$.

Problem

45. A gas mixture contains monatomic argon and diatomic oxygen. An adiabatic expansion that doubles its volume results in the pressure dropping to one-third of its original value. What fraction of the molecules are argon?

Solution

From the pressures and volumes in the described adiabatic expansion, $P_0 V_0^\gamma = (\frac{1}{3}P_0)(2V_0)^\gamma$, we can calculate that $\gamma = \ln 3 / \ln 2 = 1.58$. Then the result of Problem 43 gives $2.5 - f_{Ar} = 1/0.58$, or $f_{Ar} = 79.0\%$.

Problem

47. How much of a triatomic gas with $C_V = 3R$ would you have to add to 10 mol of monatomic gas to get a mixture whose thermodynamic behavior was like that of a diatomic gas?

Solution

Reference to the solution of Problem 43 shows that the specific heat of a mixture of two gases is $C_V = f_1 C_{V_1} + f_2 C_{V_2}$, where the f's are the number fractions of the gases. If gas 1 is monatomic ($C_V = \frac{3}{2}R$), gas 2 is triatomic (with $C_V = 3R$, as described in the text following Example 21-6), and we wish the mixture to have $C_V = \frac{5}{2}R$ appropriate to a diatomic gas, then $\frac{5}{2}R = \frac{3}{2}Rf_1 + 3Rf_2$, or $5 = 3f_1 + 6f_2$. Since $f_1 + f_2 = 1$, one finds $f_1 = \frac{1}{3}$ and $f_2 = \frac{2}{3}$. With 10 mol of gas 1, one needs 20 mol of gas 2.

Paired Problems

Problem

49. A 5.0 mol sample of ideal gas with $C_V = \frac{5}{2}R$ undergoes an expansion during which the gas does

5.1 kJ of work. If it absorbs 2.7 kJ of heat during the process, by how much does its temperature change? *Hint:* Remember that Equation 21-7 holds for *any* ideal gas process.

Solution

For any process connecting equilibrium states of an ideal gas, Equations 21-1 and 7 give $\Delta U = Q - W = nC_V \, \Delta T$, so $\Delta T = (2.7 \text{ kJ} - 5.1 \text{ kJ})/(5 \text{ mol})(\frac{5}{2} \times 8.314 \text{ J/mol·K}) = -23.1 \text{ K}$.

Problem

51. A gas with $\gamma = \frac{5}{3}$ is at 450 K at the start of an expansion that triples its volume. The expansion is isothermal until the volume has doubled, then adiabatic the rest of the way. What is the final gas temperature?

Solution

For the isothermal part of the expansion, the temperature is constant at 450 K. The adiabatic part goes from $V_1 = 2V_0$ to $V_2 = 3V_0$, so Equation 21-13b gives $T_2 = T_1(V_1/V_2)^{\gamma-1} = (450 \text{ K})(\frac{2}{3})^{(5/3)-1} = 343 \text{ K}$.

Problem

53. An ideal gas with $\gamma = 1.4$ is initially at 273 K and 100 kPa. The gas expands adiabatically until its temperature drops to 190 K. What is its final pressure?

Solution

The ideal gas law can be used to eliminate V and write the adiabatic law in terms of P and T: $PV^\gamma = P^{1-\gamma}(PV)^\gamma = P^{1-\gamma}(nRT)^\gamma$, thus $P^{1-\gamma}T^\gamma$ is constant, or so is $PT^{\gamma/(1-\gamma)}$. For this problem, $P = P_0(T_0 \div T)^{\gamma/(1-\gamma)} = (100 \text{ kPa})(273/190)^{-1.4/0.4} = 28.1 \text{ kPa}$.

Problem

55. The curved path in Fig. 21-30 lies on the 350-K isotherm for an ideal gas with $\gamma = 1.4$.
(a) Calculate the net work done on the gas as it goes around the cyclic path *ABCA*. (b) How much heat flows into or out of the gas on the segment *AB*?

Solution

(a) The work done *by* the gas in each segment of the cycle is summarized in Table 21-1. $-W_{AB} = 0$

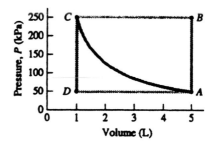

FIGURE 21-30 Problems 55 and 56.

(isovolumic), $-W_{BC} = P_B(V_B - V_C) = (250 \text{ kPa}) \times (5 \text{ L} - 1 \text{ L}) = 1000 \text{ J}$ (isobaric), $-W_{CA} = nRT_A \times \ln(V_C/V_A) = P_A V_A \ln(V_C/V_A) = (50 \text{ kPa})(5 \text{ L}) \ln(\frac{1}{5}) = -402 \text{ J}$ (isothermal). The net work done *on* the gas is $-W_{ABCA} = 0 + 1000 \text{ J} - 402 \text{ J} = 598 \text{ J}$. (b) Since V is constant, $Q_{AB} = nC_V \, \Delta T = nR(T_B - T_A)/(\gamma - 1) = (P_B V_B - P_A V_A)/(\gamma - 1) = (250 \text{ kPa} - 50 \text{ kPa})(5 \text{ L}) \div 0.4 = 2.50 \text{ kJ}$, positive for heat transferred into the gas (at constant volume, the gas must be heated in order to raise its pressure). (Note: Recall that $C_V = R/(\gamma - 1)$, as shown in the solution to Problem 43.)

Supplementary Problems
Problem

57. An 8.5-kg rock at 0°C is dropped into a well-insulated vat containing a mixture of ice and water at 0°C. When equilibrium is reached there are 6.3 g less ice. From what height was the rock dropped?

Solution

The mechanical energy of the rock (originally gravitational potential energy) melted the ice (changed its internal energy) and no heat energy was transferred ($Q = 0$). Therefore, $-W = m_{\text{rock}}gh = \Delta U = m_{\text{ice}}L_f$, or $h = m_{\text{ice}}L_f/m_{\text{rock}}g = (6.3 \text{ g})(334 \text{ J/g})/(8.5 \times 9.8 \text{ N}) = 25.3 \text{ m}$. ($W < 0$ since the rock did work on the ice-water system.)

Problem

59. Repeat Problem 8 for the case when the gas expands along a path given by $P = P_1 \left[1 + \left(\frac{V - V_1}{V_1}\right)^2\right]$. Sketch the path in the PV diagram, and determine the work done.

Solution

The path is a parabola in the PV plane, with vertex at point (V_1, P_1) and opening upwards. The work done is the area under the path between (V_1, P_1) and

$(V_2 = 2V_1, P_2 = 2P_1)$:

$$W = \int_1^2 P \, dV = \int_{V_1}^{V_2} P_1 \left[1 + \left(\frac{V - V_1}{V_1} \right)^2 \right] dV$$

$$= P_1 \left| V + \frac{V_1}{3} \left(\frac{V - V_1}{V_1} \right)^3 \right|_{V_1}^{V_2}$$

$$= P_1 \left[(V_2 - V_1) + \frac{V_1}{3} \left(\frac{V_2 - V_1}{V_1} \right)^3 \right] = \frac{4}{3} P_1 V_1.$$

Problem

61. Show that the application of Equation 21-3 to an adiabatic process results in Equation 21-14.

Solution

The work done by an ideal gas undergoing an adiabatic process from state 1 to state 2 can be found by integration of the adiabatic law, $P = P_1 V_1^\gamma / V^\gamma$.

$$W_{12} = \int_{V_1}^{V_2} P \, dV = \int_{V_1}^{V_2} (P_1 V_1^\gamma) \frac{dV}{V^\gamma}$$

$$= P_1 V_1^\gamma \left(\frac{V_2^{-\gamma+1} - V_1^{-\gamma+1}}{-\gamma + 1} \right)$$

$$= (P_1 V_1^\gamma V_1^{-\gamma+1} - P_2 V_2^\gamma V_2^{-\gamma+1}) / (\gamma - 1),$$

which is Equation 21-14. (Note: $P_1 V_1^\gamma = P_2 V_2^\gamma$.)

Problem

63. An ideal gas is taken clockwise around the circular path shown in Fig. 21-31. (a) How much work does the gas do? (b) If there are 1.3 moles of gas, what is the maximum temperature reached?

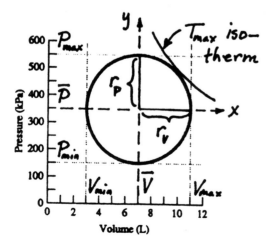

FIGURE 21-31 Problem 63 Solution.

Solution

(a) The circular path is most easily described by dimensionless variables:

$$x = (V - \bar{V})/r_V, \quad \text{and} \quad y = (P - \bar{P})/r_P,$$

where $\bar{V} = \frac{1}{2}(V_{\min} + V_{\max})$ and $\bar{P} = \frac{1}{2}(P_{\min} + P_{\max})$, and $r_V = \frac{1}{2}(V_{\max} - V_{\min})$ and $r_P = \frac{1}{2}(P_{\max} - P_{\min})$. (The "center" of the circle is $(\bar{V}, \bar{P})$, and the "radius," in volume and pressure units, is r_V or r_P, respectively.) Therefore, $x^2 + y^2 = 1$ for the path.

The work done in one clockwise cycle is (see Equations 8-1 or 22-7)

$$W = \oint P \, dV = \oint (r_P y + \bar{P}) r_V \, dx$$

$$= r_P r_V \oint y \, dx + r_V \bar{P} \oint dx.$$

The first integral is the area of the unit circle, $x^2 + y^2 = 1$, which is π, and the second integral is zero. Therefore, $W = r_P r_V \pi = \frac{1}{4} \pi (P_{\max} - P_{\min})(V_{\max} - V_{\min}) = \frac{1}{4} \pi (550 - 150) \text{ kPa} (11 - 3) \text{ L} = 2.51 \text{ kJ}$. (For those unfamiliar with integrals over closed paths, they are the difference between the integrals over the upper and lower parts, as explained in Fig. 21-19. In this case, $\oint y \, dx = \int_{-1}^1 y_+(x) \, dx - \int_{-1}^1 y_-(x) \, dx$, where $y_\pm(x) = \pm \sqrt{1 - x^2}$ are the upper and lower semicircles. Then $\oint y \, dx = 2 \int_{-1}^1 \sqrt{1 - x^2} \, dx = \pi$. The integral of a constant over a closed path is zero, since the upper and lower parts are the same. Then $\oint dx = \int_{-1}^1 dx - \int_{-1}^1 dx = 0$.)

(b) The maximum temperature reached is that of the isotherm ($PV = \text{constant}$) which is tangent to the upper semicircle in the PV diagram. In terms of the dimensionless variables, the equation of an isotherm is $xy + (\bar{P}/r_P)x + (\bar{V}/r_V)y = \text{constant}$, where $y = y_+(x) = \sqrt{1 - x^2}$ on the upper semicircle. For the particular numerical values given, $(\bar{P}/r_P = \bar{V}/r_V = \frac{7}{4})$, the equation simplifies to $xy + \frac{7}{4}(x + y) = \text{constant}$. The condition for a maximum is:

$$0 = \frac{d}{dx} \left[xy + \frac{7}{4}(x + y) \right] = y - \frac{x^2}{y} + \frac{7}{4} \left(1 - \frac{x}{y} \right)$$

$$= \left(1 - \frac{x}{y} \right) \left(x + y + \frac{7}{4} \right),$$

where we used $dy/dx = d(\sqrt{1 - x^2})/dx = -x \div \sqrt{1 - x^2} = -x/y$. The second factor, $x + y + \frac{7}{4}$, is never zero on the unit circle, so the maximum occurs for $1 - x/y = 0$, or $x_m = y_m = \sqrt{1 - x_m^2} = 1/\sqrt{2}$. The corresponding values of volume and pressure are:

$$V_m = r_V x_m + \bar{V} = \frac{1}{\sqrt{2}} \left(\frac{11 - 3}{2} \right) \text{L} + \left(\frac{11 + 3}{2} \right) \text{L}$$

$$= 9.83 \text{ L},$$

and

$$P_m = r_P y_m + \bar{P}$$
$$= \frac{1}{\sqrt{2}}\left(\frac{550 - 150}{2}\right)\text{kPa} + \left(\frac{550 + 150}{2}\right)\text{kPa}$$
$$= 491 \text{ kPa}.$$

The maximum temperature follows from the ideal gas law:

$$T_m = \frac{P_m V_m}{nR} = \frac{(491 \text{ kPa})(9.83 \text{ L})}{1.3(8.314 \text{ J/K})} = 447 \text{ K}.$$

Problem

65. Show that the work done by a van der Waals gas undergoing isothermal expansion from volume V_1 to V_2 is

$$W = nRT \ln\left(\frac{V_2 - nb}{V_1 - nb}\right) + an^2\left(\frac{1}{V_2} - \frac{1}{V_1}\right),$$

where a and b are the constants in Equation 20-5.

Solution

If we solve for P in the van der Waals equation of state, Equation 20-5, and substitute into Equation 21-3, we find

$$W = \int_{V_1}^{V_2} P \, dV = \int_{V_1}^{V_2}\left[\frac{nRT}{(V - nb)} - \frac{n^2 a}{V}\right] dV$$
$$= nRT \int_{V_1}^{V_2} \frac{dV}{V - nb} - n^2 a \int_{V_1}^{V_2} \frac{dV}{V^2}$$
$$= nRT \ln\left(\frac{V_2 - nb}{V_1 - nb}\right) + an^2\left(\frac{1}{V_2} - \frac{1}{V_1}\right),$$

where, for an isothermal process, T is a constant and can be taken out of the integral.

Problem

67. A horizontal piston-cylinder system containing n mol of ideal gas is surrounded by air at temperature T_0 and pressure P_0. If the piston is displaced slightly from equilibrium, show that it executes simple harmonic motion with angular frequency $\omega = AP_0/\sqrt{MnRT_0}$, where A and M are the piston area and mass, respectively. Assume the gas temperature remains constant.

Solution

Since the piston-cylinder system is horizontal, we do not need to consider the force of gravity on the piston. At equilibrium, the pressure forces from inside and outside the piston are equal, so the gas pressure at the equilibrium position of the piston is P_0. We also assume that the gas temperature at equilibrium is T_0,

so $P_0 V_0 = nRT_0$, where $V_0 = Ax_0$ is the volume at equilibrium. When the piston is displaced from its equilibrium position by an amount Δx (positive to the right), the horizontal force on it is $PA - P_0 A$, and Newton's second law gives an acceleration of $d^2(\Delta x) \div dt^2 = (P - P_0)A/M$.

For isothermal expansions and compressions of the gas, $PV = P_0 V_0 = PA(x_0 + \Delta x) = P_0 Ax_0$, or $P/P_0 = (1 + \Delta x/x_0)^{-1}$. For small displacements ($\Delta x \ll x_0$), $P/P_0 \approx 1 - \Delta x/x_0$ (see the binomial approximation in Appendix A), so $d^2(\Delta x)/dt^2 = (P_0 A/M)[(P/P_0) - 1] \approx -(P_0 A/Mx_0)\,\Delta x$. This is the equation for simple harmonic motion of the piston, about its equilibrium position x_0, with angular frequency $\omega^2 = P_0 A/Mx_0$. Since $P_0 V_0 = P_0 Ax_0 = nRT_0$, we may eliminate x_0 to obtain $\omega = P_0 A/\sqrt{MnRT_0}$.

(Note: In order for the gas temperature to remain constant, as assumed above, heat must flow into and out of the gas. This requires time, so the motion of the piston must be very slow. If the motion is rapid (or if the cylinder is thermally insulated), there is no time for heat transfer in the gas and the expansions and compressions are adiabatic. In this case, $PV^\gamma = P_0 V_0^\gamma = PA^\gamma(x_0 + \Delta x)^\gamma = P_0 A^\gamma x_0^\gamma$, or $P/P_0 = (1 + \Delta x/x_0)^{-\gamma}$. For $\Delta x \ll x_0, d^2(\Delta x)/dt^2 = (P_0 A/M)\times [(P/P_0) - 1] \approx (P_0 A/M)[1 - \gamma \Delta x/x_0 + \cdots - 1] = -\gamma P_0 A \, \Delta x/M$. (This represents simple harmonic motion with $\omega = \sqrt{\gamma P_0 A/Mx_0} = P_0 A\sqrt{\gamma/MnRT_0}$.)

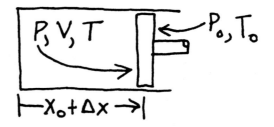

Problem 67 Solution.

Problem

69. A cylinder of cross-sectional area A is closed by a massless piston. The cylinder contains n mol of ideal gas with specific heat ratio γ, and is initially in equilibrium with the surrounding air at temperature T_0 and pressure P_0. The piston is initially at height h_1 above the bottom of the cylinder. Sand is gradually sprinkled onto the piston until it has moved downward to a final height h_2. Find the total mass of the sand if the process is (a) isothermal and (b) adiabatic.

Solution

Initially, $P_1 = P_0$ (since the piston is massless) and $T_1 = T_0$. Finally, in equilibrium with its load of sand, M, the net force on the piston is zero, or $P_2 A = Mg + P_0 A$. Therefore, $M = (P_2 - P_0)A/g$. (a) In an isothermal process, $T_2 = T_1 = T_0$, and $P_2 V_2 = P_1 V_1$. Therefore, $P_2 - P_1 = P_1[(V_1/V_2) - 1] = P_0[(h_1/h_2) - 1]$, and $M = (P_0 A/g)[(h_1/h_2) - 1]$. (b) In an adiabatic process, $P_2 V_2^\gamma = P_1 V_1^\gamma$, or $P_2 - P_1 = P_1[(V_1/V_2)^\gamma - 1]$. Thus $M = (P_0 A/g)[(h_1/h_2)^\gamma - 1]$. (Note: the given data are related by the ideal gas law, $P_0 A h_1 = nRT_0$.)

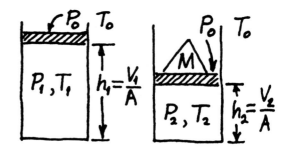

Problem 69 Solution.

CHAPTER 22   THE SECOND LAW OF THERMODYNAMICS

ActivPhysics can help with these problems: Activity 8.14.

Section 22-1:   Reversibility and Irreversibility

Problem

1. The egg carton shown in Fig. 22-27 has places for one dozen eggs. (a) How many distinct ways are there to arrange six eggs in the carton? (b) Of these, what fraction correspond to all six eggs being in the left half of the carton? Treat the eggs as distinguishable, so an interchange of two eggs gives rise to a new state.

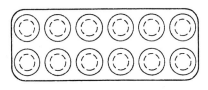

FIGURE 22-27 Problem 1.

Solution

(a) There are twelve places for first egg, eleven for the second, etc., so the number of arrangements (states) of six distinguishable eggs into twelve places is $12{\times}11{\times}10{\times}9{\times}8{\times}7 = 12!/6! \approx 6.65{\times}10^5$. (b) If limited to the left side of the carton only, there are 6! arrangements, so the fraction is $6!/(12!/6!) = 1/924$.

Problem

3. Estimate the energy that could be extracted by cooling the world's oceans by 1°C. How does your estimate compare with humanity's yearly energy consumption of about $2.5{\times}10^{20}$ J?

Solution

The volume of the oceans is about $1.35{\times}10^{18}$ m^3 (the average depth is 3.73 km over 71% of the earth's surface). The heat extracted by cooling this volume of water by 1°C is $Q = \rho V c\,\Delta T = (10^3$ kg/m$^3){\times}$ $(1.35 \times 10^{18}$ m$^3)(4184$ J/kg·K)(1 K) $\simeq 5.65{\times}10^{24}$ J, or about 23,000 times the world's annual energy consumption.

Sections 22-2 and 22-3:   The Second Law and its Applications

Problem

5. What are the efficiencies of reversible heat engines operating between (a) the normal freezing and boiling points of water, (b) the 25°C temperature at the surface of a tropical ocean and deep water at 4°C, and (c) a 1000°C candle flame and room temperature?

Solution

The efficiency of a reversible engine, operating between two absolute temperatures, $T_h > T_c$, is given by Equation 22-3. (a) $e = 1 - T_c/T_h = 1 - 273/373 = 26.8\%$. (b) $e = (T_h - T_c)/T_h = \Delta T/T_h = 21/298 = 7.05\%$. (c) With room temperature at $T_c = 20$°C, $e = 980/1273 = 77.0\%$.

Problem

7. A reversible Carnot engine operating between helium's melting point and its 4.25-K boiling point has efficiency of 77.7%. What is the melting point?

Solution

We can solve Equation 22-3 for the low temperature to find $T_c = (1 - e)T_h = (1 - 0.777)(4.25$ K) $= 0.948$ K.

Problem

9. The maximum temperature in a nuclear power plant is 570 K. The plant rejects heat to a river where the temperature is 0°C in the winter and 25°C in the summer. What are the maximum possible efficiencies for the plant in these seasons? Why might the plant not achieve these efficiencies?

Solution

The winter and summer thermodynamic efficiencies are $1 - (T_c/T_h)$, or $1 - (273/570) = 52.1\%$ and $1 - (298/570) = 47.7\%$, respectively. As explained in Section 22-3, irreversible processes, transmission losses, etc., make actual efficiencies less than the theoretical maxima.

Problem

11. A power plant's electrical output is 750 MW. Cooling water at 15°C flows through the plant at 2.8×10^4 kg/s, and its temperature rises by 8.5°C. Assuming the plant's only energy loss is to the cooling water and that the cooling water is effectively the low-temperature reservoir, find (a) the rate of energy extraction from the fuel, (b) the plant's efficiency, and (c) its highest temperature.

Solution

(a) In order to raise the temperature of the cooling water by 8.5 K, heat must be exhausted to it at a rate of $c(dm/dt) \Delta T = (4.184$ kJ/kg·K$)(2.8 \times 10^4$ kg/s$) \times$ (8.5 K) = 996 MW (see Equation 19-4). If this is also all the heat rejected by the power plant, dQ_c/dt, then since the work output, dW/dt, is given, the heat input to the plant (extracted from its fuel) is $dQ_h/dt = dQ_c/dt + dW/dt =$ 996 MW + 750 MW = 1.75 GW. (b) The plant's actual efficiency (from the definition of efficiency in terms of rates) is $e = (dW/dt)/(dQ_h/dt) =$ 750 MW/1.75 GW = 43.0%. (c) If the power plant is considered to operate like an ideal Carnot engine, then $T_h/T_c = Q_h/Q_c = (dQ_h/dt)/(dQ_c/dt) = 1.75$ GW $\div$ 996 MW = 1.75 (the energy rate per cycle and the energy rate per second are proportional). If $T_c =$ 15°C = 288 K, then $T_h = 1.75(288$ K$) = 505$ K = 232°C. The actual highest temperature would be somewhat greater than this, because the actual efficiency is always less than the Carnot efficiency.

Problem

13. The electric power output of all the thermal electric power plants in the United States is about 2×10^{11} W, and these plants operate at an average efficiency around 33%. What is the rate at which all these plants use cooling water, assuming an average 5°C rise in cooling-water temperature? Compare with the 1.8×10^7 kg/s average flow at the mouth of the Mississippi River.

Solution

The total rate at which heat is exhausted by all power plants is

$$\frac{dQ_c}{dt} = \frac{d}{dt}(Q_h - W) = \frac{dW}{dt}\left(\frac{1}{e} - 1\right)$$

$$= (2 \times 10^{11} \text{ W})\left(\frac{1}{33\%} - 1\right) = 4 \times 10^{11} \text{ W}.$$

The mass rate of flow at which water could absorb this amount of energy, with only a 5°C temperature rise, is

given by:

$$\frac{dQ_c}{dt} = \frac{dm}{dt} c_{\text{water}} \Delta T, \quad \text{or}$$

$$\frac{dm}{dt} = \frac{4 \times 10^{11} \text{ W}}{(4184 \text{ J/kg·K})(5°C)} = 1.91 \times 10^7 \text{ kg/s},$$

or about 1 Mississippi (a self-explanatory unit of river flow).

Problem

15. A Carnot engine absorbs 900 J of heat each cycle and provides 350 J of work. (a) What is its efficiency? (b) How much heat is rejected each cycle? (c) If the engine rejects heat at 10°C, what is its maximum temperature?

Solution

(a) The efficiency of the engine (by definition) is $e = W/Q_h = 350$ J/900 J = 38.9%, where W and Q_h are the work done and heat absorbed per cycle. (b) These are related to the heat rejected per cycle by the first law of thermodynamics (since ΔU per cycle is zero), or $Q_c = Q_h - W = 900$ J $- 350$ J $= 550$ J. (c) For a Carnot engine operating between two temperatures, $T_h/T_c = Q_h/Q_c$, so $T_h = (283$ K$) \times$ (900/550) = 463 K = 190°C. (Carnot's theorem applies to the ratio of absolute temperatures.)

Problem

17. How much work does a refrigerator with a COP of 4.2 require to freeze 670 g of water already at its freezing point?

Solution

The amount of heat that must be extracted in order to freeze the water is $Q_c = mL_f = (0.67$ kg$) \times$ (334 kJ/kg) = 224 kJ. The work consumed by the refrigerator while extracting this heat is $W = Q_c/\text{COP} = 224$ kJ/4.2 = 53.3 kJ. (See Equation 22-4.)

Problem

19. A 4.0 L sample of water at 9.0°C is put into a refrigerator. The refrigerator's 130-W motor then runs for 4.0 min to cool the water to the refrigerator's low temperature of 1.0°C. (a) What is the COP of the refrigerator? (b) How does this compare with the maximum possible COP if the refrigerator exhausts heat at 25°C?

Solution

(a) The heat extracted from the water is $Q_c = mc \Delta T = \rho V c \Delta T = (10^3$ kg/m$^3)(4 \times 10^{-3}$ m$^3) \times$ (4.184 kJ/kg·K)(9°C $- 1$°C) = 134 kJ, while the work input is $W = \mathcal{P}t = (130 \text{ W})(4 \times 60 \text{ s}) = 31.2$ kJ. Therefore, the actual COP is (Equation 22-4) $Q_c/W = 134/31.2 = 4.29$. (b) This is about 38% of the maximum possible COP for a reversible refrigerator operating between $T_c = 274$ K (1°C) and $T_h = 298$ K (25°C), which is $T_c/(T_h - T_c) = 274/24 = 11.4$ (Equation 22-5).

Problem

21. A heat pump consumes electrical energy at the rate P_e. Show that it delivers heat at the rate $(\text{COP} + 1)P_e$.

Solution

For each cycle of operation of the heat pump, $Q_h = Q_c + W$ and $\text{COP} = Q_c/W = (Q_h/W) - 1$. Therefore, $Q_h = (1 + \text{COP})W$, which if written in terms of rates, is the relation stated in the question.

Problem

23. A heat pump transfers heat between the interior of a house and the outside air. In the summer the outside air averages 26°C, and the pump operates by chilling water to 5°C for circulation throughout the house. In winter the outside air averages 2°C, and the pump operates by heating water to 80°C for circulation throughout the house. (a) Find the coefficients of performance in summer and winter. How much work does the pump require (b) for each joule of heat removed from the house in summer and (c) for each joule supplied to the house in winter?

Solution

(a) If the heat pump is reversible, the summertime COP is $T_c/(T_h - T_c) = (273 + 5)/(26 - 5) = 13.2$, and the winter-time COP is $275/78 = 3.53$. (See Equation 22-5; if the heat pump is not reversible, then its COP cannot be found from just the hot and cold operating temperatures.) From the definition of COP and the first law, $W = Q_c/\text{COP} = Q_h/(1 + \text{COP})$. Therefore, (b) for each joule of heat removed in the summer, $W = 1 \text{ J}/13.2 = 7.55 \times 10^{-2}$ J is required, while (c) for each joule of heat supplied in the winter, $W = 1 \text{ J}/(1 + 3.53) = 0.221$ J is required.

Problem

25. A 0.20-mol sample of an ideal gas goes through the Carnot cycle of Fig. 22-29. Calculate (a) the heat Q_h absorbed, (b) the heat Q_c rejected, and (c) the work done. (d) Use these quantities to determine efficiency. (e) Find the maximum and minimum temperatures, and show explicitly that

the efficiency as defined in Equation 22-1 is equal to the Carnot efficiency of Equation 22-3.

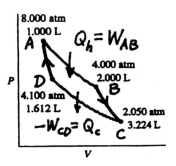

FIGURE 22-29 Problem 25 (Diagram is not to scale).

Solution

From the discussion of the efficiency of a Carnot engine in Section 22-2, (a) $Q_h = nRT_A \ln(V_B/V_A) = P_A V_A \ln(V_B/V_A) = (8)(1)(101.3 \text{ J})\ln 2 = 561.7$ J, and (b) $Q_c = P_C V_C \ln(V_C/V_D) = (2.050)(3.224) \times (101.3 \text{ J})\ln(3.224/1.612) = 464.1$ J (we used 101.3 for the conversion factor of L·atm to J). (c) The work done in one cycle (from the first law) is $W = Q_h - Q_c = 97.66$ J, resulting in an efficiency of (d) $e = W/Q_h = 0.1739$. (Note: For the Carnot cycle, $T_A = T_B$ and $T_C = T_D$, so for the adiabatic segments, $W_{BC} + W_{DA} = 0$. Thus, $W = W_{AB} + W_{BC} + W_{CD} + W_{DA} = Q_h - Q_c$, explicitly.) We find the maximum and minimum temperatures from the ideal gas law:

$$T_A = P_A V_A/nR$$
$$= (8)(1)(101.3 \text{ J})/(0.2)(8.314 \text{ J/K}) = 487.4 \text{ K},$$

and

$$T_C = (2.050)(3.224)(101.3 \text{ J})/(0.2)(8.314 \text{ J/K})$$
$$= 402.6 \text{ K}.$$

These imply a Carnot efficiency of $e = 1 - T_C/T_A = 0.1739$, exactly as before. Equations 22-1 and 22-3 are identical because $Q_c/Q_h = T_C/T_A = 0.8261$, explicitly. (We did not round off until after completing all the calculations, and we labeled the states as in Fig. 22-6.)

Problem

27. Use appropriate energy flow diagrams to show that the existence of a perfect heat engine would permit the construction of a perfect refrigerator, thus violating the Clausius statement of the second law.

Solution

If it were possible to construct a perfect heat engine (one which would extract heat and perform an equivalent amount of work), then it could be coupled to a real refrigerator in such a way that the work output of the engine equals the work input to the refrigerator, as shown. The net effect of this arrangement is to produce a perfect refrigerator (a cyclic device whose sole effect is the transfer of heat, $Q_c + Q_h - Q_c = Q_h$, from a cold reservoir to a hot one), in violation of the Clausius statement of the second law. This completes the proof of the equivalence of the Kelvin-Planck and Clausius statements in Section 22-2.

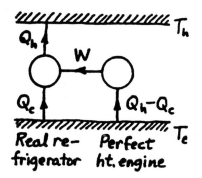

Problem 27 Solution.

Section 22-4: The Thermodynamic Temperature Scale

Problem

29. A Carnot engine operating between a vat of boiling sulfur and a bath of water at its triple point has an efficiency of 61.95%. What is the boiling point of sulfur?

Solution

From the efficiency of a reversible engine, $e = 1 - T_c \div T_h$, and the triple point temperature 273.16 K, we find $T_h = T_c/(1 - e) = 273.16 \text{ K}/(1 - 61.95\%) = 718 \text{ K}$ (in agreement with Table 20-1, to three-figure accuracy).

Problem

31. Calculate the entropy change associated with melting 1.0 kg of ice at 0°C.

Solution

Since the temperature is constant during a change of phase, Equation 22-8 gives $\Delta S = \Delta Q/T = mL_f/T = (1 \text{ kg})(334 \text{ kJ/kg})/273 \text{ K} = 1.22 \text{ kJ/K}$.

Problem

33. A 2.0-kg sample of water is heated to 35°C. If the entropy change is 740 J/K, what was the initial temperature?

Solution

Since the specific heat of water is approximately constant under normal conditions and no phase changes occur, Equation 22-9 can be solved for T_1 to yield $T_1 = T_2 e^{-\Delta S/mc} = (308 \text{ K})\exp\{-(740 \text{ J/K}) \div (2 \text{ kg})(4.184 \text{ kJ/kg·K})\} = 282 \text{ K} = 8.93°\text{C}$.

Problem

35. A shallow pond contains 94,000 kg of water. In winter it's entirely frozen. By how much does the entropy of the pond increase when the ice, already at 0°C, melts and then heats to its summer temperature of 15°C?

Solution

During the melting at $T_1 = 0°\text{C}$, $\Delta S_1 = \Delta Q/T_1 = mL_f/T_1$, and during the warming to $T_2 = 15°\text{C}$, $\Delta S_2 = mc \ln(T_2/T_1)$. The total change is $\Delta S = \Delta S_1 + \Delta S_2 = m[(L_f/T_1) + c\ln(T_2/T_1)] = (9.4 \times 10^4 \text{ kg})[(334 \text{ kJ}/273 \text{ kg·K}) + (4.184 \text{ kJ/kg·K}) \ln(288/273)] = 136 \text{ MJ/K}$.

Problem

37. The temperature of n moles of ideal gas is changed from T_1 to T_2 while the gas volume is held constant. Show that the corresponding entropy change is $\Delta S = nC_V \ln(T_2/T_1)$.

Solution

From the first law of thermodynamics $(dQ = dU + dW)$ and the properties of an ideal gas $(dU = nC_V \, dT$ and $PV = nRT)$, an infinitesimal entropy change is $dS = \frac{dQ}{T} = nC_V \frac{dT}{T} + \frac{P}{T}dV = nC_V \frac{dT}{T} + nR\frac{dV}{V}$. If we integrate from state 1 (T_1, V_1) to state 2 (T_2, V_2), we obtain $\Delta S = nC_V \ln(T_2/T_1) + nR \ln(V_2/V_1)$. For an isovolumic process (in which the gas does no work), ΔS is as given in the problem. (Of course, we could have started with $dQ = nC_V \, dT$ at constant volume, but we wanted to display ΔS for a general ideal gas process, for use in other problems.)

Problem

39. A 5.0-mol sample of an ideal diatomic gas $(C_V = \frac{5}{2}R)$ is initially at 1.0 atm pressure and 300 K. What is the entropy change if the gas is heated to 500 K (a) at constant volume, (b) at constant pressure, and (c) adiabatically?

Solution

(a) From Problem 37, $\Delta S_V = nC_V \ln(T_2/T_1) = (5 \text{ mol})(2.5 \times 8.314 \text{ J/mol·K})\ln(500/300) = 53.1 \text{ J/K}$.

(b) From the general expression in the solution to Problem 37, with $V_2/V_1 = T_2/T_1$ at constant pressure and $C_P = C_V + R$, $\Delta S_P = nC_P \ln(T_2/T_1) = (C_P/C_V)\Delta S_V = 1.4(53.1 \text{ J/K}) = 74.3 \text{ J/K}$. (c) For an adiabatic process, $dQ = T\,dS = 0$, so $\Delta S = 0$. (An adiabatic process is one at constant entropy.)

Problem

41. A 250-g sample of water at 80°C is mixed with 250 g of water at 10°C. Find the entropy changes for (a) the hot water, (b) the cool water, and (c) the system.

Solution

The equilibrium temperature for the mixture, assuming all the heat lost by the hot water is gained by the cold, is $T_{eq} = 45°C$. (a) $\Delta S_{\text{hot water}} = mc \ln(T_{eq}/T_{\text{hot}}) = (0.25 \text{ kg})(4.184 \text{ kJ/kg·K}) \times \ln(318/353) = -109 \text{ J/K}$, (b) $\Delta S_{\text{cold water}} = (0.25 \text{ kg})(4.184 \text{ kJ/kg·K})\ln(318/283) = 122 \text{ J/K}$, and (c) $\Delta S_{\text{tot}} = -109 \text{ J/K} + 122 \text{ J/K} = 12.7 \text{ J/K}$.

Problem

43. A 5.0-mol sample of ideal monatomic gas undergoes the cycle shown in Fig. 22-31, in which the process BC is isothermal. Calculate the entropy change associated with each of the three steps, and show explicitly that there is zero net entropy change over the full cycle.

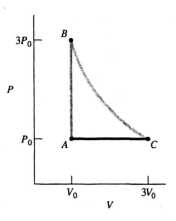

FIGURE 22-31 Problem 43.

Solution

For an ideal monatomic gas undergoing an isovolumic process $(dW = 0)$, $dQ = dU = nC_V\,dT = \frac{3}{2}nR\,dT$, and the entropy change is

$$\Delta S_{AB} = \int_A^B \frac{dQ}{T} = \int_A^B \frac{3}{2}nR\frac{dT}{T} = \frac{3}{2}nR\ln\left(\frac{T_B}{T_A}\right).$$

For the isothermal process $(dU = 0)$, $dQ = dW = P\,dV$, and

$$\Delta S_{BC} = \int_B^C \frac{dQ}{T} = \int_B^C \frac{P}{T}\,dV = \int_B^C nR\frac{dV}{V}$$
$$= nR\ln\left(\frac{V_C}{V_B}\right).$$

For the final isobaric process, $dQ = nC_P\,dT = \frac{5}{2}nR\,dT$, and $\Delta S_{CA} = \frac{5}{2}nR\ln(T_A/T_C)$. Therefore, the total entropy change for one cycle is $\Delta S = nR[\frac{3}{2}\ln(T_B/T_A) - \frac{5}{2}\ln(T_C/T_A) + \ln(V_C/V_B)]$. But $T_C = T_B$, while $P_B V_B = P_C V_C$ and $P_B/T_B = P_A/T_A$ imply $V_C/V_B = P_B/P_C = P_B/P_A = T_B/T_A$, so the logarithms are equal and $\Delta S = 0$ as expected. Numerically, $\Delta S_{AB} = (5 \text{ mol})(1.5)(8.314 \text{ J/mol·K})\times \ln 3 = 68.5 \text{ J/K}$, $\Delta S_{BC} = (5 \text{ mol})(8.314 \text{ J/mol·K})\times \ln 3 = 45.7 \text{ J/K}$, $\Delta S_{CA} = 2.5(5 \text{ mol})\times (8.314 \text{ J/mol·K})\ln(\frac{1}{3}) = -114.2 \text{ J/K}$, and $\Delta S_{\text{tot}} = 0$.

Problem

45. Ideal gas occupying 1.0 cm^3 is placed in a 1.0-m^3 vacuum chamber, where it expands adiabatically. If 6.5 J of energy become unavailable to do work, what was the initial gas pressure?

Solution

From Equations 22-10, 11 and the ideal gas law, $nRT = E_{\text{unavailable}}/\ln(V_2/V_1) = 6.5 \text{ J}/\ln(10^6) = 0.470 \text{ J} = P_1 V_1$. Therefore, $P_1 = 0.470 \text{ J}/(10^{-6} \text{ m}^3) = 470 \text{ kPa}$.

Paired Problems

Problem

47. Cooling water circulates through a reversible Carnot engine at 3.2 kg/s. The water enters at 23°C and leaves at 28°C; the average temperature is essentially that of the engine's cool reservoir. If the engine's mechanical power output is 150 kW, what are (a) its efficiency and (b) its highest temperature?

Solution

(a) From the rate of flow and temperature rise of the cooling water, the rate of heat exhausted by the engine can be calculated: $(dQ_c/dt) = (dm/dt)c\,\Delta T = (3.2 \text{ kg/s})(4.184 \text{ kJ/kg·K})(28°C - 23°C) = 66.9 \text{ kW}$. Then $(dQ_h/dt) = (dQ_c/dt) + (dW/dt) = 66.9 \text{ kW} + 150 \text{ kW}$ and $e = (dW/dt)/(dQ_h/dt) = 150 \text{ kW} \div 216.9 \text{ kW} = 69.1\%$. (b) For a Carnot engine with $T_c = \frac{1}{2}(23°C + 28°C) = 298.5 \text{ K}$, $T_h = T_c/(1 - e) = (298.5 \text{ K})/(1 - 0.691) = 967 \text{ K} = 694°C$.

Problem

49. Which would provide the greatest increase in efficiency of a Carnot engine, a 10 K increase in the maximum temperature or a 10 K decrease in the minimum temperature?

Solution

If we differentiate the efficiency with respect to T_c or T_h, respectively, we obtain: $de_c = -dT_c/T_h$, and $de_h = T_c \, dT_h/T_h^2$. If $dT_h = -dT_c$, then $de_h = (T_c/T_h)de_c < de_c$, since $T_c/T_h < 1$. The fact that a decrease in T_c produces a greater increase in efficiency than an increase of the same magnitude in T_h can also be demonstrated by direct substitution of $T_c - \Delta T$ or $T_h + \Delta T$ into Equation 22-3.

Problem

51. It costs \$180 to heat a house with electricity in a typical winter month. (Electric heat simply converts all the incoming electrical energy to heat.) What would be the monthly heating bill following conversion to an electrically powered heat pump system with COP = 2.1?

Solution

The same electrical energy W, as used for direct conversion in electric heating, would produce heat $Q_h = W + Q_c = (1 + \text{COP})W$ if used to run a heat pump. (A heat pump gives more heat for the money than electric heat.) Therefore, the cost of running a heat pump is a factor $(1 + \text{COP})^{-1}$ less, or $\$180(1 + 2.1)^{-1} = \$58.1$ for the house in this question.

Problem

53. A reversible engine contains 0.20 mol of ideal monatomic gas, initially at 600 K and confined to 2.0 L. The gas undergoes the following cycle:

- Isothermal expansion to 4.0 L.
- Isovolumic cooling to 300 K.
- Isothermal compression to 2.0 L.
- Isovolumic heating to 600 K.

(a) Calculate the net heat added during the cycle and the net work done. (b) Determine the engine's efficiency, defined as the ratio of the work done to only the heat *absorbed* during the cycle.

Solution

The P-V diagram for the cycle is as shown. For the isothermal expansion, $Q_{AB} = W_{AB} = nRT_A \ln(V_B/V_A) > 0$; for the isovolumic cooling, $W_{BC} = 0$, $Q_{BC} = \Delta U_{BC} = nC_V \, \Delta T_{BC} = \frac{3}{2}nR \times (T_C - T_B) < 0$; for the isothermal compression, $Q_{CD} =$

$W_{CD} = nRT_C \ln(V_D/V_C) < 0$; and for the final isovolumic heating $W_{DA} = 0$, $Q_{DA} = \Delta U_{DA} = \frac{3}{2}nR \times (T_A - T_D) > 0$. For these processes, it is given that $V_B = 2V_A = V_C = 2V_D = 4$ L, $T_A = T_B = 600$ K, and $T_C = T_D = 300$ K. (a) In a cyclic process ($\Delta U = 0$), the net heat added equals the net work done, $Q_\text{net} = W_\text{net} = nRT_A \ln(V_B/V_A) + nRT_C \ln(V_D/V_C) = nR(T_A - T_C)\ln(V_B/V_A) = (0.2 \text{ mol})(8.314 \text{ J/mol·K}) \times (300 \text{ K})\ln 2 = 346$ J. (Note explicitly, that since $\Delta T_{BC} = -\Delta T_{DA}$, $W_{BC} + W_{DA} = 0 = \Delta U_{BC} + \Delta U_{DA} = Q_{BC} + Q_{DA}$, and therefore $W_\text{net} = W_{AB} + W_{CD} = Q_{AB} + Q_{CD} = Q_\text{net}$.) (b) The heat absorbed during the cycle (just the positive values of heat) is $Q_+ = Q_{AB} + Q_{DA} = nRT_A \ln(V_B/V_A) + \frac{3}{2}nR(T_A - T_B) = (0.2 \text{ mol})(3.314 \text{ J/mol·K})[(600 \text{ K}) \ln 2 + 1.5(300 \text{ K})] = 1.44$ kJ. (Note: $Q_- = -Q_{BC} - Q_{CD} = 1.09$ kJ is the heat exhausted per cycle, and $Q_\text{net} = Q_+ - Q_-$.) The efficiency, as defined in this problem, is $W_\text{net}/Q_+ = 346$ J/1.44 kJ = 24.0%. (Note: A Carnot engine operating between 600 K and 300 K has efficiency $1 - 300/600 = 50\%$. This is not a contradiction of Carnot's theorem, because the engine in this problem does *not* absorb and exhaust heat at constant temperatures.)

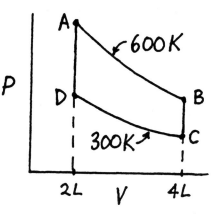

Problem 53 Solution.

Problem

55. You dump three 10-kg buckets of 10°C water into an empty tub, then add one 10-kg bucket of 70°C water. By how much does the entropy of the water increase?

Solution

Mixing 30 kg of water at 10°C = 283 K with 10 kg of water at 70°C = 343 K produces water at an equilibrium temperature given by $30(T_\text{eq} - 283 \text{ K}) + 10(T_\text{eq} - 343 \text{ K}) = 0$, or $T_\text{eq} = 298$ K. (This assumes there is no heat transfer to the tub or the surroundings.) The total entropy change of the water

is $\Delta S = m_1 c \ln(T_{eq}/T_1) + m_2 c \ln(T_{eq}/T_2) =$
$(4.184 \text{ kJ/kg·K})[(30 \text{ kg})\ln(298/283) + (10 \text{ kg})\ln \times$
$(298/343)] = 6.48 \text{ kJ/K} - 5.88 \text{ kJ/K} = 598 \text{ J/K}.$

Supplementary Problems

Problem

57. You're lying in a bathtub of water at 42°C. Suppose, in violation of the second law of thermodynamics, that the water spontaneously cooled to room temperature (20°C) and that the energy so released was transformed into your gravitational potential energy. Estimate the height to which you would rise above the bathtub.

Solution

A person taking a bath uses, on average, about 40 gal, or (40 gal)(3.785×10⁻³ m³/gal)(10³ kg/m³) = 151 kg, of water (see Appendix C). (In contrast, 5 min under a low-flow shower head consumes about 15 gal of water.) The amount of thermal energy that would be released by an average bathtub full of water, which cooled from 42°C to 20°C, is $\Delta Q = mc_w \Delta T = (151 \text{ kg}) \times$ (4184 J/kg·K)(22 K) = 13.9 MJ (see Equation 19-5 and Table 19-1). This amount is rather large compared to the increments of gravitational potential energy for ordinary objects near the Earth's surface, $\Delta U = mg \Delta y$ (see Equation 8-3). For a person of average mass 65 kg, it corresponds to a height difference of Δy = (13.9 MJ)/(6×9.81 N) = 21.9 km! (This energy is nearly half of the roughly 31.2 MJ required to launch 1 kg into a near Earth orbit (see Problem 9-45).)

Problem

59. A solar-thermal power plant is to be built in a desert location where the only source of cooling water is a small creek with average flow of 100 kg/s and an average temperature of 30°C. The plant is to cool itself by boiling away the entire creek. If the maximum temperature achieved in the plant is 500 K, what is the maximum electric power output it can sustain without running out of cooling water?

Solution

The maximum heatflow the creek could absorb is:
$$\frac{dQ_c}{dt} = \frac{dm}{dt}(c_W \Delta T + L_v)$$
$$= \left(10^2 \frac{\text{kg}}{\text{s}}\right)\left[\left(4.184 \frac{\text{kJ}}{\text{kg·K}}\right)\right.$$
$$\left. \times (100°\text{C} - 30°\text{C}) + 2257 \frac{\text{kJ}}{\text{kg}}\right] = 255 \text{ MW}.$$

If the plant had the maximum thermodynamic efficiency ($Q_c/Q_h = T_c/T_h$), operating between $T_c = (273 + 30)$ K and $T_h = 500$ K, with the above rate of heat exhaust, its power output would be

$$\frac{dW}{dt} = \frac{d}{dt}(Q_h - Q_c) = \frac{dQ_c}{dt}\left(\frac{T_h}{T_c} - 1\right)$$
$$= 255 \text{ MW}\left(\frac{500}{303} - 1\right) = 166 \text{ MW}.$$

Problem

61. Gasoline engines operate approximately on the **Otto cycle**, consisting of two adiabatic and two constant-volume segments. The Otto cycle for a particular engine is shown in Fig. 22-33. (a) If the gas in the engine has specific heat ratio γ, find the engine's efficiency, assuming all processes are reversible. (b) Find the maximum temperature, in terms of the minimum temperature $T_{\min}$. (c) How does the efficiency compare with that of a Carnot engine operating between the same two temperature extremes? *Note:* Fig. 22-33 neglects the intake of fuel-air and the exhaust of combustion products, which together involve essentially no net work.

Solution

It is convenient to solve this problem beginning with part (b), because we will need to express the temperatures of all the numbered points in Fig. 22-33 in terms of T_1, the minimum. This is accomplished by use of the adiabatic and ideal gas laws, Equations 21-13a and b, and 20-2, respectively. First,

$$\frac{T_3}{T_4} = \left(\frac{V_4}{V_3}\right)^{\gamma-1} = 5^{\gamma-1} = \left(\frac{V_1}{V_2}\right)^{\gamma-1} = \frac{T_2}{T_1}.$$

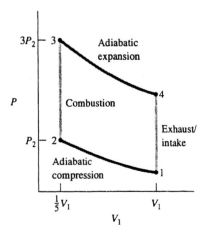

FIGURE 22-33 Problems 61 and 62.

Second,

$$\frac{P_3}{P_4} = \left(\frac{V_4}{V_3}\right)^\gamma = \left(\frac{V_1}{V_2}\right)^\gamma = \frac{P_2}{P_1}.$$

Last,

$$\frac{T_3}{T_2} = \frac{P_3}{P_2} = 3 = \frac{P_4}{P_1} = \frac{T_4}{T_1}.$$

Therefore, $T_2 = 5^{\gamma-1}T_1$, $T_4 = 3T_1$, and (the maximum temperature) $T_3 = 5^{\gamma-1}T_4 = 3 \times 5^{\gamma-1}T_1$. (a) Since no heat is transferred on the adiabatic segments, the heat input is $Q_h = Q_{23} = nC_V(T_3 - T_2) = nC_V 5^{\gamma-1} \times (3-1)T_1 = 2 \times 5^{\gamma-1}nC_V T_1$, and the heat exhaust is $Q_c = -Q_{41} = -nC_V(T_1 - T_4) = 2nC_V T_1$. Therefore, the efficiency is $e = 1 - Q_c/Q_h = 1 - 5^{1-\gamma}$. (c) A Carnot engine operating between T_3 and T_1 has efficiency $1 - T_1/T_3 = 1 - \frac{1}{3} \times 5^{1-\gamma}$, so $e_{Otto} < e_{Carnot}$.

Problem

63. A heat pump designed for southern climates extracts heat from outside air and delivers air at 40°C to the inside of a house. (a) If the average outside temperature is 5°C, what is the average COP of the heat pump? (b) Suppose the pump is used in a northern climate where the average winter temperature is −10°C. Now what is the COP? (c) Two *identical* houses, one in the north and one in the south, are heated by this pump. Both houses maintain indoor temperatures of 19°C. What is the ratio of electric power consumption in the two houses? *Hint:* Think about heat loss as well as COP!

Solution

(a) We assume the heat pump operates on a reversible Carnot cycle, so $COP_s = T_c/(T_h - T_c) = (273 + 5) \div (40 - 5) = 7.94$, where the subscript "s" is for southern. (b) Similarly, $COP_n = (273 - 10)/50 = 5.26$. (c) The heat flow needed from the pump (to balance the heat loss from the house) is proportional to the inside/outside temperature difference (see Equation 19-10), so for identical northern and southern houses, $H_n/H_s = [19°C - (-10°C)] \div (19°C - 5°C) = 2.07$. If we eliminate Q_c from Equation 22-4, we obtain $Q_h = W(1 + COP)$. Now, $dQ_h/dt = H$ is the heat flow from the pump, while $dW/dt = \mathcal{P}$ is the power consumption, so substitution into the ratio of heat losses yields $2.07 = \mathcal{P}_n(1 + COP_n)/\mathcal{P}_s(1 + COP_s)$, or $\mathcal{P}_n/\mathcal{P}_s = 2.07(1 + 7.94)/(1 + 5.26) = 2.96$.

Problem

65. A Carnot engine extracts heat from a block of mass m and specific heat c that is initially at temperature T_{h0} but which has no heat source to maintain that temperature. The engine rejects heat to a reservoir at a constant temperature T_c. The engine is operated so its mechanical power output is proportional to the temperature difference $T_h - T_c$:

$$P = P_0 \frac{T_h - T_c}{T_{h0} - T_c},$$

where T_h is the instantaneous temperature of the hot block and P_0 is the initial power output. (a) Find an expression for T_h as a function of time, and (b) determine how long it takes for the engine's power output to reach zero.

Solution

(a) In time dt, the engine extracts heat $dQ_h = -mc\, dT_h$ from the block, and does work $dW = \mathcal{P}\, dt$. Since it is a Carnot engine, $dW = e_{max}\, dQ_h = [(T_h - T_c)/T_h](-mc\, dT_h) = \mathcal{P}\, dt$. The power is also assumed to be proportional to $T_h - T_c$, so the equation becomes $-mc\, dT_h/T_h = \mathcal{P}_0\, dt/(T_{h0} - T_c)$. Integrating from $t = 0$ and T_{h0} to t and T_h, we obtain

$$\int_{T_{h0}}^{T_h} \frac{dT'_h}{T'_h} = \ln\left(\frac{T_h}{T_{h0}}\right) = -\int_0^t \frac{\mathcal{P}_0\, dt}{mc(T_{h0} - T_c)}$$
$$= -\frac{\mathcal{P}_0 t}{mc(T_{h0} - T_c)},$$

or $T_h = T_{h0} \exp\{-\mathcal{P}_0 t/mc(T_{h0} - T_c)\}$. (b) The power output is zero for $T_h = T_c$. This occurs at time $t_0 = (mc/\mathcal{P}_0)(T_{h0} - T_c)\ln(T_{h0}/T_c)$. (Note: The expression for $\mathcal{P}$ was originally assumed valid for $T_h \geq T_c$, or for times $t \leq t_0$. If we allow $T_h < T_c$, or $t > t_0$, then $dW = \mathcal{P}\, dt < 0$ becomes work input to an "engine" which acts like a refrigerator cooling the block.)

Problem

67. An ideal diatomic gas undergoes the cyclic process described in Fig. 22-34. Fill in the blank spaces in the table below:

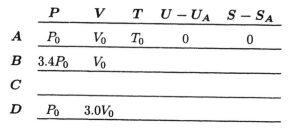

	P	V	T	$U - U_A$	$S - S_A$
A	P_0	V_0	T_0	0	0
B	$3.4P_0$	V_0			
C					
D	P_0	$3.0V_0$			

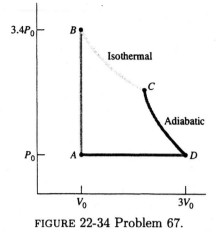

FIGURE 22-34 Problem 67.

Solution

We first calculate the blank P, V, and T's, using the adiabatic and ideal gas laws, with $\gamma = 1.4$. For states B and D:

$$T_B = (P_B V_B / P_A V_A) T_A = 3.4 T_0, \quad \text{and}$$
$$T_D = (P_D V_D / P_A V_A) T_A = 3 T_0.$$

For state C,

$$T_C = T_B,$$
$$P_C V_C^\gamma = P_D V_D^\gamma = P_0 (3 V_0)^\gamma, \quad \text{and}$$
$$P_C V_C = P_B V_B = 3.4 P_0 V_0.$$

Division yields

$$V_C^{\gamma-1} = \frac{3^\gamma}{3.4} V_0^{\gamma-1}, \quad \text{or}$$

$$V_C = \left(\frac{3^\gamma}{3.4}\right)^{1/(\gamma-1)} V_0 = \frac{3^{3.5}}{3.4^{2.5}} V_0 = 2.19 V_0.$$

Then

$$P_C = P_B (V_B T_C / V_C T_B)$$
$$= (3.4 P_0)(1/2.19)(1) = 1.55 P_0.$$

The internal energies and entropies can be calculated from $\Delta U = nC_V \Delta T$ (Equation 21-7), and $\Delta S = nC_V \ln(T_2/T_1) + nR \ln(V_2/V_1)$ (see the solution to Problem 37, or Equation 22-9 for an isobaric or isovolumic process, and Equation 22-10 for an isothermal one), where $C_V = \frac{5}{2}R$. Thus, $U_B - U_A = nC_V(T_B - T_A) = \frac{5}{2}nR(3.4 - 1)T_0 = \frac{5}{2}(2.4)(nRT_0) = 6P_0V_0$, $U_C - U_B = 0$ (or $U_C - U_A = 6P_0V_0$) and, $U_D - U_A = \frac{5}{2}nR(3-1)T_0 = 5P_0V_0$, while $S_B - S_A = nC_V \ln(T_B/T_A) = \frac{5}{2}nR \ln(3.4) = 3.06nR$, $S_C - S_A = nC_V \ln(T_C/T_A) + nR \ln(V_C/V_A) = 3.06nR + nR \times \ln(2.19) = 3.85nR$, and $S_D - S_C = 0$ ($dS = dQ/T = 0$ on an adiabat), or alternatively, $S_D - S_A = nC_V \times \ln(T_D/T_A) + nR \ln(V_D/V_A) = nC_P \ln(T_D/T_A) = \frac{7}{2}nR \ln 3$. Of course, $nR = P_0V_0/T_0$, so all the tabulated results can be expressed in terms of the given parameters.

	P	V	T	$U - U_A$	$S - S_A$
A	P_0	V_0	T_0	0	0
B	$3.4P_0$	V_0	$3.4T_0$	$6P_0V_0$	$3.06nR$
C	$1.55P_0$	$2.19V_0$	$3.4T_0$	$6P_0V_0$	$3.85nR$
D	P_0	$3.0V_0$	$3T_0$	$5P_0V_0$	$3.85nR$

PART 3   CUMULATIVE PROBLEMS

Problem

1. Figure 1 shows the thermodynamic cycle of a diesel engine. Note that this cycle differs from that of a gasoline engine (see Fig. 22-33) in that combustion takes place isobarically. As with the gasoline engine, the compression ratio r is the ratio of maximum to minimum volume; $r = V_1/V_2$. In addition, the so-called *cutoff ratio* is defined by $r_c = V_3/V_2$. Find an expression for the engine's efficiency, in terms of the ratios r and r_c and the specific heat ratio γ. Although your expression suggests that the diesel engine might be less efficient than the gasoline engine (see Problem 61 of Chapter 22), the diesel's higher compression ratio more than compensates, giving it a higher efficiency.

Solution

From Table 21-1, the work done and heat absorbed during the four processes comprising the diesel cycle are:

$1 \to 2$ (adiabatic) $W_{12} = (P_1V_1 - P_2V_2)/(\gamma - 1)$,
$$Q_{12} = 0,$$

$2 \to 3$ (isobaric) $W_{23} = P_2(V_3 - V_2)$,
$$Q_{23} = nC_P(T_3 - T_2) \equiv Q_h,$$

$3 \to 4$ (adiabatic) $W_{34} = (P_3V_3 - P_4V_4)/(\gamma - 1)$,
$$Q_{34} = 0,$$

$4 \to 1$ (isovolumic) $W_{41} = 0$,
$$Q_{41} = nC_V(T_1 - T_4) \equiv -Q_c.$$

For the whole cycle, the work done is

$$W = \frac{P_1V_1 - P_2V_2 + P_3V_3 - P_4V_4}{(\gamma - 1)} + P_3V_3 - P_2V_2$$
$$= \frac{\gamma(P_3V_3 - P_2V_2) - P_4V_4 + P_1V_1}{(\gamma - 1)},$$

while the heat added can be written as $Q_h = nC_P(T_3 - T_2) = \gamma(P_3V_3 - P_2V_2)/(\gamma - 1)$, where we used the ideal gas law, $nT = PV/R$, and $C_P/R = C_P/(C_P - C_V) = \gamma/(\gamma - 1)$. Therefore,

$$W = Q_h - \frac{(P_4V_4 - P_1V_1)}{(\gamma - 1)} = Q_h - \frac{(P_4V_4 - P_1V_1)Q_h}{\gamma(P_3V_3 - P_2V_2)}$$

and the efficiency is $e = W/Q_h = 1 - (P_4V_4 - P_1V_1) \div \gamma(P_3V_3 - P_2V_2)$. The adiabatic law can now be used to express every product in terms of P_2V_2 and the compression and cutoff ratios: $P_2 = P_3$, $V_1 = V_4$, $V_1/V_2 = r$, $V_3/V_2 = r_c$, $P_1V_1^\gamma = P_2V_2^\gamma$, $P_3V_3^\gamma = P_4V_4^\gamma$, so $P_1V_1 = P_2V_2r^{1-\gamma}$, $P_3V_3 = P_2V_2r_c$, and $P_4V_4 = P_2V_2r^{1-\gamma}r_c^\gamma$. Finally, $e = 1 - r^{1-\gamma}(r_c^\gamma - 1)/\gamma(r_c - 1)$.

Problem

3. Equation 21-4 gives the work done by an ideal gas undergoing an isothermal expansion from volume V_1 to volume V_2. Find the analogous expression for a van der Waals gas described by Equation 20-7. Is the work done equal to the heat transferred to the gas in this case? Why or why not?

Solution

An expression for the work done by a van der Waals gas undergoing an isothermal expansion is derived in the solution to Problem 21-65. The van der Waals equation includes the effects of intermolecular forces, which contribute to the potential energy of a molecule, so we should not expect the internal energy, U, to be a function of T only (it depends on V and T). Therefore, $Q = \Delta U + W \neq W$ when a van der Waals gas undergoes an isothermal process.

Problem

5. The ideal Carnot engine shown in Fig. 4 operates between a heat reservoir and a block of ice with mass M. An external energy source maintains the reservoir at a constant temperature T_h. At time $t = 0$ the ice is at its melting point T_0, but it is insulated from everything except the engine, so it is free to change state and temperature. The engine is operated in such a way that it extracts heat from the reservoir at a constant rate P_h. (a) Find an expression for the time t_1 at which the ice is all melted, in terms of the quantities given and

any other appropriate thermodynamic parameters. (b) Find an expression for the mechanical power output of the engine as a function of time for times $t > t_1$. (c) Your expression in (b) holds only up to some maximum time t_2. Why? Find an expression for t_2.

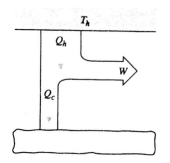

FIGURE 4 Cumulative Problem 5.

Solution

(a) The ice acts as a constant temperature cold reservoir at $T_c = T_0 = 273$ K, while it is melting for times $0 \leq t \leq t_1$. The Carnot engine exhausts heat at a constant rate, over this time interval, so the simplified form of Equation 22-2 gives $P_c = (T_c/T_h)P_h$, (where the first and second laws of thermodynamics have been written in terms of rate of heat flow or power, as in Example 22-2). The total heat exhausted is just sufficient to melt all the ice, therefore $P_ct_1 = (T_0/T_h)P_ht_1 = ML_f$, or $t_1 = ML_fT_h/P_hT_0$. (Here, L_f is the heat of fusion of water and Equation 20-6 was used.) (b) After the ice is melted, the temperature of the cold reservoir increases with time. So does the rate of heat exhausted, while the mechanical power of the engine, $P = P_h - P_c$, decreases. From Equation 19-5 in terms of rates, $P_cdt = (T_c/T_h)P_hdt = McdT_c$, or $dT_c/T_c = (P_h/McT_h)\,dt$. This equation holds for a time interval $t_1 \leq t \leq t_2$ (see part (c) below), where $T_c = T_0$ at $t = t_1$, and can be integrated to give $\ln(T_c/T_0) = (P_h/McT_h)(t - t_1)$, or $T_c = T_0\exp\{P_h(t - t_1)/McT_h\}$. The power output of the Carnot engine is therefore $P = eP_h = (1 - T_c/T_h)P_h = [1 - (T_0/T_h)\exp\{P_h(t - t_1)/McT_h\}]P_h$, where e is the Carnot efficiency (Equation 22-3) and $\exp\{...\}$ is the exponential function. (c) The Carnot engine operates as described above only as long as $T_c < T_h$. When $T_c = T_h$ at time t_2, the power output has dropped to zero. Then, from part (b), $\ln(T_h/T_0) = (P_h/McT_h)(t_2 - t_1)$, or $t_2 = t_1 + (McT_h/P_h)\times \ln(T_h/T_0)$.

CHAPTER 34   MAXWELL'S EQUATIONS AND ELECTROMAGNETIC WAVES

Section 34-2:   Ambiguity in Ampère's Law

Problem

1. A uniform electric field is increasing at the rate of 1.5 V/m·μs. What is the displacement current through an area of 1.0 cm² at right angles to the field?

Solution

Maxwell's displacement current is $\varepsilon_0 \partial\phi_E/\partial t = (8.85\times10^{-12}$ F/m$)(1.5$ V/m·μs$)(1$ cm²$) = 1.33$ nA. (See Equations 34-1 and 24-2.)

Problem

3. A parallel-plate capacitor of plate area A and spacing d is charging at the rate dV/dt. Show that the displacement current in the capacitor is equal to the conduction current flowing in the wires feeding the capacitor.

Solution

The displacement current is $I_D = \varepsilon_0 \partial\phi_E/\partial t$. For a parallel-plate capacitor, $E = q/\varepsilon_0 A$, so $I_D = \varepsilon_0\ \partial(EA)/\partial t = \varepsilon_0\partial(q/\varepsilon_0)/\partial t = dq/dt$. But dq/dt is just the conduction current (the rate at which charge is flowing onto the capacitor plates); hence $I_D = I$.

Problem

5. A parallel-plate capacitor has circular plates with radius 50 cm and spacing 1.0 mm. A uniform electric field between the plates is changing at the rate 1.0 MV/m·s. What is the magnetic field between the plates (a) on the symmetry axis, (b) 15 cm from the axis, and (c) 150 cm from the axis?

Solution

(a) As explained in Example 34-1, cylindrical symmetry and Gauss's law for magnetism require that the **B**-field lines be circles around the symmetry axis, as in Fig. 34-5. For a radius, r, less than the radius of the plates, R, the displacement current is $I_D = \varepsilon_0 d\phi_E/dt = \varepsilon_0(d/dt)\int \mathbf{E}\cdot d\mathbf{A} = \varepsilon_0\pi r^2(dE/dt)$, where the integral is over a disk of radius r centered between

the plates. Maxwell's form of Ampère's law gives $\oint \mathbf{B}\cdot d\boldsymbol{\ell} = 2\pi r B = \mu_0 I_D$, where the line integral is around the circumference of the disk. Thus, $B = \frac{1}{2}\mu_0\varepsilon_0 r(dE/dt) = r(dE/dt)/2c^2$, where c is the speed of light (Equation 34-16). On the symmetry axis, $r = 0$, so $B = 0$. (b) For $r = 15$ cm $< R, B = \frac{1}{2}(0.15$ m$)(10^6$ V/m·s$)/(3\times10^8$ m/s$)^2 = 8.33\times10^{-13}$ T. (c) For $r > R$, the displacement current is $I_D = \varepsilon_0\pi R^2(dE/dt)$, so $B = (dE/dt)R^2/2c^2 r$. At $r = 150$ cm$, B = (10^6$ V/m·s$)(50$ cm$)^2/2(3\times10^8$ m/s$)^2\times (150$ cm$) = 9.26\times10^{-13}$ T.

Section 34-4:   Electromagnetic Waves

Problem

7. At a particular point the instantaneous electric field of an electromagnetic wave points in the $+y$ direction, while the magnetic field points in the $-z$ direction. In what direction is the wave propagating?

Solution

For electromagnetic waves in vacuum, the directions of the electric and magnetic fields, and of wave propagation, form a right-handed coordinate system, as shown. (The vector relationship is summarized in Equation 34-20b.) Therefore, the given wave is headed in the $-x$-direction.

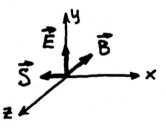

Problem 7 Solution.

Problem

9. The electric field of a radio wave is given by $\mathbf{E} = E\sin(kz - \omega t)(\hat{\mathbf{i}}+\hat{\mathbf{j}})$. (a) What is the peak amplitude of the electric field? (b) Give a unit vector in the direction of the magnetic field at a place and time where $\sin(kz - \omega t)$ is positive.

Solution

(a) The peak amplitude is the magnitude of $E(\hat{\imath}+\hat{\jmath})$, which is $E\sqrt{2}$. Note that $\hat{\imath}+\hat{\jmath}=\sqrt{2}\hat{n}$, where $\hat{n}$ is a unit vector $45°$ between the positive x and y axes.
(b) When $\mathbf{E}$ is parallel to $\hat{n}$ (for $\sin(kz-\omega t)$ positive) $\mathbf{B}$ points $45°$ into the second quadrant (so that $\mathbf{E}\perp\mathbf{B}$, and $\mathbf{E}\times\mathbf{B}$ is in the $+z$ direction). Thus, $\mathbf{B}$ is parallel to the unit vector $(-\hat{\imath}+\hat{\jmath})/\sqrt{2}$.

Problem

11. Show that it is impossible for an electromagnetic wave in a vacuum to have a time-varying component of its electric field in the direction of its magnetic field. *Hint:* Assume $\mathbf{E}$ does have such a component, and show that you cannot satisfy both Gauss and Faraday.

Solution

Consider a wave propagating in the x direction through a vacuum (no charges or currents present). Gauss's laws for electricity and magnetism require the field lines to continue forever in the y-z plane (no E_x or B_x). We may choose the z direction parallel to the magnetic field, $\mathbf{B}=B_z\hat{k}$. Suppose $\mathbf{E}=E_y\hat{\jmath}+E_z\hat{k}$. The discussion of Faraday's law leading to Equation 34-12b shows that $\partial E_y/\partial x=-\partial B_z/\partial t$. But consider a corresponding loop in the x-z plane. Then $-\partial E_z/\partial x=-\partial B_y/\partial t=0$, since there is no B_y by assumption. Because all the space-time dependence in the wave occurs in the combination $kx-\omega t$ (see Problem 10), $\omega\partial E_z/\partial t=-k\partial E_z/\partial x=0$. Then E_z must be a constant and is therefore not a part of the wave. (Similar consideration of Ampère's law over the loop in the x-y plane gives $\varepsilon_0\mu_0\partial E_z/\partial t=0$ directly, with the same conclusion regarding E_z.)

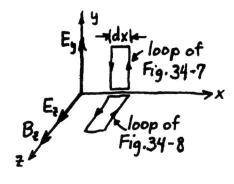

Problem 11 Solution.

Section 34-5: The Speed of Electromagnetic Waves

Problem

13. Your intercontinental telephone call is carried by electromagnetic waves routed via a satellite in geosynchronous orbit at an altitude of 36,000 km. Approximately how long does it take before your voice is heard at the other end?

Solution

Assuming the satellite is approximately overhead, we can estimate the round-trip travel time by $\Delta t = \Delta r/c = (2\times36{,}000\text{ km})/(3\times10^5\text{ km/s}) = 0.24$ s.

Problem

15. Roughly how long does it take light to go 1 foot?

Solution

In $\Delta t = 1$ ns, light travels about $\Delta r = c\,\Delta t = (3\times10^8\text{ m/s})(10^{-9}\text{ s}) = 30$ cm, or about one foot.

Problem

17. "Ghosts" on a TV screen occur when part of the signal goes directly from transmitter to receiver, while part takes a longer route, reflecting off mountains or buildings (Fig. 34-31). The electron beam in a 50-cm-wide TV tube "paints" the picture by scanning the beam from left to right across the screen in about 10^{-4} s. If a "ghost" image appears displaced about 1 cm from the main image, what is the difference in path lengths of the direct and indirect signals?

Solution

The time it takes for the electron beam to sweep across 1 cm of the TV screen is 1 cm$/(50$ cm$/10^{-4}$ s$) = 2\times10^{-6}$ s, which equals the time delay of the ghost signal. Therefore, the path difference is $\Delta r = c\,\Delta t = (3\times10^8\text{ m/s})(2\times10^{-6}\text{ s}) = 600$ m.

Problem

19. Problem 69 shows that the speed of electromagnetic waves in a transparent dielectric is given by $1/\sqrt{\kappa\varepsilon_0\mu_0}$, where κ is the dielectric constant described in Chapter 26. An experimental measurement gives 1.97×10^8 m/s for the speed of light in a piece of glass. What is the dielectric constant of this glass at optical frequencies?

Solution

Since $c = 1/\sqrt{\varepsilon_0\mu_0}$ (speed of light in vacuum), we can write $v = c/\sqrt{\kappa}$ for the speed of light in a dielectric.

Then $\kappa = (c/v)^2 = (3/1.97)^2 = 2.32$. (Note: $\sqrt{\kappa}$ at optical frequencies is called the index of refraction; see Section 35-3.)

Section 34-6:   Properties of Electromagnetic Waves

Problem

21. A 60-Hz power line emits electromagnetic radiation. What is the wavelength?

Solution

The wavelength in a vacuum (or air) is $\lambda = c/f = (3\times10^8$ m/s$)/(60$ Hz$) = 5\times10^6$ m, almost as large as the radius of the Earth.

Problem

23. A CB radio antenna is a vertical rod 2.75 m high. If this length is one-fourth of the CB wavelength, what is the CB frequency?

Solution

From Equation 34-17b, $f = c/\lambda = (3\times10^8$ m/s$)\div$ $(4\times2.75$ m$) = 27.3$ MHz.

Problem

25. What would be the electric field strength in an electromagnetic wave whose magnetic field equaled that of Earth, about 50 μT?

Solution

For a wave in free space, Equation 34-18 gives $E = cB = (3\times10^8$ m/s$)(0.5\times10^{-4}$ T$) = 15$ kV/m.

Problem

27. A radio receiver can detect signals with electric fields as low as 320 μV/m. What is the corresponding magnetic field?

Solution

From Equation 34-18 for waves in free space, $B = E/c = (320$ μV/m$)/(3\times10^8$ m/s$) = 1.07$ pT.

Section 34-8:   Polarization

Problem

29. Polarized light is incident on a sheet of polarizing material, and only 20% of the light gets through. What is the angle between the electric field and the polarization axis of the material?

Solution

From the law of Malus (Equation 34-19), $S/S_0 = \cos^2\theta = 20\%$, or $\theta = \cos^{-1}(\sqrt{0.2}) = 63.4°$.

Problem

31. A polarizer blocks 75% of a polarized light beam. What is the angle between the beam's polarization and the polarizer's axis?

Solution

Equation 34-19 gives $\theta = \cos^{-1}\sqrt{S/S_0} = \cos^{-1}\sqrt{1-75\%} = \cos^{-1}\sqrt{\frac{1}{4}} = 60°$.

Problem

33. Unpolarized light of intensity S_0 passes first through a polarizer with its polarization axis vertical, then through one with its axis at 35° to the vertical. What is the light intensity after the second polarizer?

Solution

Only 50% (one half the intensity) of the unpolarized light is transmitted through the first polarizer, and the second cuts this down by $\cos^2 35°$. Therefore $\frac{1}{2}\cos^2 35° = 33.6\%$ of the unpolarized intensity gets through both polarizers.

Problem

35. Unpolarized light with intensity S_0 passes through a stack of five polarizing sheets, each with its axis rotated 20° with respect to the previous one. What is the intensity of the light emerging from the stack?

Solution

Only $\frac{1}{2}$ (or 50%) of the incident unpolarized intensity gets through the first polarizing sheet, while $\cos^2 20°$ (or 88.3%) is passed through each of the succeeding four sheets. The net percentage emerging is $\frac{1}{2}(\cos^2 20°)^4 = 30.4\%$.

Problem

37. Polarized light with average intensity S_0 passes through a sheet of polarizing material which is rotating at 10 rev/s. At time $t = 0$ the polarization axis is aligned with the incident polarization. Write an expression for the transmitted intensity as a function of time.

Solution

Because the frequency of light is much greater than that of the rotating polarizer (5×10^{14} Hz $\gg$ 10 Hz), the law of Malus relates the average light intensities (see discussion leading to Equation 34-21a). Thus, $S = S_0\cos^2\theta$. For $\theta = \omega t$, where $\omega = 2\pi\times10$ s^{-1}, $S = S_0\cos^2(20\pi$ s$^{-1})t = \frac{1}{2}S_0[1 + \cos(40\pi$ s$^{-1})t]$.

Section 34-10: Energy in Electromagnetic Waves

Problem

39. What would be the average intensity of a laser beam so strong that its electric field produced dielectric breakdown of air (which requires $E_p = 3\times10^6$ V/m)?

Solution

Equation 34-21b for the average intensity of electromagnetic waves gives $\bar{S} = E_p^2/2\mu_0 c = (3\times10^6 \text{ V/m})^2(8\pi\times10^{-7} \text{ H/m})^{-1}(3\times10^8 \text{ m/s})^{-1} = 11.9 \text{ GW/m}^2$.

Problem

41. A radio receiver can pick up signals with peak electric fields as low as 450 μV/m. What is the average intensity of such a signal?

Solution

From Equation 34-21b, $\bar{S} = E_p^2/2\mu_0 c = (450 \ \mu\text{V/m})^2/(8\pi\times10^{-7} \text{ H/m})(3\times10^8 \text{ m/s}) = 2.69\times10^{-10} \text{ W/m}^2$.

Problem

43. A laser blackboard pointer delivers 0.10 mW average power in a beam 0.90 mm in diameter. Find (a) the average intensity, (b) the peak electric field, and (c) the peak magnetic field.

Solution

(a) If the average power is spread uniformly over the beam area, $\bar{S} = 0.1 \text{ mW}/\frac{1}{4}\pi(0.9 \text{ mm})^2 = 157 \text{ W/m}^2$.
(b) Equation 34-21b gives $E_p = \sqrt{2\mu_0 c\bar{S}} = 344$ V/m, and (c) Equation 34-18 gives $B_p = E_p/c = 1.15 \ \mu$T.

Problem

45. The United States' safety standard for continuous exposure to microwave radiation is 10 mW/cm^2. The glass door of a microwave oven measures 40 cm by 17 cm and is covered with a metal screen that blocks microwaves. What fraction of the oven's 625-W microwave power can leak through the door window without exceeding the safe exposure to someone right outside the door? Assume the power leaks uniformly through the window area.

Solution

The power corresponding to the safety standard of intensity, uniformly distributed over the window area,

is (10 mW/cm^2)(40$\times$17 cm^2) = 6.8 W, which is 1.09% of the microwave's 625 W power output.

Problem

47. Use the fact that sunlight intensity at Earth's orbit is 1368 W/m^2 to calculate the Sun's total power output.

Solution

If the Sun is emitting isotropically, its power output is $\mathcal{P} = 4\pi r^2\bar{S}$ (from Equation 34-22). Using values of comparable accuracy for the Earth's average orbital distance, we find $\mathcal{P} = 4\pi(1.496\times10^{11} \text{ m})^2 \times (1368 \text{ W/m}^2) = 3.85\times10^{26}$ W.

Problem

49. During its 1989 encounter with Neptune, the Voyager II spacecraft was 4.5×10^9 km from Earth. Its images of Neptune were broadcast by a radio transmitter with a mere 21-W average power output. What would be (a) the average intensity and (b) the peak electric field received at Earth if the transmitter broadcast equally in all directions? (The received signal was actually somewhat stronger because Voyager used a directional antenna.)

Solution

(a) The average intensity at a distance r from an isotropic emitter is (Equation 34-22) $\bar{S} = \mathcal{P}/4\pi r^2 = 21 \text{ W}/4\pi(4.5\times10^{12} \text{ m})^2 = 8.25\times10^{-26} \text{ W/m}^2$.
(b) This corresponds to a peak electric field of only (Equation 34-21b) $E_p = \sqrt{2\mu_0 c\bar{S}} = 7.89\times10^{-12}$ V/m. (The one-way travel time queried in the caption of Fig. 34-32 is $r/c = 4$ h, 10 min.)

Problem

51. At 1.5 km from the transmitter, the peak electric field of a radio wave is 350 mV/m. (a) What is the transmitter's power output, assuming it broadcasts uniformly in all directions? (b) What is the peak electric field 10 km from the transmitter?

Solution

(a) Equations 34-22 and 21b can be combined to express the average power output of an isotropic transmitter in terms of the peak electric field at a distance r, $\mathcal{P} = 4\pi r^2(E_p^2/2\mu_0 c) = (1.5 \text{ km})^2 \times (350 \text{ mV/m})^2/(2\times10^{-7} \times 3\times10^8 \text{ H/s}) = 4.59$ kW.
(b) Since $r^2 E_p^2$ is a constant, $E_p' = (r/r')E_p = (1.5/10)(350 \text{ mV/m}) = 52.5$ mV/m at a distance of 10 km.

Problem

53. A typical fluorescent lamp is a little over 1 m long and a few cm in diameter. How do you expect the light intensity to vary with distance (a) near the lamp but not near either end and (b) far from the lamp?

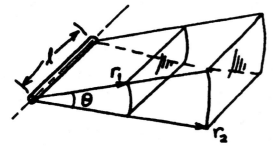

Problem 53 Solution.

Solution

(a) Near the lamp, but far from its ends, light waves travel approximately radially outwards from the tube axis. The power crossing two co-axial cylindrical patches is the same, but the area of each patch is proportional to the radius. Therefore, the intensity varies as $1/r$. ($S_1 A_1 = S_2 A_2 = S_1 \theta r_1 \ell = S_2 \theta r_2 \ell$.) This is the same relation as depicted in the solution to Problem 16-44. (b) Very far away, the lamp appears as a point source, and Equation 34-22 holds, so the intensity varies like $1/r^2$.

Section 34-11: Wave Momentum and Radiation Pressure

Problem

55. What is the radiation pressure exerted on a light-absorbing surface by a laser beam whose intensity is 180 W/cm^2?

Solution

The radiation pressure generated by a totally absorbed electromagnetic wave of given average intensity (from Equation 34-24) is $P_{\text{rad}} = \bar{S}/c = (180 \text{ W/cm}^2)/(3 \times 10^8 \text{ m/s}) = 6$ mPa.

Problem

57. The average intensity of noonday sunlight is about 1 kW/m^2. What is the radiation force on a solar collector measuring 60 cm by 2.5 m if it is oriented at right angles to the incident light and absorbs all the light?

Solution

For sunlight incident normally on a perfect absorber, $P_{\text{rad}} = \bar{S}/c$ (Equation 34-24). Therefore, the force on

the solar collector is $P_{\text{rad}} A = (1 \text{ kW/m}^2) \times (0.6 \times 2.5 \text{ m}^2)/(3 \times 10^8 \text{ m/s}) = 5 \ \mu$N.

Problem

59. A 65-kg astronaut is floating in empty space. If the astronaut shines a 1.0-W flashlight in a fixed direction, how long will it take the astronaut to accelerate to a speed of 10 m/s?

Solution

The reaction force of the light emitted on the flashlight equals the rate at which momentum is carried away by the beam, or $F = dp/dt = (dU/dt)/c = \mathcal{P}/c$. Such a force could accelerate a mass m from rest to a speed v in time $t = v/a = mv/F = mcv/\mathcal{P}$. For the values given for the astronaut and flashlight, $t = (65 \text{ kg}) \times (3 \times 10^8 \text{ m/s})(10 \text{ m/s})/(1 \text{ W}) = 1.95 \times 10^{11}$ s $= 6.18 \times 10^3$ y (impractically long).

Paired Problems

Problem

61. Find the peak electric and magnetic fields 1.5 m from a 60-W light bulb that radiates equally in all directions.

Solution

For an isotropic source of electromagnetic waves (in a medium with vacuum permittivity and permeability) Equations 34-21b and 22 give $\bar{S} = \mathcal{P}/4\pi r^2 = E_p^2/2\mu_0 c$, therefore $E_p = \sqrt{2\mu_0 c\mathcal{P}/4\pi r^2} = (2 \times 10^{-7} \times 3 \times 10^8 \times 60)^{1/2}(\text{ V/m})/(1.5 \text{ m}) = 40$ V/m. Then Equation 34-18 gives $B_p = E_p/c = 133$ nT.

Problem

63. Unpolarized light is incident on two polarizers with their axes at 45°. What fraction of the incident light gets through?

Solution

50% of the incident unpolarized light (a random mixture of all polarizations) is transmitted by the first polarizer, and $\cos^2 45° = 50\%$ of that (see Equation 34-19) by the second, for a total of $0.5 \times 0.5 = 25\%$ for both.

Problem

65. What is the radiation force on the door of a microwave oven if 625 W of microwave power hits the door at right angles and is reflected?

Solution

The radiation pressure for normally incident, perfectly reflected electromagnetic waves is $2\bar{S}/c$. We suppose that the microwave power is uniformly spread over the area of the door (as for plane waves), so $\bar{S} = \mathcal{P}/A$. Then the force on the door is simply $P_{\text{rad}}A = (2\bar{S}/c)A = 2\mathcal{P}/c = 2(625 \text{ W})/(3\times10^8 \text{ m/s}) = 4.17 \ \mu\text{N}$.

Problem

67. A 60-W light bulb is 6.0 cm in diameter. What is the radiation pressure on an opaque object at the bulb's surface?

Solution

Suppose that the filament in the bulb is small enough to be considered as an isotropic point source. Then the radiation pressure on an opaque (perfectly absorbing) object is $P_{\text{rad}} = \bar{S}/c$ and $\bar{S} = \mathcal{P}/4\pi r^2$. Thus $P_{\text{rad}} = (60 \text{ W}/4\pi)(3 \text{ cm})^{-2}(3\times10^8 \text{ m/s})^{-1} = 17.7 \ \mu\text{Pa}$.

Supplementary Problems

Problem

69. Maxwell's equations in a dielectric resemble those in vacuum (Equations 34-6 through 34-9), but with ϕ_E in Ampère's law replaced by $\kappa\phi_E$, where κ is the dielectric constant introduced in Chapter 26. Show that the speed of electromagnetic waves in such a dielectric is $c/\sqrt{\kappa}$.

Solution

The effect of a linear, isotropic, homogeneous dielectric medium in Gauss's law is to replace ε_0 by $\kappa\varepsilon_0$. Maxwell defined the displacement current in a dielectric analogously, as $\kappa\varepsilon_0 d\phi_E/dt$. Therefore, Maxwell's equations in a dielectric medium (containing no free charge or conduction currents) are just those in Table 34-2 with $\kappa\varepsilon_0$ replacing ε_0. The discussion in Sections 34-4 through 6 applies to waves in a dielectric medium, with the same replacement. In particular, the wave speed (Equation 34-16) becomes $1/\sqrt{\kappa\varepsilon_0\mu_0} = c/\sqrt{\kappa}$. (In Section 35-3, $\sqrt{\kappa}$ is defined as the index of refraction of the medium.)

Problem

71. A radar system produces pulses consisting of 100 full cycles of a sinusoidal 70-GHz electromagnetic wave. The average power while the transmitter is on is 45 MW, and the waves are confined to a beam 20 cm in diameter. Find (a) the peak electric field, (b) the wavelength, (c) the total energy in a pulse, and (d) the total momentum in a pulse. (e) If the transmitter produces 1000 pulses per second, what is its average power output?

Solution

(a) The average intensity of a pulse is the average power during a pulse divided by the beam area, $\bar{S} = \mathcal{P}/\pi R^2$, and the peak electric field is therefore $E_p = \sqrt{2\mu_0 c\bar{S}} = (1/R)\sqrt{2\mu_0 c\mathcal{P}/\pi} = [(8\times10^{-7} \text{ H/m})\times (3\times10^8 \text{ m/s})(45 \text{ MW})]^{1/2}/(0.1 \text{ m}) = 1.04 \text{ MV/m}$. (b) The wavelength is $\lambda = c/f = (3\times10^8 \text{ m/s})\div (70 \text{ GHz}) = 4.29 \text{ mm}$. (c) 100 full cycles has a duration of $100/f = 100/(70 \text{ GHz}) = 1.43 \text{ ns}$, so the total energy in a pulse is $\mathcal{P}t = (45 \text{ MW})(1.43 \text{ ns}) = 64.3 \text{ mJ}$. (d) From Equation 34-23, the momentum per pulse is $(64.3 \text{ mJ})/(3\times10^8 \text{ m/s}) = 2.14\times10^{-10} \text{ kg}\cdot\text{m/s}$. (e) The average power output (which includes the time between pulses) is $(1000 \text{ pulses/s})(64.3 \text{ mJ/pulse}) = 64.3 \text{ W}$. (This is, of course, much less than the average power during a pulse, since pulses are emitted for only $10^3\times1.43 \text{ ns} = 1.43 \ \mu\text{s}$ each second. Thus $\mathcal{P}_{\text{out}} = \mathcal{P}_{\text{pulse}} \times 1.43 \ \mu\text{s/s}$, as above.)

Problem

73. The peak electric field measured at 8.0 cm from a light source is 150 W/m^2, while at 12 cm it measures 122 W/m^2. Describe the shape of the source.

Solution

The intensity is proportional to the square of the peak electric field (Equation 34-21b), so the given data implies that the ratio of intensities is proportional to that of the inverse distances, $(150/122)^2 = 1.51 \approx (12/8)$. Thus, $\bar{S}r$ is roughly constant. The intensity near a long, cylindrically symmetric source, where r is the axial distance, has this space dependence (see Problem 53).

Problem

75. Studies of the origin of the solar system suggest that sufficiently small particles might be blown out of the solar system by the force of sunlight. To see how small such particles must be, compare the force of sunlight with the force of gravity, and solve for the particle radius at which the two are equal. Assume the particles are spherical and have density 2 g/cm^3. Why do you not need to worry about the distance from the Sun?

Solution

The force due to radiation pressure (away from the Sun) on a totally absorbing spherical particle (radius R, cross-sectional area πR^2) is $P_{\text{rad}}\pi R^2$, where

$P_{\text{rad}} = \bar{S}/c$, and $\bar{S} = \mathcal{P}_\odot/4\pi r^2$ is the intensity of Sunlight at a distance r from the Sun. The force of the Sun's gravity on the particle (toward the Sun) is $GM_\odot(\frac{4}{3}\pi R^3\rho)/r^2$, where ρ is the particle's density. The two forces are equal in magnitude for particles with

$$R\rho = 3\mathcal{P}_\odot/16\pi GM_\odot c$$
$$= \frac{3(3.85\times10^{26}\text{ W}/16\pi)}{(6.67\times10^{-11}\text{ N·m}^2/\text{kg}^2)(1.99\times10^{30}\text{ kg})(3\times10^8\text{ m/s})}$$
$$= 5.77\times10^{-5}\text{ g/cm}^2.$$

(Note that since both forces are proportional to r^{-2}, the result is independent of r.) For particles with density 2 g/cm^3, $R = 2.89\times10^{-5}$ cm $= 0.289$ μm. Particles of the same density but smaller radius would be swept away by the solar radiation pressure.

PART 4   CUMULATIVE PROBLEMS

Problem

1. An air-insulated parallel-plate capacitor has plate area 100 cm^2 and spacing 0.50 cm. The capacitor is charged and then disconnected from the charging battery. A thin-walled, nonconducting box of the same dimensions as the capacitor is filled with water at 20.00°C. The box is released at the edge of the capacitor and moves without friction into the capacitor (Fig. 1). When it reaches equilibrium the water temperature is 21.50°C. What was the original voltage on the capacitor?

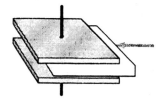

FIGURE 1 Cumulative Problem 1.

Solution

We assume that the entire difference between the initial and final values of the electrostatic energy stored in the capacitor is eventually dissipated as heat in the water (the dielectric medium), as mentioned following Equation 26-12. Thus, $U_0 - U = mc\,\Delta T$. From Equation 26-12, $U_0 - U = U_0 - U_0/\kappa = \frac{1}{2}C_0V_0^2(\kappa-1)/\kappa$, where $C_0 = \varepsilon_0 A/d = (8.85\text{ pF/m})\times(10^{-2}\text{ m}^2)/(5\times10^{-3}\text{ m}) = 17.7$ pF, and $\kappa = 78$ for water; see Table 26-1. The amount of water is $m = (1\text{ g/cm}^3)(100\text{ cm}^2)(0.5\text{ cm}) = 50$ g, so putting

everything together and solving for V_0, we find:

$$V_0 = \sqrt{\frac{2mc\,\Delta T}{C_0(\kappa-1)/\kappa}}$$
$$= \sqrt{\frac{2(50\text{ g})(4.184\text{ J/g·°C})(1.5°C)}{(17.7\text{ pF})(77/78)}} = 5.99\text{ MV}.$$

Problem

3. Five wires of equal length 25 cm and resistance 10 Ω are connected, as shown in Fig. 3. Two solenoids, each 10 cm in diameter, extend a long way perpendicular to the page. The magnetic fields of both solenoids point out of the page; the field strength in the left-hand solenoid is increasing at 50 T/s while that in the right-hand solenoid is decreasing at 30 T/s. Find the current in the resistance wire shared by both triangles. Which way does the current flow?

Solution

The increasing (decreasing) magnetic flux in the left-hand (right-hand) triangle in Fig. 3 gives rise to a clockwise (counterclockwise) induced emf in loop 1 (2), so the circuit behaves like the one shown in Fig. 28-18, but with both batteries reversed. Then the solution to

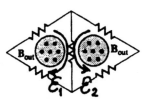

FIGURE 3 Cumulative Problem 3 Solution.

Problem 28-33 gives the current in the middle wire as

$$I_3 = -(\mathcal{E}_2 R_1 + \mathcal{E}_1 R_2)/(R_1 R_2 + R_2 R_3 + R_3 R_1).$$

The minus sign means that the direction of the current is opposite to that shown in Fig. 28-18, i.e., downward. There are two wires in the left and right branches and one in the middle, so the corresponding resistances are $R_1 = R_2 = 2R_3 = 2(10\ \Omega)$. Then I_3 becomes $-(\mathcal{E}_1 + \mathcal{E}_2)/4(10\ \Omega)$. The magnitudes of the emf's are given by Faraday's law, $\mathcal{E} = |d\phi/dt| = \pi r^2 |dB/dt|$, and both solenoids have the same cross-sectional area, so $I_3 = -\pi(5\ \text{cm})^2(50\ \text{T/s} + 30\ \text{T/s})/4(10\ \Omega) = -15.7\ \text{mA}$.

Problem

5. A coaxial cable consists of an inner conductor of radius a and an outer conductor of radius b; the space between the conductors is filled with insulation of dielectric constant κ (Fig. 4). The cable's axis is the z axis. The cable is used to carry electromagnetic energy from a radio transmitter to a broadcasting antenna. The electric field between the conductors points radially from the axis, and is given by $E = E_0(a/r)\cos(kz - \omega t)$. The magnetic field encircles the axis, and is given by $B = B_0(a/r)\cos(kz - \omega t)$. Here $E_0, B_0, k,$ and ω are constants. (a) Show, using appropriate closed surfaces and loops, that these fields satisfy Maxwell's equations. Your result shows that the cable acts as a "waveguide," confining an electromagnetic wave to the space between the conductors. (b) Find an expression for the speed at which the wave propagates along the cable.

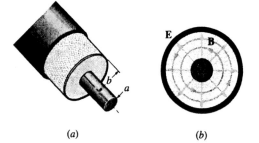

(a)   (b)

FIGURE 4 Cumulative Problem 5.

Solution

The method for (a) demonstrating that the given fields in a coaxial cable (so-called transverse electric and magnetic waves, or TEM-waves) satisfy Maxwell's equations and for (b) finding their speed is the same as that used in Sections 34-4 and 5, except that cylindrical coordinates r, θ, z, and Maxwell's equations in the dielectric (see solution to Problem 34-69) must

be used. Consider an infinitesimal volume of dielectric at a point (r, θ, z) bounded by mutually orthogonal coordinate displacements $dr, r\ d\theta, dz$. The dielectric contains no free charges or conduction currents, so the given radial electric field and circulating magnetic field satisfy Gauss's laws for electricity and magnetism in the dielectric.

In Faraday's law, take a CCW loop and sides dr and dz, at fixed θ, so that the normal to the area it bounds is parallel to **B**, as shown. Then, since $\mathbf{E} \perp d\mathbf{z}$ and $\mathbf{B} \perp d\mathbf{r}$ and $d\mathbf{z}$,

$$\oint \mathbf{E} \cdot d\ell = -E\ dr + \left(E + \frac{\partial E}{\partial z}\ dz\right) dr = \frac{\partial E}{\partial z}\ dz\ dr$$

$$= -\frac{d\phi_B}{dt} = -\frac{d}{dt}(B\ dz\ dr) = -\frac{\partial B}{\partial t}\ dz\ dr,$$

or $\partial E/\partial z = -(E_0 ak/r)\sin(kz - \omega t) = -\partial B/\partial t = -(B_0 a\omega/r)\sin(kz - \omega t)$. Thus, $E_0 k = B_0 \omega$ (same as Equation 34-14).

In Ampere's law, take a CCW loop with sides $r\ d\theta$ and dz, at fixed r, so that the normal to its area is parallel to **E**. Then, since $\mathbf{B} \perp d\mathbf{z}$ and $\mathbf{E} \perp r\ d\theta$ and $d\mathbf{z}$,

$$\oint \mathbf{B} \cdot d\ell = Br\ d\theta - \left(B + \frac{\partial B}{\partial z}\ dz\right) r\ d\theta = -\frac{\partial B}{\partial z} r\ d\theta\ dz$$

$$= \kappa\varepsilon_0\mu_0\frac{d\phi_E}{dt} = \kappa\varepsilon_0\mu_0\frac{d}{dt}(Er\ d\theta\ dz)$$

$$= \kappa\varepsilon_0\mu_0\frac{\partial E}{\partial t}r\ d\theta\ dz,$$

or $-\partial B/\partial z = (B_0 ak/r)\sin(kz - \omega t) = \kappa\varepsilon_0\mu_0 \times (\partial E/\partial t) = \kappa\varepsilon_0\mu_0(E_0 a\omega/r)\sin(kz - \omega t)$. Thus, $B_0 k = \kappa\varepsilon_0\mu_0 E_0\omega$ (same as Equation 34-15 except for κ).

Therefore, Maxwell's equations are satisfied provided E_0, B_0, k and ω are related by $B_0\omega = E_0 k$ and $B_0 k = E_0\omega\kappa\varepsilon_0\mu_0$. The wave speed follows by dividing these equations to eliminate the amplitudes. Then $\omega/k = k/\omega\kappa\varepsilon_0\mu_0$, or $(\omega/k)^2 = 1/\kappa\varepsilon_0\mu_0 = v^2$, and $v = 1/\sqrt{\kappa\varepsilon_0\mu_0} = c/\sqrt{\kappa}$.

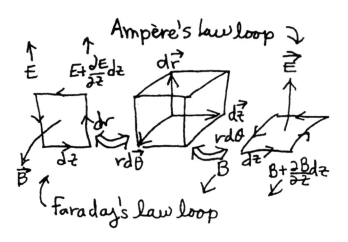

Cumulative Problem 5 Solution.

PART 5   OPTICS

CHAPTER 35   REFLECTION AND REFRACTION

ActivPhysics can help with these problems:
Activities 15.1, 15.2

Section 35-2:   Reflection

Problem

1. Through what angle should you rotate a mirror in order that a reflected ray rotate through 30°?

Solution

Since $\theta_1 = \theta_1'$ for specular reflection, (Equation 35-1) a reflected ray is deviated by $\phi = 180° - 2\theta_1$ from the incident direction. If rotating the mirror changes θ_1 by $\Delta\theta_1$, then the reflected ray is deviated by $\Delta\phi = |-2\Delta\theta_1|$ or twice this amount. Thus, if $\Delta\phi = 30°$, $|\Delta\theta_1| = 15°$.

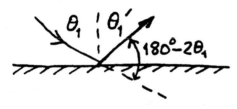

Problem 1 Solution.

Problem

3. To what angular accuracy must two ostensibly perpendicular mirrors be aligned in order that an incident ray returns on a path within 1° of its incident direction?

Solution

A ray incident on the first mirror at a grazing angle α is deflected through an angle 2α (this follows from the law of reflection). It strikes the second mirror at a grazing angle β, and is deflected by an additional angle 2β. The total deflection is $2\alpha + 2\beta = 2(180° - \theta)$. If this is to be within $180° \pm 1°$, then the angle between the mirrors, θ, must be within $90° \pm \frac{1}{2}°$.

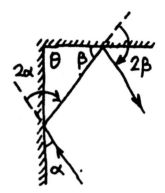

Problem 3 Solution.

Problem

5. Suppose the angle in Fig. 35-33 is changed to 75°. A ray enters the mirror system parallel to the axis. (a) How many reflections does it make? (b) Through what angle is it turned when it exits the system?

Solution

Now, after the first reflection, the ray leaves the top mirror at a grazing angle of $37\frac{1}{2}°$, and so makes a grazing angle of $180° - 75° - 37\frac{1}{2}° = 67\frac{1}{2}°$ with the bottom mirror. It is therefore deflected through an angle of $2(37\frac{1}{2}°) + 2(67\frac{1}{2})° = 210°$ CW, as it exits the system, after being reflected once from each mirror.

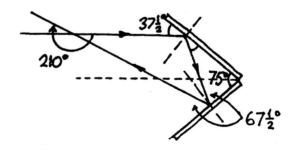

FIGURE 35-33 Problem 5 Solution.

Problem

7. Two plane mirrors make an angle ϕ. A light ray enters the system and is reflected once off each mirror. Show that the ray is turned through an angle $360° - 2\phi$.

Solution

The diagram in the solution to Problem 3 shows that the deflection of a ray, reflected once from each of two mirrors making an angle ϕ, is $2(180° - \phi) = 360° - 2\phi$. (Of course, there are conditions on ϕ and α, the grazing angle for the first mirror, if there is to be just one reflection from each mirror.)

Section 35-3: Refraction

Problem

9. Information in a compact disc is stored in "pits" whose depth is essentially one-fourth of the wavelength of the laser light used to "read" the information. That wavelength is 780 nm in air, but the wavelength on which the pit depth is based is measured in the $n = 1.55$ plastic that makes up most of the disc. Find the pit depth.

Solution

Equation 35-4 and the reasoning in Example 35-4 show that the wavelength in the plastic is $\lambda = \lambda_{\text{air}}/n = 780$ nm$/1.55 = 503$ nm. The pit depth is one quarter of this, or 126 nm.

Problem

11. A light ray propagates in a transparent material at 15° to the normal to the surface. When it emerges into the surrounding air, it makes a 24° angle with the normal. What is the refractive index of the material?

Solution

Snell's law (Equation 35-3), with air as medium 1, gives $n_2 = n_1 \sin\theta_1/\sin\theta_2 = 1 \times \sin 24°/\sin 15° = 1.57$.

Problem

13. A block of glass with $n = 1.52$ is submerged in one of the liquids listed in Table 35-1. For a ray striking the glass with incidence angle 31.5°, the angle of refraction is 27.9°. What is the liquid?

Solution

With the unknown liquid as medium 1, and the glass as medium 2, Snell's law gives $n_1 = n_2 \sin\theta_2/\sin\theta_1 = 1.52 \times \sin 27.9°/\sin 31.5° = 1.361$. This is the same as ethyl alcohol.

Problem

15. You look at the center of one face of a solid cube of glass, on a line of sight making a 55° angle with the normal to the cube face. What is the minimum refractive index of the glass for which you will see through the opposite face of the cube?

Solution

The angle of refraction in the glass, given by $\sin\theta_2 = \sin 55°/n_2$, must be less than $\tan^{-1}(\frac{1}{2}) = 26.6°$, for the ray to emerge from the opposite face (see diagram). Therefore, $n_2 \geq \sin 55°/\sin 26.6° = 1.83$.

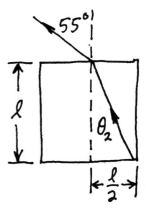

Problem 15 Solution.

Problem

17. You're standing 2.3 m horizontally from the edge of a 4.5-m-deep lake, with your eyes 1.7 m above the water surface. A diver holding a flashlight at the lake bottom shines the light so you can see it. If the light in the water makes a 42° angle with the vertical, at what horizontal distance is the diver from the edge of the lake?

Solution

Snell's law gives the angle of refraction (θ_1) in terms of the angle of incidence ($\theta_2 = 42°$) for the light path from the flashlight to your eye. These can be related to the other given distances by means of a carefully drawn diagram. Thus, $\theta_1 = \sin^{-1}(n_2 \sin\theta_2/n_1) = \sin^{-1}(1.333 \sin 42°) = 63.1°$, where we used indices of refraction from Table 35-1, with $n_1 \approx 1$ for air. The geometry of the diagram makes the horizontal distances apparent: $\tan\theta_1 = (2.3 \text{ m} + x_1)/(1.7 \text{ m})$, or $x_1 = (1.7 \text{ m})\tan 63.1° - 2.3 \text{ m} = 1.05 \text{ m}$, and $\tan\theta_2 = x_2/(4.5 \text{ m})$, or $x_2 = (4.5 \text{ m})\tan 42° = 4.05 \text{ m}$. The total horizontal distance from the edge is $x_1 + x_2 = 5.11$ m.

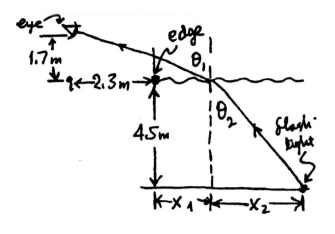

Problem 17 Solution.

Problem

19. A light ray is propagating in a crystal where its wavelength is 540 nm. It strikes the interior surface of the crystal with an incidence angle of 34° and emerges into the surrounding air at 76° to the surface normal. Find (a) the light's frequency and (b) its wavelength in air.

Solution

The index of refraction of the crystal (Equation 35-3) is $n_2 = \sin 76°/\sin 34° = 1.74$ (relative to air, with $n_1 \approx 1$). (a) The frequency of the light is $f = v_2/\lambda_2 = c/n_2\lambda_2 = (3 \times 10^8 \text{ m/s})/(1.74 \times 540 \text{ nm}) = c/(937 \text{ nm}) = 3.20 \times 10^{14}$ Hz, where we used the velocity (Equation 35-2) and wavelength of light in the crystal. (b) Of course, $\lambda_1 = n_2\lambda_2 = 937$ nm is the wavelength of the light in air (Equation 35-4). (Obviously, $f = v_1/\lambda_1$ is an alternative approach for part (a), since $v_1 \approx c$ in air.)

Section 35-4:   Total Internal Reflection

Problem

21. Find the critical angle for total internal reflection in (a) ice, (b) polystyrene, and (c) rutile. Assume the surrounding medium is air.

Solution

For $n_{air} \approx 1$, the critical angle for total internal reflection in a medium of refractive index n is $\theta_c = \sin^{-1}(1/n)$. (Air is medium-2 in Equation 35-5.) From Table 35-1, $n = 1.309$ (ice), 1.49 (polystyrene), and 2.62 (rutile), so $\theta_c = \sin^{-1}(1/1.309) = 49.8°$, 42.2° and 22.4°, respectively, for these media.

Problem

23. What is the critical angle for light propagating in glass with $n = 1.52$ when the glass is immersed in (a) water, (b) benzene, and (c) diiodomethane?

Solution

The critical angle in medium-1, at an interface with medium-2, is $\theta_c = \sin^{-1}(n_2/n_1)$, where $n_1 > n_2$ (Equation 35-5). (a) For glass ($n_1 = 1.52$) immersed in water ($n_2 = 1.333$), $\theta_c = \sin^{-1}(1.333/1.52) = 61.3°$. (b) The same glass immersed in benzene has $\theta_c = \sin^{-1}(1.501/1.52) = 80.9°$. (c) Since the index of refraction of diiodomethane ($n_2 = 1.738$) is not smaller than that for this glass, there is no total internal reflection for light propagating in the glass. (However, for light originating in the liquid, $\theta_c' = \sin^{-1}(1.52 \div 1.738) = 61.0°$ at the glass interface.)

Problem

25. Light propagating in a medium with refractive index n_1 encounters a parallel-sided slab with index n_2. On the other side is a third medium with index $n_3 < n_1$. Show that the condition for avoiding internal reflection at *both* interfaces is that the incidence angle at the n_1-n_2 interface be less than the critical angle for an n_1-n_3 interface. In other words, the index of the intermediate material doesn't matter.

Solution

Since medium-2 has parallel interfaces with media-1 and 3, the angle of refraction at the 1-2 interface equals the angle of incidence at the 2-3 interface, as shown. (The normals to the interfaces are also parallel, so the alternate angles, marked θ_2, are equal.) Thus Snell's law implies $n_1 \sin\theta_1 = n_2 \sin\theta_2 = n_3 \sin\theta_3$, so that the angles in media-1 and 3 are related as if media-2 were not present. Of course, there are conditions on the intensity of the light transmitted

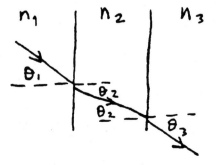

Problem 25 Solution.

through medium-2 which do depend on n_2 and the critical angle, if any, at the 1-2 interface. If $n_2 < n_1$, the phenomenon of frustrated total reflection (i.e., transmission of light for angles greater than the critical angle) may occur if the thickness of the slab is on the order of a few wavelengths of the incident light.

Problem

27. What is the minimum refractive index for which total internal reflection will occur as shown in Fig. 35-15a? Assume the surrounding medium is air and that the prism is an isosceles right triangle.

Solution

Figure 35-15a shows a 45° right-triangle prism with critical angle less than 45°. Thus, $\theta_c = \sin^{-1}(\frac{1}{n}) < 45°$, or $n > 1/\sin 45° = \sqrt{2}$. (We used $n_2 = 1$ for air, and $n_1 = n$ for the prism, in Equation 35-5.)

Problem

29. What is the speed of light in a material for which the critical angle at an interface with air is 61°?

Solution

From Equations 35-5 and 2, $\sin \theta_c = n_{\text{air}}/n \approx \frac{1}{n} = v/c$, so $v = c \sin \theta_c = (3 \times 10^8 \text{ m/s}) \sin 61° = 2.62 \times 10^8$ m/s. (The critical angle and the speed of light in a material are both related to the index of refraction.)

Problem

31. A compound lens is made from crown glass ($n = 1.52$) bonded to flint glass ($n = 1.89$). What is the critical angle for light incident on the flint-crown interface?

Solution

The critical angle for light incident in the glass of higher index of refraction (flint glass) is $\theta_c = \sin^{-1}(n_{\text{crown}}/n_{\text{flint}}) = \sin^{-1}(1.52/1.89) = 53.5°$.

Problem

33. A scuba diver sets off a camera flash a distance h below the surface of water with refractive index n. Show that light emerges from the water surface through a circle of diameter $2h/\sqrt{n^2 - 1}$.

Solution

Light from the flash will strike the water surface at the critical angle for a distance $r = h \tan \theta_c$ from a point directly over the flash. Therefore, the diameter of the circle through which light emerges is $2r = 2h \tan \theta_c$.

But $\sin \theta_c = 1/n$ (Equation 33-5 at the water-air interface), and $\tan^2 \theta_c = (\csc^2 \theta_c - 1)^{-1}$ (a trigonometric identity), so we can write $2r = 2h \div \sqrt{n^2 - 1}$.

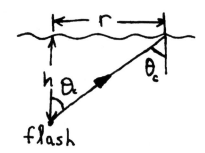

Problem 33 Solution.

Section 35-5: Dispersion

Problem

35. Suppose the red and blue beams of the preceding problem are now propagating in the same direction *inside* the glass. For what range of incidence angles on the glass-air interface will one beam be totally reflected and the other not?

Solution

The critical angle for blue light is less than for red light, $\theta_{c,\text{blue}} = \sin^{-1}(1/1.680) = 36.5°$, and $\theta_{c,\text{red}} = \sin^{-1}(1/1.621) = 38.1°$. For incidence angles between these values, blue light will be totally reflected, while some red light is refracted at the glass-air interface.

Problem

37. Two of the prominent spectral lines—discrete wavelengths of light—emitted by glowing hydrogen are hydrogen-α at 656.3 nm and hydrogen-β at 486.1 nm. Light from glowing hydrogen passes through a prism like that of Fig. 35-22, then falls on a screen 1.0 m from the prism. How far apart will these two spectral lines be? Use Fig. 35-20 for the refractive index.

Solution

The angular dispersion of H_α and H_β light in the prism of Fig. 35-22 can be found from the analysis in Example 35-6. For normal incidence on the prism, rays emerge with refraction angles of $\sin^{-1}(n \sin 40°)$. From Fig. 35-20, we estimate that $n_\alpha = 1.517$ and $n_\beta = 1.528$, so the angular dispersion is $\gamma = 79.2° - 77.2° = 1.98°$. We can assume that the size of the prism is small compared to the distance, r, to the screen, so the separation on the screen corresponding to γ is $\Delta x = \gamma \cdot r = (1.98°)(\pi/180°)(1 \text{ m}) = 3.45$ cm.

Section 35-6:   Reflection and Polarization

Problem

39. Find the polarizing angle for diamond when light is incident from air.

Solution

Equation 35-6 gives the polarizing angle, for light in air reflected from diamond; $\theta_p = \tan^{-1}(2.419/1) = 67.5°$.

Problem

41. What is the polarizing angle for light incident from below on the surface of a pond?

Solution

In Equation 35-6, n_2 is the index of refraction of the reflecting medium, so $\theta_p = \tan^{-1}(n_{air}/n_{water}) = \tan^{-1}(1/1.333) = 36.9°$.

Paired Problems

Problem

43. Light propagating in air strikes a transparent crystal at incidence angle 35°. If the angle of refraction is 22°, what is the speed of light in the crystal?

Solution

Combining Equations 35-2 and 3 (or using the form of Snell's law preceding Equation 35-2), we find $v = c/n = c\sin\theta_2/\sin\theta_1 = (3\times10^8 \text{ m/s})\sin 22°/\sin 35° = 1.96\times10^8$ m/s. (Note: $n_{air} \approx 1$.)

Problem

45. A cylindrical tank 2.4 m deep is full to the brim with water. Sunlight first hits part of the tank bottom when the rising Sun makes a 22° angle with the horizon. Find the tank's diameter.

Solution

The rays of sunlight which first hit the bottom of the tank just skim the opposite edge of the rim, as sketched. The diameter and depth of the tank (d and h) are related to the angle of refraction as shown, $\tan\theta_2 = d/h$. Combining this with Snell's law (Equation 35-3), we find $d = h\tan\theta_2 = h\tan[\sin^{-1}\times(n_1\sin\theta_1/n_2)] = (2.4 \text{ m})\tan[\sin^{-1}(\sin 68°/1.333)] = 2.32$ m. (Note: $n_1 = 1$ for air and $n_2 = 1.333$ for water; see Table 35-1.)

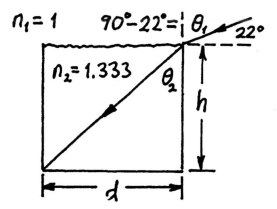

Problem 45 Solution.

Problem

47. Light is incident from air on the flat wall of a polystyrene water tank. If the incidence angle is 40°, what angle does the light make with the tank normal in the water?

Solution

If the plastic wall of the tank has parallel faces, it does not affect the angle of refraction in the water (see solution to Problem 25). Then $n_1\sin\theta_1 = n_3\sin\theta_3$, or $\theta_3 = \sin^{-1}(n_1\sin\theta_1/n_3) = \sin^{-1}(\sin 40°/1.333) = 28.8°$. (Media-1, 2, and 3 are air, polystyrene, and water, respectively, in the solution to Problem 25.)

Problem

49. Light strikes a right-angled glass prism ($n = 1.52$) in a direction parallel to the prism's base, as shown in Fig. 35-39. The point of incidence is high enough that the refracted ray hits the opposite sloping side. (a) Through which side of the prism does the beam emerge? (b) Through what angle has it been deflected?

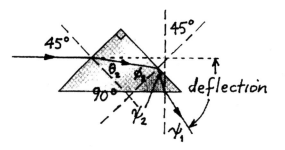

FIGURE 35-39 Problem 49 Solution.

Solution

The prism geometry of Fig. 35-39 and Snell's law imply $\phi_2 = 90° - \theta_2 = 90° - \sin^{-1}(\sin 45°/1.52) = 62.3°$, which is greater than the critical angle for total reflection from the glass-air interface, $\theta_c = \sin^{-1}(1 \div 1.52) = 41.1°$. Therefore, the incident light is totally reflected in the glass, as shown superposed on Fig. 35-39, and hits the base of the prism at an incidence angle of $\psi_2 = \phi_2 - 45° = 17.3°$. Its angle of refraction in air, after emerging, is $\psi_1 = \sin^{-1} \times (1.52 \sin 17.3°) = 26.8°$, giving it a net deflection of $90° - 26.8° = 63.2°$, measured clockwise from its original direction.

Problem

51. Repeat Problem 20 for the case $n = 1.75$, $\alpha = 40°$, and $\theta_1 = 25°$.

Solution

A general treatment of refraction through a prism of index of refraction $n_2 = n$, surrounded by air of index $n_1 = 1$, for the geometry of Fig. 35-36, is given in the solution to Problem 55. For $n = 1.75$, $\alpha = 40°$, and $\theta_1 = 25°$, the other angles defined there are:

$\theta_2 = \sin^{-1}(\sin \theta_1/n) = \sin^{-1}(\sin 25°/1.75) = 14.0°$,
$\phi_2 = \alpha - \theta_2 = 40° - 14.0° = 26.0°$,
$\phi_1 = \sin^{-1}(n \sin \phi_2) = \sin^{-1}(1.75 \sin 26.0°) = 50.2°$,
and $\delta = \theta_1 + \phi_1 - \alpha = 35.2°$.

(Note that ϕ_2 is less than the critical angle for this prism, which is $\sin^{-1}(1/1.75) = 34.8°$.)

Supplementary Problems
Problem

53. A cubical block is made from two equal-size slabs of materials with different refractive indices, as shown in Fig. 35-40. Find the index of the right-hand slab if a light ray is incident on the center of the left-hand slab and then describes the path shown.

Solution

In Fig. 35-40, the incident ray appears to hit the cube at the center of a side and the thickness of each material is the same, so $x_1 = \ell \tan \theta_1$, $x_2 = \ell \tan \theta_2$, and $x_1 + x_2 = \ell$. Thus $\tan \theta_1 + \tan \theta_2 = 1$, where θ_1 and θ_2 are the angles of refraction in the two materials, as shown. From Snell's law, $\sin 35° = n_1 \times \sin \theta_1 = n_2 \sin \theta_2$, so θ_1 and θ_2 can be eliminated in terms of the indices of refraction of the two materials, and since n_1 is given, n_2 can be easily determined. With the aid of a calculator, the intermediate steps are $\theta_1 = \sin^{-1}(\sin 35°/1.43) = 23.6°$, $\theta_2 = \tan^{-1}(1 -$

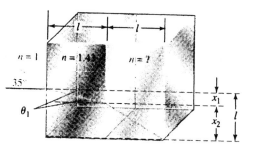

FIGURE 35-40 Problem 53 Solution.

$\tan \theta_1) = 29.3°$, and $n_2 = \sin 35°/\sin \theta_2 = 1.17$. In order to write the solution compactly for general values of n_1 and n_2, first notice that $\tan \theta = \sin \theta \div \cos \theta = \sin \theta/\sqrt{1 - \sin^2 \theta} = 1/\sqrt{\csc^2 \theta - 1}$, and that $n_1 \csc 35° = \csc \theta_1$ and $n_2 \csc 35° = \csc \theta_2$ (recall that the cosecant is the reciprocal of the sine). Then

$$\tan \theta_1 + \tan \theta_2 = 1 = \left(1/\sqrt{n_1^2 \csc^2 35° - 1}\right) + \left(1/\sqrt{n_2^2 \csc^2 35° - 1}\right).$$

Since $n_1 = 1.43$, one finds $\sqrt{n_2^2 \csc^2 35° - 1} = 1.78$, and $n_2 = 1.17$.

Problem

55. Light is incident with incidence angle θ_1 on a prism with apex angle α and refractive index n, as shown in Fig. 35-36. Show that the angle δ through which the outgoing beam deviates from the incident beam is given by

$$\delta = \theta_1 - \alpha + \sin^{-1}\left\{n \sin\left[\alpha - \sin^{-1}\left(\frac{\sin \theta_1}{n}\right)\right]\right\}.$$

Assume the surrounding medium has $n = 1$.

Solution

It is an exercise in ray tracing to determine the angles shown superposed on Fig. 35-36; from Snell's law and plane geometry: $\theta_2 = \sin^{-1}(\sin \theta_1/n)$ (Snell's law for the first refraction, with $n_1 = 1$ and $n_2 = n$), $\phi_2 = \alpha - \theta_2$ (α is the exterior angle to the triangle formed by the ray segment in the prism and the normals to the surfaces), $\phi_1 = \sin^{-1}(n \sin \phi_2)$ (Snell's law for the second refraction), and finally, $\delta = \theta_1 - \theta_2 + \phi_1 - \phi_2 = \theta_1 + \phi_1 - \alpha$ (the total deflection is the sum of the deflections at each refraction, clockwise deflection positive in Fig. 35-36). Writing down these steps in reverse order, substituting for each angle, one gets

$$\delta = \theta_1 + \sin^{-1}\left\{n \sin\left[\alpha - \sin^{-1}\left(\frac{\sin \theta_1}{n}\right)\right]\right\} - \alpha.$$

(Note: Problems 20, 36, 49–52, and also Problems 27, 28, 30, 37 and 38, involve ray tracing through prisms, in which a similar, but not identical, analysis is useful. Of course, ϕ_1 must be a real angle, i.e., less than 90°, or total internal reflection occurs instead of the second refraction. This is determined by the given values of n, α and θ_1.)

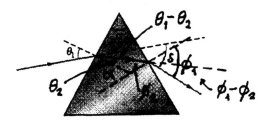

FIGURE 35-36 Problem 55 Solution.

Problem

57. Show that a three-dimensional corner reflector (three mirrors in three mutually perpendicular planes, or a solid cube in which total internal reflection occurs) turns an incident light ray through 180°, so it returns in the direction from which it came. *Hint:* Let $\mathbf{q} = q_x\hat{\mathbf{i}} + q_y\hat{\mathbf{j}} + q_z\hat{\mathbf{k}}$ be a vector in the direction of propagation. How does this vector get changed on reflection by a mirror in a plane defined by two of the coordinate axes?

Solution

A single plane mirror reverses the direction of just the normal component of a ray striking its surface. For example, a ray incident in the direction $\hat{\mathbf{q}} = \hat{\mathbf{i}}\cos\alpha_x + \hat{\mathbf{j}}\cos\alpha_y + \hat{\mathbf{k}}\cos\alpha_z$, on a mirror normal to the x-axis, is reflected into the direction $-\hat{\mathbf{i}}\cos\alpha_x + \hat{\mathbf{j}}\cos\alpha_y + \hat{\mathbf{k}}\cos\alpha_z$. (In our notation, $\hat{\mathbf{q}}$ is a unit vector, and $\cos^2\alpha_x + \cos^2\alpha_y + \cos^2\alpha_z = 1$.) If the ray also strikes mirrors which are normal to the y- and z-axes, as in a corner reflector, it emerges in the direction $\hat{\mathbf{q}}' = -\hat{\mathbf{q}}$, or opposite to the initial direction. In order to strike all three mirrors, the direction cosines of the incident ray must have magnitudes greater than some minimum non-zero value, depending on the size of the reflector (i.e., $|\cos\alpha_i| > 0$ for $i = x$, y, and z).

Problem

59. (a) Differentiate the result of the preceding problem to show that the maximum value of ϕ occurs when the incidence angle θ is given by $\cos^2\theta = \frac{1}{3}(n^2 - 1)$. (b) Use this result and that of the preceding problem to find $\phi_{\max}$ in water with $n = 1.333$.

Solution

One can differentiate ϕ, with respect to θ, directly, by using $d[\sin^{-1}(x/a)]/dx = 1/\sqrt{a^2 - x^2}$ (see the integral table in Appendix A.) Then

$$\frac{d\phi}{d\theta} = \frac{4}{\sqrt{n^2 - \sin^2\theta}}\frac{d(\sin\theta)}{d\theta} - 2 = \frac{4\cos\theta}{\sqrt{n^2 - \sin^2\theta}} - 2.$$

The condition for a maximum, $d\phi/d\theta = 0$, implies that $2\cos\theta_m = \sqrt{n^2 - \sin^2\theta_m}$, or $4\cos^2\theta_m = n^2 - (1 - \cos^2\theta_m)$, so $\cos^2\theta_m = \frac{1}{3}(n^2 - 1)$. If this value of θ is substituted into the expression for ϕ, after noting that $\sin^2\theta_m = \frac{1}{3}(4 - n^2)$, one gets $\phi_{\max} = 4\sin^{-1}\times(\sqrt{(4 - n^2)/3n^2}) - 2\cos^{-1}\sqrt{(n^2 - 1)/3}$, which equals 42.1° for $n = 1.333$. (This is the average angle, above the anti-solar direction, that an observer sees a rainbow, because n is the average index of refraction for visible wavelengths.)

Problem

61. *Fermat's principle* states that the path of a light ray between two points is such that the time to traverse that path is an extremum (either a minimum or maximum) when compared with the times for nearby paths. Consider two points A and B on the same side of a reflecting surface, and show that a light ray traveling from A to B via a point on the reflecting surface will take the least time if its path obeys the law of reflection. Thus, the law of reflection (Equation 35-1) follows from Fermat's principle.

Solution

Take the x-z plane to be the reflecting surface, and the x-y plane to contain the points A and B, with the y-axis through A. Suppose a ray traveling from A to B

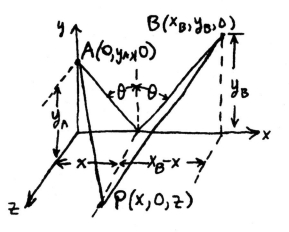

Problem 61 Solution.

via the surface is reflected at point $P(x, 0, z)$, as shown. (It is assumed that the path of a ray between two points in the same medium, with no intervening reflections or refractions, is a straight line, which also follows from Fermat's principle.) Since the ray propagates in only one medium, the time to traverse the path APB is proportional to the total distance $(t = D/v)$, where $D = AP + PB = \sqrt{x^2 + y_A^2 + z^2} + \sqrt{(x_B - x)^2 + y_B^2 + z^2}$. The conditions for D to be an extremum (a minimum in this case) are $\partial D/\partial z = 0$ and $\partial D/\partial x = 0$. The first condition requires that $(z/\sqrt{x^2 + y_A^2 + z^2}) + (z/\sqrt{(x_B - x)^2 + y_B^2 + z^2}) = 0$,

which is satisfied only for $z = 0$. (Thus, the incident ray, the normal to the surface, and the reflected ray all lie in the same plane, called the plane of incidence.) With $z = 0$, the second condition requires that $(x/\sqrt{x^2 + y_A^2}) - (x_B - x)/\sqrt{(x_B - x)^2 + y_B^2} = 0$. But $\sin\theta = x/\sqrt{x^2 + y_A^2}$, and $\sin\theta' = (x_B - x) \div \sqrt{(x_B - x)^2 + y_B^2}$, therefore $\sin\theta - \sin\theta' = 0$ which is the law of reflection. (Note: If A and B are on opposite sides of the x-z plane in media where the velocity of light is different, differentiation of $t = (AP/v) + (PB/v')$ leads to $(\sin\theta/v) - (\sin\theta'/v') = 0$, which is the subject of the next problem.)

CHAPTER 36   IMAGE FORMATION AND OPTICAL INSTRUMENTS

ActivPhysics can help with these problems:
All activities in Section 15

Sections 36-1 and 36-2:   Plane and Curved Mirrors

Problem

1. A shoe store uses small floor-level mirrors to let customers view prospective purchases. At what angle should such a mirror be inclined so that a person standing 50 cm from the mirror with eyes 140 cm off the floor can see her feet?

Solution

A small mirror (M) on the floor intercepts rays coming from a customer's shoes (O), which are traveling nearly parallel to the floor. The angle to the customer's eye (E) from the mirror is twice the angle of reflection, so $\tan 2\alpha = h/d$, or $\alpha = \frac{1}{2}\tan^{-1} \times (140/50) = 35.2°$, for the given distances. Therefore, the plane of the mirror should be tilted by 35.2° from the vertical to provide the customer with a floor-level view of her shoes.

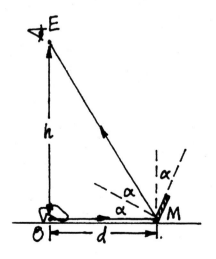

Problem 1 Solution.

Problem

3. (a) What is the focal length of a concave mirror if an object placed 50 cm in front of the mirror has a real image 75 cm from the mirror? (b) Where and what type will the image be if the object is moved to a point 20 cm from the mirror?

Solution

(a) The mirror equation relates the given distances (both positive for a real object and image) to the focal length: $f^{-1} = (50 \text{ cm})^{-1} + (75 \text{ cm})^{-1}$, or $f = 30$ cm. (See Equation 36-2.) (b) A second application of the mirror equation yields $(\ell')^{-1} = (30 \text{ cm})^{-1} - (20 \text{ cm})^{-1}$, or $\ell' = -60$ cm. A negative distance indicates a virtual, erect image located behind the mirror. (Fig. 36-8c and Table 36-1 confirm these results.)

Problem

5. An object is five focal lengths from a concave mirror. (a) How do the object and image heights compare? (b) Is the image upright or inverted?

Solution

(a) One can solve Equation 36-2 for ℓ', and substitute into Equation 36-1, to yield $h'/h = -\ell'/\ell = -f/(\ell - f) = -f/(5f - f) = -\frac{1}{4}$. (b) A negative magnification applies to a real, inverted image.

Problem

7. A virtual image is located 40 cm behind a concave mirror with focal length 18 cm. (a) Where is the object? (b) By how much is the image magnified?

Solution

(a) The mirror equation (Equation 36-2) gives $\ell = f\ell'/(\ell' - f) = (18 \text{ cm})(-40 \text{ cm})/(-58 \text{ cm}) = 12.4$ cm (positive distances are in front of the mirror, negative distances behind). (b) Equation 36-1 gives $M = -\ell'/\ell = +40 \text{ cm}/12.4 \text{ cm} = 3.22$.

Problem

9. A 12-mm-high object is 10 cm from a concave mirror with focal length 17 cm. (a) Where, (b) how high, and (c) what type is its image?

Solution

For an object on the mirror's axis, Equations 36-2 and 1 give (a) $\ell' = f\ell/(\ell - f) = (17 \times 10 \text{ cm})/(10 - 17) =$

−24.3 cm (i.e., behind the mirror). (c) A negative image distance indicates a virtual image. (b) $M = -\ell'/\ell = 24.3/10 = 2.43 = h'/h$, so the image is upright and 2.43×12 mm $= 29.1$ mm high.

Problem

11. An object's image in a 27-cm-focal-length concave mirror is upright and magnified by a factor of 3. Where is the object?

Solution

An upright image in a concave mirror must be virtual, so $M = +3 = -\ell'/\ell$. The mirror equation gives $(1/\ell) + (1/\ell') = (1/\ell) - (1/3\ell) = 1/f$, or $\ell = (\frac{2}{3})f = (\frac{2}{3})(27$ cm$) = 18$ cm (positive in front of the mirror).

Problem

13. When viewed from Earth, the moon subtends an angle of 0.5° in the sky. How large an image of the moon will be formed by the 3.6-m-diameter mirror of the Canada-France-Hawaii telescope, which has a focal length of 8.5 m?

Solution

The main mirror of a telescope is concave, since only such a mirror collects light from a distant object into a real image. Inspection of Fig. 36-8a (partially redrawn below) shows that the angular size of the object and image are equal ($h/\ell = h'/\ell' \approx \theta =$ size ÷ distance). Since the object distance is astronomical, $1/\ell \approx 0 \approx 1/f - 1/\ell'$, or $\ell' \approx f$. Thus, the image distance equals the focal length, and its size is $\theta \times f = \frac{1}{2}° \times (\pi/180°) \times 8.5$ m $= 7.42$ cm. (See Problem 6.)

Problem 13 Solution.

Problem

15. You look into a reflecting sphere 80 cm in diameter and see an image of your face at one-third its normal size (Fig. 36-46). How far are you from the sphere's surface?

Solution

The sphere reflects like a convex mirror of focal length $f = R/2 = -40$ cm$/2 = -20$ cm. (Only a convex mirror produces a reduced, upright, virtual image.)

The equation in the solution to Problem 5(a) can be used to find the object distance in terms of f and the magnification, $\ell = f(1 - h/h') = f(1 - 1/M) = -20$ cm$(1 - 3) = 40$ cm.

Section 36-3: Lenses

Problem

17. A light bulb is 56 cm from a convex lens, and its image appears on a screen located 31 cm on the other side of the lens. (a) What is the focal length of the lens? (b) By how much is the image enlarged or reduced?

Solution

(a) The object and image distances are both positive, for a real image formed by a single lens (recall that only a real image can appear on a screen), so the lens equation gives $f^{-1} = (56$ cm$)^{-1} + (31$ cm$)^{-1} = (20.0$ cm$)^{-1}$. (b) Equation 36-4 gives a magnification of $M = -31/56 = -0.554$, so the inverted image is reduced to nearly 55% of the actual size of the bulb.

Problem

19. A lens with 50-cm focal length produces a real image the same size as the object. How far from the lens are image and object?

Solution

For a real image the same size as the object, $h' = -h$, so $M = -1 = -\ell'/\ell$, or $\ell' = \ell$. The lens equation (Equation 36-5) then gives $(1/\ell) + (1/\ell') = 2/\ell = 1/f$, or $\ell = \ell' = 2f = 100$ cm.

Problem

21. A simple camera uses a single converging lens to focus an image on its film. If the focal length of the lens is 45 mm, what should be the lens-to-film distance for the camera to focus on an object 80 cm from the lens?

Solution

Set $\ell = 80$ cm and $f = 45$ mm in the lens equation and solve for ℓ'. The result is $\ell' = \ell f/(\ell - f) = (80 \times 45$ cm$)/(800 - 45) = 4.77$ cm.

Problem

23. How far from a page should you hold a lens with 32-cm focal length in order to see the print magnified 1.6 times?

Solution

When a virtual, upright image is formed by a converging lens (a diverging lens always produces a reduced image), the magnification is positive, $M = 1.6 = -f/(\ell - f)$. (Use Equations 36-5 and 4.) Therefore, $\ell = (M - 1)f/M = 0.6$ (32 cm)/1.6 = 12 cm.

Problem

25. The largest refracting telescope in the world, at Yerkes Observatory, has a 1-m-diameter lens with focal length 12 m (Fig. 36-47). If an airplane flew 1 km above the telescope, where would its image occur in relation to the images of the very distant stars?

Solution

Very distant stars ($\ell = \infty$) produce images at the focus, $\ell' = f = 12$ m. For an airplane 1 km away, $\ell' = \ell f/(\ell - f) = (1 \text{ km})(12 \text{ m})/(988 \text{ m}) = 12.1$ m, or 14.6 cm farther than the focal point. ($\ell' - f = f^2 \div (\ell - f) = (144/988)$ m can be calculated more accurately.)

Problem

27. A lens has focal length $f = 35$ cm. Find the type and height of the image produced when a 2.2-cm-high object is placed at distances (a) $f + 10$ cm and (b) $f - 10$ cm.

Solution

The lens equation and magnification for a thin (converging, i.e., positive f) lens, Equations 36-4 and 5, give $M = -\ell'/\ell = -f/(\ell - f)$, so $h' = Mh = -fh \div (\ell - f)$. (a) If $f = 35$ cm and $\ell = f + 10$ cm, then $h' = -(35 \text{ cm})(2.2/10) = -7.7$ cm. A negative image height signifies a real, inverted image. (b) If $\ell = f - 10$ cm, then $h' = -(35 \text{ cm})(2.2)/(-10) = +7.7$ cm, which represents a virtual, erect image of the same size.

Problem

29. A candle and a screen are 70 cm apart. Find two points between candle and screen where you could put a convex lens with 17 cm focal length to give a sharp image of the candle on the screen.

Solution

Since ℓ and ℓ' are both positive for a real image, and the distance $a \equiv \ell + \ell' = 70$ cm is fixed, the lens equation can be rewritten as a quadratic, $af = (\ell + \ell')f = \ell\ell' = \ell(a - \ell) = \ell'(a - \ell')$. The solutions for ℓ or ℓ' are $\frac{1}{2}a(1 \pm \sqrt{1 - 4f/a}) = (35 \text{ cm})(1 \pm \sqrt{1 - (4 \times 17)/70}) = 29.1$ cm or 40.9 cm, which are the desired lens locations. (Note that this situation has a real solution only if $0 < 4f \le a$.)

Section 36-4   Refraction in Lenses: The Details

Problem

31. You're standing in a wading pool and your feet appear to be 30 cm below the surface. How deep is the pool?

Solution

The image formed by a single refracting interface between two media, for paraxial rays, is described by Equation 36-6, with sign conventions for distances defined in the paragraph following. For the flat surface of the wading pool, $R = \infty$, $n_1 = 1.333$ for water, ℓ is the depth of the pool (your feet, the object, are on the bottom), $n_2 = 1$ for air, and $\ell' = -30$ cm (for a virtual image at the apparent depth). Thus, $(1.333/\ell) + (1/(-30 \text{ cm})) = (n_2 - n_1)/\infty = 0$, or $\ell = 40$ cm. (This problem could also be solved directly from Snell's law, as in the previous chapter, without the paraxial ray approximation.)

Problem

33. Use Equation 36-6 to show that an object at the center of a glass sphere will appear to be its actual distance—one radius—from the edge. Draw a ray diagram showing why this result makes sense.

Solution

Solving for ℓ' in Equation 36-6 gives us $\ell' = n_2 R\ell \div [(n_2 - n_1)\ell - n_1 R]$. If the object is at the center of a glass sphere ($\ell = |R|$ and R is negative for a concave surface toward the object, i.e., $R = -|R|$) and viewed from the air outside ($n_2 = 1$), one obtains $\ell' = -|R|^2/[(1 - n_1)|R| + n_1|R|] = -|R|$. This represents a virtual image, on the same side of the surface as the object, a distance $|R|$ from the surface, or at the center, coincident with the object. This is to be expected, because all the rays from an object at the center of curvature, strike the surface normally and are not refracted. The diagram is hardly necessary to understand this.

Problem 33 Solution.

Problem

35. Rework Example 36-6 for a fish 15 cm from the *far* wall of the tank.

Solution

As in Example 36-6, use Equation 36-6 with $R = -35$ cm, $n_1 = 1.333$, $n_2 = 1$, but with $\ell = 70$ cm $- 15$ cm $= 55$ cm (as distance from the near wall). Then $\ell' = [(1 - 1.333)/(-35 \text{ cm}) - 1.333/55 \text{ cm}]^{-1} = -67.9$ cm. In this case, the object is closer to the refracting surface than its image (see sketch and compare with Fig. 36-25b).

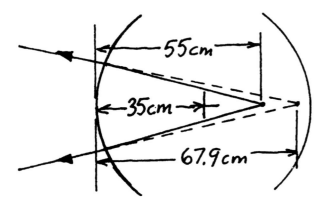

Problem 35 Solution.

Problem

37. Two specks of dirt are trapped in a crystal ball, one at the center and the other halfway to the surface. If you peer into the ball on a line joining the two specks, the outer one appears to be only one-third of the way to the other. What is the refractive index of the ball?

Solution

The outer speck appears $\frac{1}{3}$ the distance to the center of the ball, $\ell' = -|R|/3$, since the speck at the center appears at the center (see Problem 33.) The actual distance of the outer speck is given as $\ell = |R|/2$, so Equation 36-6 (with n_1 for the ball's material, $n_2 = 1$ for air, and $R = -|R|$ for a concave surface toward the object) gives $(n_1/\frac{1}{2}|R|) + (1/(-\frac{1}{3}|R|)) = (1 - n_1) \div (-|R|)$. This simplifies to $2n_1 - 3 = n_1 - 1$, or $n_1 = 2$.

Problem

39. A contact lens is in the shape of a convex meniscus (see Fig. 36-28); the inner surface is curved to fit the eye, with a curvature radius of 7.80 mm. The lens is made from plastic with refractive index $n = 1.56$. If it's to have a focal length of 44.4 cm, what should be the curvature radius of its outer surface?

Solution

The lensmaker's formula (Equation 36-8) relates the four quantities mentioned in this problem. The sign conventions used here for a convex meniscus lens require $R_1 < R_2$ and $R_1 R_2 > 0$; i.e., R_1 and R_2 are either both positive or both negative, depending on whether one takes the light coming from the left, as we choose here, or right side of the lens, in Fig. 36-28. Then $R_2 = 7.80$ mm, and $R_1^{-1} = (n-1)^{-1}f^{-1} + R_2^{-1} = (0.56 \times 44.4 \text{ cm})^{-1} + (7.80 \text{ mm})^{-1} = (7.56 \text{ mm})^{-1}$. (To test your understanding of the sign conventions, try taking the light coming from the right, using $R_1 = -7.80$ mm. Also note that for a concave meniscus lens, $R_1 > R_2$ and $R_1 R_2 > 0$.)

Problem

41. An object is 28 cm from a double convex lens with $n = 1.5$ and curvature radii 35 cm and 55 cm. Where and what type is the image?

Solution

The focal length of the lens, $f^{-1} = (n - 1)(R_1^{-1} - R_2^{-1}) = (1.5 - 1)[(35 \text{ cm})^{-1} + (55 \text{ cm})^{-1}] = (42.8 \text{ cm})^{-1}$ (from Equation 36-8) is greater than the object distance, so the lens equation gives a virtual, erect image located at $\ell' = \ell f/(\ell - f) = (28 \times 42.8 \text{ cm}) \div (28 - 42.8) = -81.1$ cm (negative ℓ' being on the same side of the lens as the object).

Problem

43. A plano-convex lens has curvature radius 20 cm and is made from glass with $n = 1.5$. Use the generalized lensmaker's formula given in Problem 73 to find the focal length when the lens is (a) in air, (b) submerged in water ($n = 1.333$) and (c) embedded in glass with $n = 1.7$. Comment on the sign of your answer to (c).

Solution

In the generalized lensmaker's formula, $n_r = n_{\text{lens}} \div n_{\text{ext}}$ is the index of refraction of the lens relative to the external medium. For a plano-convex lens, $R_1 = 20$ cm and $R_2 = \infty$ (or $R_1 = \infty$ and $R_2 = -20$ cm), so $f = 20 \text{ cm}/(n_r - 1)$. (a) In air, the relative index of refraction of the lens is 1.5/1, so $f = 40$ cm. (b) In water, $n_r = 1.5/1.333$ and $f = 160$ cm. (c) In a medium of higher index of refraction, the relative index is less than one, so the lens acts as a diverging lens with $f = 20 \text{ cm}/[(1.5/1.7) - 1] = -170$ cm.

Problem

45. Two plano-convex lenses are geometrically identical, but one is made from crown glass

($n = 152$), the other from flint glass. An object at 45 cm from the lens focuses to a real image at 85 cm with the crown-glass lens and at 53 cm with the flint-glass lens. Find (a) the curvature radius (common to both lenses) and (b) the refractive index of the flint glass.

Solution

From the lens equation, we calculate the focal lengths of the lenses to be $f_c^{-1} = (45 \text{ cm})^{-1} + (85 \text{ cm})^{-1} = (29.4 \text{ cm})^{-1}$ for the crown glass and $f_f^{-1} = (45 \text{ cm})^{-1} + (53 \text{ cm})^{-1} = (24.3 \text{ cm})^{-1}$ for the flint glass. The lens maker's formula, with the crown glass data, gives the radius of curvature, $R = (n_c - 1)f = (1.52 - 1)(29.4 \text{ cm}) = 15.3 \text{ cm}$ (see solution to Problem 43). The same formula gives the index of refraction of the flint glass, with data for this lens, as $n_f = 1 + R/f = 1 + 15.3/24.3 = 1.63$.

Problem

47. An object placed 15 cm from a plano-convex lens made of crown glass focuses to a virtual image twice the size of the object. If the lens is replaced with an identically shaped one made from diamond, what type of image will appear and what will be its magnification? See Table 35-1.

Solution

Equations 36-5 and 4 for the magnification (which is positive for a virtual image) give $M_g = 2 = -\ell'/\ell = f_g/(f_g - \ell)$ for the crown glass lens, so $f_g = 2\ell = 30 \text{ cm}$. The focal length of a diamond lens with the same radii of curvature is $f_d = (n_g - 1)f_g/(n_d - 1) = 30 \text{ cm} (1.520 - 1)/(2.419 - 1) = 11.0 \text{ cm}$ (use Equation 36-8 and Table 35-1). An object 15 cm from the diamond lens produces a real, inverted image (negative M) magnified by $M_d = 11.0/(11.0 - 15) = -2.74$.

Section 36-5: Optical Instruments

Problem

49. Grandma's new reading glasses have 3.8-diopter lenses to provide full correction of her farsightedness. Her old glasses were 2.5 diopters. (a) Where is the near point for her unaided eyes? (b) Where will be the near point if she wears her old glasses?

Solution

(a) The new correction is designed to make an object placed at the standard near point, $\ell = 25 \text{ cm}$, appear (as a virtual image) to be at the near point for unaided vision, $\ell' = -\text{near point}$. Therefore, $(f_{\text{cor}})^{-1} =$ ($25 \text{ cm})^{-1} + (-\text{near point})^{-1}$, or $(\text{near point})^{-1} = (0.25 \text{ m})^{-1} - 3.8 \text{ diopters} = 0.2 \text{ diopters} = (5 \text{ m})^{-1}$. (b) The old correction, $(f_{\text{cor}})^{-1} = 2.5 \text{ diopters}$, would not bring an object, placed at the standard 25 cm, to a virtual image at the near point of 5 m, but only from $\ell^{-1} = (f_{\text{cor}})^{-1} - \ell'^{-1} = 2.5 \text{ diopters} - (-5 \text{ m})^{-1} = (37.0 \text{ cm})^{-1}$, which is the near point when wearing the old correction.

Problem

51. A camera's zoom lens covers the focal length range from 38 mm to 110 mm. You point the camera at a distant object and photograph it first at 38 mm and then with the camera zoomed out to 110 mm. Compare the sizes of its images on the two photos.

Solution

The image size can be determined from the lens equation, $h'/h = -\ell'/\ell = -f/(\ell - f)$. The ratio of the image sizes, for two different focal lengths, is $h_1'/h_2' = [-f_1/(\ell - f_1)]/[-f_2/(\ell - f_2)] \approx f_1/f_2$, if $\ell \gg f_1$ or f_2 (as for a distant object). Then the image size at 110 mm is approximately $110/38 = 2.89$ times larger than at 38 mm.

Problem

53. The maximum magnification of a simple magnifier occurs with the image at the 25-cm near point. Show that the angular magnification is then given by $m = 1 + \frac{25 \text{ cm}}{f}$, where f is the focal length.

Solution

Another way of using a magnifier is to arrange for the virtual image to be at the near point, as shown (instead of at ∞, as in Fig. 36-38b). From the diagram and the lens equation, $\beta \approx \tan \beta = h'/(-\ell') = h/\ell = h[(1/f) - (1/\ell')] = h[(1/f) + (1/25 \text{ cm})]$. Thus, with the same definition of angular magnification as before (Equation 36-9), $m = \beta/\alpha = h[(1/f) + (1/25 \text{ cm})] \div (h/25 \text{ cm}) = 1 + (25 \text{ cm}/f)$. This is the maximum magnification obtainable with a simple magnifier, because the image can't be seen clearly if it's closer

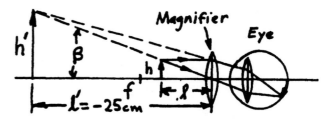

Problem 53 Solution.

than the near point (i.e., $\beta \approx h'/|\ell'|$ and $|\ell'| \geq 25$ cm). Incidentally, the most effective way to use a magnifier is to hold it close to your eye, moving the object up to it until a sharp image is seen.

Problem

55. A 300-power compound microscope has a 4.5-mm-focal-length objective lens. If the distance from objective to eyepiece is 10 cm, what should be the focal length of the eyepiece?

Solution

For a 300×microscope, with $f_0 = 4.5$ mm and $L = 100$ mm, we can solve Equation 36-10 for $f_e = (100/4.5)(25 \text{ cm}/300) = 1.85$ cm.

Problem

57. A Cassegrain telescope like that shown in Fig. 36-42b has 1.0-m focal length, and the convex secondary mirror is located 0.85 m from the primary. What should be the focal length of the secondary in order to put the final image 0.12 m behind the front surface of the primary mirror?

Solution

Reference to Fig. 36-42b shows that parallel rays reflected by the objective mirror converge toward a point, 1 m − 0.85 m = 15 cm behind the secondary mirror, and behave as if they came from a virtual object, with $\ell = -15$ cm in the mirror equation. The final image is located a distance $\ell' = 85$ cm + 12 cm = 97 cm from the secondary mirror, whose required focal length is therefore $f^{-1} = \ell^{-1} + \ell'^{-1} = (-15 \text{ cm})^{-1} + (97 \text{ cm})^{-1} = (-17.7 \text{ cm})^{-1}$. (Recall that a convex mirror has negative focal length.)

Paired Problems

Problem

59. (a) How far from a 1.2-m-focal-length concave mirror should you place an object in order to get an inverted image 1.5 times the size of the object? (b) Where will the image be?

Solution

(a) Equation 36-1 for the mirror's magnification can be combined with Equation 36-2 to yield $-1/M = (\ell/f) - 1$, so $\ell = f(1 - 1/M)$. For a concave mirror with $f = 1.2$ m > 0, and a real image with $M = -1.5$, one finds $\ell = (1.2 \text{ m})(1 + 1/1.5) = 2.0$ m. (b) From Equation 36-1, $\ell' = -M\ell = 1.5(2.0 \text{ m}) = 3.0$ m. (A real image is, of course, in front of the mirror.)

Problem

61. Find the focal length of a concave mirror if an object 15 cm from the mirror has a virtual image 2.5 times the object's actual size.

Solution

The equation in part (a) of the solution to Problem 59, with M positive for an upright, virtual image, gives $f = \ell/(1 - 1/M) = (15 \text{ cm})/(1 - 1/2.5) = 25$ cm.

Problem

63. How far from a 1.6-m-focal-length concave mirror should you place an object to get an upright image magnified by a factor of 2.5?

Solution

The analysis in the solutions to Problems 59 and 61 shows that $\ell = f(1 - 1/M) = (1.6 \text{ m})(1 - 1/2.5) = 96$ cm.

Problem

65. An object and its lens-produced real image are 2.4 m apart. If the lens has 55-cm focal length, what are the possible values for the object distance and magnification?

Solution

If the distance between the object and the real image is $L = \ell + \ell'$ (all positive), the lens equation, $\ell^{-1} + (L - \ell)^{-1} = f^{-1}$, can be rewritten as $\ell(L - \ell) = Lf$. This quadratic in ℓ has solutions $\ell = (L/2) \pm \sqrt{(L/2)^2 - Lf} = 1.2 \text{ m} \pm \sqrt{(1.2 \text{ m})^2 - (2.4 \text{ m})(0.55 \text{ m})} = 85.4$ cm and 154.6 cm. The corresponding magnifications are $M = -f \div (\ell - f) = -1.81$ and -0.552, respectively (see the similar equation in the solution to Problem 5(a)). (Since the image and object distances satisfy the same quadratic, $\ell(L - \ell) = (L - \ell')\ell' = Lf$, their numerical values are conjugates. Compare with the solution to problem 29.)

Problem

67. An object is 68 cm from a plano-convex lens whose curved side has curvature radius 26 cm. The refractive index of the lens is 1.62. Where and of what type is the image?

Solution

The focal length of the lens is given by Equation 36-8, with $R_1 = 26$ cm and $R_2 = \infty$ (or $R_1 = \infty$ and $R_2 = -26$ cm), so $f^{-1} = (n - 1)/R_1 = (1.62 - 1)/26$ cm = $(41.9 \text{ cm})^{-1}$. An object at $\ell = 68$ cm is imaged at

$\ell'^{-1} = f^{-1} - \ell^{-1} = (41.9 \text{ cm})^{-1} - (68 \text{ cm})^{-1} = (109 \text{ cm})^{-1}$. This is a real, inverted image, on the opposite side of the lens from the object.

Supplementary Problems

Problem

69. My contact lens prescription calls for +2.25-diopter lenses with an inner curvature radius of 8.6 mm to fit my cornea. (a) If the lenses are made from plastic with $n = 1.56$, what should be the outer curvature radius? (b) Wearing these lenses, I hold a newspaper 30 cm from my eyes. Where is its image as viewed through the lenses?

Solution

(a) This prescription calls for a converging lens (positive dioptric power) of focal length $1/(2.25 \text{ m}^{-1}) = 44.4$ cm, with a convex meniscus shape (Fig. 36-28). The analysis in the solution to Problem 39 shows that the outer curvature radius (of the first surface to intercept light coming to the eye) is $R_1^{-1} = (n-1)^{-1}f^{-1} + R_2^{-1} = (0.56)^{-1}(2.25 \text{ m}^{-1}) + (8.60 \text{ mm})^{-1} = (8.31 \text{ mm})^{-1}$. (b) The lens equation gives the distance of the image of the newspaper formed by just the contact lens as $(\ell')^{-1} = f^{-1} - \ell^{-1} = 2.25 \text{ m}^{-1} - (30 \text{ cm})^{-1} = (-92.3 \text{ cm})^{-1}$. The negative sign indicates a virtual, erect image in front of the lens. (Of course, the contact lens and the eye together form a real image on the retina.)

Problem

71. Show that identical objects placed equal distances on either side of the focal point of a concave mirror or converging lens produce images of equal size. Are the images of the same type?

Solution

A concave mirror or a converging lens are both represented by positive focal lengths in the lens or mirror equations. For either, the object and image sizes are related by $h'/h = -\ell'/\ell = -f/(\ell - f)$. One can easily see that for $\ell - f = \pm x$ (where $0 < x < f$ is implicit in the statement of this problem), the image size is the same. However, for $\ell = f + x$, the image is real ($h' < 0$), and for $\ell = f - x$, it is virtual ($h' > 0$). (A lens has two symmetrically placed focal points; this problem makes sense for the one on the same side of the lens as the object.)

Problem

73. Generalize the derivation of the lensmaker's formula (Equation 36-8) to show that a lens of

refractive index n_{lens} in an external medium with index n_{ext} has focal length given by

$$\frac{1}{f} = \left(\frac{n_{\text{lens}}}{n_{\text{ext}}} - 1\right)\left(\frac{1}{R_1} - \frac{1}{R_2}\right).$$

Solution

Refraction at the two lens surfaces in Fig. 36-27, when the surrounding medium has index of refraction n_{ext} (instead of $n_1 = 1$), is described by equations analogous to the two preceding Equation 36-7:

$$\frac{n_{\text{ext}}}{\ell_1} + \frac{n_{\text{lens}}}{\ell_1'} = \frac{n_{\text{lens}} - n_{\text{ext}}}{R_1},$$

and

$$\frac{n_{\text{lens}}}{t - \ell_1'} + \frac{n_{\text{ext}}}{\ell_2'} = \frac{n_{\text{ext}} - n_{\text{lens}}}{R_2}.$$

(These are just Equation 36-6 applied to the left- and right-hand surfaces.) For $t \to 0$, there is no distinction between distances measured from either surface, so adding the equations and dropping the subscripts 1 and 2, we find $(n_{\text{ext}}/\ell) + (n_{\text{ext}}/\ell') = (n_{\text{lens}} - n_{\text{ext}}) \times (R_1^{-1} - R_2^{-1})$. Division by n_{ext} gives the sought-for generalization of Equation 36-8. Note that $n_{\text{lens}}/n_{\text{ext}}$ is the relative index of refraction.

Problem

75. A Newtonian telescope like that of Fig. 36-42c has a primary mirror with 20-cm diameter and 1.2-m focal length. (a) Where should the flat diagonal mirror be placed to put the focus at the edge of the telescope tube? (b) What shape should the flat mirror have to minimize blockage of light to the primary?

Solution

(a) The focal point of the primary mirror is 1.2 m from the mirror apex, and the radius of the telescope tube (presumably the same diameter as the mirror) is 0.1 m. Since the total distance of the light path from the primary mirror to the focus is not changed by the insertion of the secondary mirror, the secondary mirror should be (at least) 0.1 m closer than the focal point, or 1.1 m from the primary mirror apex. (b) The cone of rays reflected by the circular primary mirror is sliced by the plane of the secondary mirror into an ellipse (recall the definition of conic sections), which is the shape which blocks the least amount of incoming light.

Problem

77. Just before Equation 36-7 are two equations describing refraction at the two surfaces of a lens with thickness t. Combine these equations to show

that the object distance ℓ and image distance ℓ' for such a lens are related by

$$\frac{1}{\ell} + \frac{1}{\ell'} - \frac{[(n-1)\ell - R_1]^2 t}{\ell R_1[t(\ell + R_1) + n\ell(R_1 - t)]} = (n-1)\left(\frac{1}{R_1} - \frac{1}{R_2}\right).$$

Solution

Combine the two equations by adding them to obtain

$$\frac{1}{\ell_1} + \frac{1}{\ell'_2} + n\left(\frac{1}{\ell'_1} + \frac{1}{t - \ell'_1}\right) = \frac{1}{\ell_1} + \frac{1}{\ell'_2} + \frac{nt}{\ell'_1(t - \ell'_1)}$$
$$= (n-1)\left(\frac{1}{R_1} - \frac{1}{R_2}\right).$$

Eliminate ℓ'_1 from the third term in the middle member of the above equation, by using either of the original two equations, with the following result:

$$\frac{nt}{\ell'_1(t - \ell'_1)} = -\frac{[(n-1)\ell_1 - R_1]^2 t}{\ell_1 R_1[t(\ell_1 + R_1) + n\ell_1(R_1 - t)]}$$
$$= -\frac{[(n-1)\ell'_2 + R_2]^2 t}{\ell'_2 R_2[t(R_2 - \ell'_2) + n\ell'_2(R_2 + t)]}.$$

Then the desired relation between ℓ_1 and ℓ'_2 (with t, n, R, and R_2 as parameters) is achieved. (Note that the object distance $\ell_1 = \ell$, and the image distance $\ell'_2 = \ell'$, are measured from different lens surfaces. The

subscripts 1 and 2 are retained as a reminder of this.) For example, from the first of the original equations,

$$\frac{n}{\ell'_1} = \frac{n-1}{R_1} - \frac{1}{\ell_1} = \frac{(n-1)\ell_1 - R_1}{\ell_1 R_1}.$$

Then

$$\ell'_1 = \frac{n\ell_1 R_1}{[(n-1)\ell_1 - R_1]}$$

and

$$t - \ell'_1 = -\frac{n\ell_1(R_1 - t) + t(R_1 + \ell_1)}{[(n-1)\ell_1 - R_1]}.$$

Multiplication and division by nt produces the first expression for the third term above. The other expression comes from a similar treatment of the second original equation,

$$\frac{n}{t - \ell'_1} = -\frac{(n-1)}{R_2} - \frac{1}{\ell'_2}.$$

Then

$$t - \ell'_1 = -\frac{n\ell'_2 R_2}{[(n-1)\ell'_2 + R_2]},$$

and

$$\ell'_1 = \frac{n\ell'_2(R_2 + t) + t(R_2 - \ell'_2)}{[(n-1)\ell'_2 + R_2]},$$

and the second expression for $nt/\ell'_1(t - \ell'_1)$ follows.

CHAPTER 37   INTERFERENCE AND DIFFRACTION

ActivPhysics can help with these problems:
Activities in Section 16, Physical Optics

Section 37-2:   Double-Slit Interference

Problem

1. A double-slit system is used to measure the wavelength of light. The system has slit spacing $d = 15$ μm and slit-to-screen distance $L = 2.2$ m. If the $m = 1$ maximum in the interference pattern occurs 7.1 cm from screen center, what is the wavelength?

Solution

The experimental arrangement and geometrical approximations valid for Equation 37-2a are satisfied for the situation and data given, so $\lambda = y_{\text{bright}}\, d/mL =$ (7.1 cm/2.2 m)(15 μm/1) = 484 nm. (In particular, $\lambda \ll d$ and $\theta_1 = 3.23\times10^{-2} = 1.85°$ is small.)

Problem

3. A double-slit experiment has slit spacing 0.12 mm.
   (a) What should be the slit-to-screen distance L if the bright fringes are to be 5.0 mm apart when the slits are illuminated with 633-nm laser light?
   (b) What will be the fringe spacing with 480-nm light?

Solution

The particular geometry of this type of double-slit experiment is described in the paragraphs preceding Equations 37-2a and b. (a) The spacing of bright fringes on the screen is $\Delta y = \lambda L/d$, so $L =$ (0.12 mm)(5 mm)/(633 nm) = 94.8 cm. (b) For two different wavelengths, the ratio of the spacings is $\Delta y'/\Delta y = \lambda'/\lambda$; therefore $\Delta y' = (5$ mm)(480/633) = 3.79 mm.

Problem

5. The green line of gaseous mercury at 546 nm falls on a double-slit apparatus. If the fifth dark fringe is at 0.113° from the centerline, what is the slit separation?

Solution

The interference minima fall at angles given by Equation 37-1b; therefore $d = (4 + \frac{1}{2})\lambda/\sin\theta =$

4.5(546 nm)$/\sin 0.113° = 1.25$ mm. (Note that $m = 0$ gives the first dark fringe.)

Problem

7. Light shines on a pair of slits whose spacing is three times the wavelength. Find the locations of the first- and second-order bright fringes on a screen 50 cm from the slits. *Hint:* Do Equations 37-2 apply?

Solution

Since $d = 3\lambda$, the angles are not small, and Equations 37-2 do not apply. The interference maxima occur at angles given by Equation 37-1a, $\theta = \sin^{-1}(m\lambda/d) = \sin^{-1}(m/3)$, so only two orders are present, for values of $m = 1$ and 2 ($\theta < 90°$). If we assume that the slit/screen geometry is as shown in Fig. 37-6, then $y = L\tan\theta = L\tan(\sin^{-1}(m/3)) = Lm/\sqrt{9 - m^2}$. (Consider a right triangle with hypotenuse of 3 and opposite side m, or use $\tan\theta = \sin\theta/\sqrt{1 - \sin^2\theta}$.) For $m = 1$ and 2, and $L = 50$ cm, this gives $y_1 = (50$ cm)$(1/\sqrt{8}) = 17.7$ cm, and $y_2 = (50$ cm)$(2/\sqrt{5}) = 44.7$ cm.

Problem

9. For a double-slit experiment with slit spacing 0.25 mm and wavelength 600 nm, at what angular position is the path difference equal to one-fourth of the wavelength?

Solution

If we set the path difference equal to a quarter wavelength, we obtain $d\sin\theta = \lambda/4$, or $\theta \approx \sin\theta = 600$ nm/4(0.25 mm) = 6×10^{-4} rad $\simeq 0.0344°$.

Problem

11. Laser light at 633 nm falls on a double-slit apparatus with slit separation 6.5 μm. Find the separation between (a) the first and second and (b) the third and fourth bright fringes, as seen on a screen 1.7 m from the slits.

Solution

Since $d \sim 10\lambda$ for this interference process, the small-angle approximation is not particularly accurate, especially for higher orders. The angular position and position on the screen (for the usual slit/screen configuration) for bright fringes are $\theta_m = \sin^{-1}(m\lambda/d)$ and $y_m = L\tan\theta_m$, so the separation of two bright fringes on the screen is $\Delta y_{m_1 m_2} = y_{m_2} - y_{m_1} = L[\tan(\sin^{-1}(m_2\lambda/d)) - \tan(\sin^{-1}(m_1\lambda/d))]$. (a) For $L = 1.7$ m, $d = 6.5$ μm, $\lambda = 633$ nm, $m_1 = 1$ and $m_2 = 2$, one finds $\Delta y_{12} = 17.1$ cm. (b) For $m_1 = 3$ and $m_2 = 4$, and the same other data, one finds $\Delta y_{34} = 20.0$ cm. (The approximate separation implied by Equation 37-2a is $\Delta y = \lambda L/d = 16.6$ cm.)

Section 37-3: Multiple-Slit Interference and Diffraction Gratings

Problem

13. In a 5-slit system, how many minima lie between the zeroth-order and first-order maxima?

Solution

In an N-slit system with slit separation d (illuminated by normally incident plane waves), the main maxima occur for angles $\sin\theta = m\lambda/d$, and minima for $\sin\theta = m'\lambda/Nd$ (excluding m' equal to zero or multiples of N). Between two adjacent maxima, say $m' = mN$ and $(m + 1)N$, there are $N - 1$ minima. (The number of integers between mN and $(m + 1)N$ is $(m + 1)N - mN - 1 = N - 1$, because the limits are not included.) For $N = 5$, the number of minima is 4.

Problem

15. A 5-slit system with 7.5-μm slit spacing is illuminated with 633-nm light. Find the angular positions of (a) the first two maxima and (b) the third and sixth minima.

Solution

(a) Primary maxima occur at angles $\theta = \sin^{-1}(m\lambda/d)$. The first two (after the central peak, $m = 0$) are for $m = 1$ and 2 at $\theta_1 = \sin^{-1}(633\text{ nm}/7.5\text{ }\mu\text{m}) = 4.84°$ and $\theta_2 = \sin^{-1}(2\times633\text{ nm}/7.5\text{ }\mu\text{m}) = 9.72°$. (b) Minima occur at angles $\theta' = \sin^{-1}(m'\lambda/Nd)$, where $m' = \pm1, \pm2, \dots$, but excluding multiples of $N = 5$, in this case. The third minimum is for $m' = 3$, and the sixth for $m' = 7$ (because $m' = 5$ doesn't count). Then $\theta'_3 = \sin^{-1}(3\lambda/5d) = 2.90°$ and $\theta'_7 = \sin^{-1}(7\lambda/5d) = 6.79°$. (These minima would be difficult to observe because the secondary maxima between them are faint.)

Problem

17. Green light at 520 nm is diffracted by a grating with 3000 lines per cm. Through what angle is the light diffracted in (a) first and (b) fifth order?

Solution

For light normally incident on a diffraction grating, maxima occur at angles $\theta = \sin^{-1}(m\lambda/d)$, where d is the grating spacing (equal to the reciprocal of the number of lines per meter), and m is the order. (a) In first order, $\theta_1 = \sin^{-1}(520\text{ nm}\times3000/\text{cm}) = 8.97°$, and (b) in fifth order, $\theta_5 = \sin^{-1}(5\sin 8.97°) = 51.3°$.

Problem

19. Light is incident normally on a grating with 10,000 lines per cm. What is the maximum order in which (a) 450-nm and (b) 650-nm light will be visible?

Solution

The grating condition is $\sin\theta = m\lambda/d$, and, of course, for the diffracted light to be visible, $\theta < 90°$, or $m\lambda/d < 1$. Therefore, the highest order visible is the greatest integer m less than d/λ. For this grating, $d = 1$ cm$/10^4 = 10^3$ nm, so for $\lambda = 450$ nm and 650 nm, the highest visible orders are less than $10^3/450 = 2.22$ and $10^3/650 = 1.54$, or second and first, respectively.

Problem

21. A solar astronomer is studying the Sun's 589-nm sodium spectral line with a 2500-line/cm grating spectrometer whose fourth-order dispersion puts the wavelength range from 575 nm to 625 nm on a detector. The astonomer is interested in observing simultaneously the so-called calcium-K line, at 393 nm. What order dispersion will put this line also on the detector?

Solution

In fourth order on a grating with spacing $d = 1$ cm$/2500 = 4000$ nm, the wavelength range 575 nm to 625 nm lies in the angular range $\theta = \sin^{-1}(4\lambda/d) = \sin^{-1}(0.575) = 35.1°$ to $\sin^{-1}(0.625) = 38.7°$. The Ca-K line of order m also lies in the range if $0.575 < m\lambda_K/d = m(0.393/4) < 0.625$, or $5.85 < m < 6.36$, which is satisfied for $m = 6$.

Problem

23. Estimate the number of lines per cm in the grating used to produce Fig. 37-15.

Solution

The number of lines per cm ($1/d$ in cm^{-1}) is easily estimated from the angular position of the central 550-nm line in a particular order, as shown in the figure; that is, $1/d = \sin\theta/m\lambda$. For example, in fifth order, this line is at $\theta = 61°$ (average of right and left values), so $1/d = \sin 61°/5(550 \text{ nm}) = 3.18 \times 10^3/\text{cm}$ or about 3200 lines/cm.

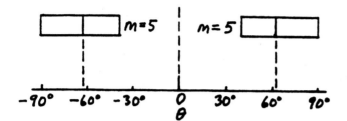

FIGURE 37-15 Problem 23 Solution.

Problem

25. When viewed in sixth-order, the 486.1-nm hydrogen-β spectral line is flanked by another line that appears at the position of 484.3 nm in the sixth-order spectrum. Actually the line is from a different order of the spectrum. What are the possible visible wavelengths of this line?

Solution

To appear at the same angular position as wavelength 484.3 nm in sixth order, the possible other wavelengths and orders must satisfy $m\lambda = 6(484.3 \text{ nm})$. (Then $d\sin\theta$ is the same.) If λ is in the visible range, then $400 \text{ nm} < \lambda = 6(484.3 \text{ nm})/m < 700 \text{ nm}$, or $6(484.3 \div 700) = 4.15 < m < 7.26 = 6(484.3/400)$. Thus, $m = 5$ and 7 are possible orders, corresponding to wavelengths $6(484.3 \text{ nm})/m = 415$ nm, and 581 nm respectively.

Problem

27. Echelle spectroscopy uses relatively course gratings in high order. Compare the resolving power of an 80-line/mm echelle grating used in twelfth order with a 600-line/mm grating used in first order, assuming the two have the same width.

Solution

If the echelle and grating have the same width, then the number of lines in each is proportional to the given spacings, $N/N' = 80/600$. The ratio of the resolving powers (Equation 37-6) is then $mN/m'N' = 12 \times 80/1 \times 600 = 1.6$, so the echelle has about 60% greater resolving power than the grating.

Problem

29. You wish to resolve the calcium-H line at 396.85 nm from the hydrogen-ε line at 397.05 nm

in a first-order spectrum. To the nearest hundred, how many lines should your grating have?

Solution

From Equation 37-6, $N = \lambda/m \; \Delta\lambda \approx 397/(1 \times 0.2) = 1985 \approx 2000$ lines. (This is the number of lines that must be illuminated.)

Section 37-4:   Thin Films and Interferometers

Problem

31. Find the minimum thickness of a soap film $(n = 1.33)$ in which 550-nm light will undergo constructive interference.

Solution

The condition for constructive interference from a soap film is Equation 37-8a, in which the minimum thickness corresponds to the integer $m = 0$. Thus, $2nd_{\min} = \frac{1}{2}\lambda$, or $d_{\min} = \lambda/4n = 550 \text{ nm}/4(1.33) = 103$ nm. (Recall that Equation 37-8a applies to normal incidence on a thin film in air.)

Problem

33. Monochromatic light shines on a glass wedge with refractive index 1.65, and enhanced reflection occurs where the wedge is 450 mm thick. Find all possible values for the wavelength in the visible range.

Solution

Equation 37-8a gives the condition for constructive interference (enhanced reflection) from a given thickness of glass surrounded by air, so $\lambda = 4nd/(2m+1) = 4(1.65)(450 \text{ nm})/(2m+1) = 2970 \text{ nm}/(2m+1)$. Integers giving wavelengths in the visible range (400 to 700 nm) are $m = 2$ and 3, corresponding to $\lambda = 594$ nm and 424 nm, respectively.

Problem

35. As a soap bubble $(n = 1.33)$ evaporates and thins, the reflected colors gradually disappear. (a) What is its thickness just as the last vestige of color vanishes? (b) What is the last color seen?

Solution

The minimum thickness of the bubble, which produces interference colors, is $d_{\min} = \lambda_{\min}/4n$, where $\lambda_{\min}$ is the shortest visible wavelength, normally 400 nm violet light. (See the solution to Problem 31.) Thus, $d_{\min} = 400 \text{ nm}/4(1.33) = 75.2$ nm.

Problem

37. Light reflected from a thin film of acetone ($n = 1.36$) on a glass plate ($n = 1.5$) shows maximum reflection at 500 nm and minimum at 400 nm. Find the minimum possible film thickness.

Solution

The index of refraction of acetone is less than that of glass, so there are 180° phase changes at both boundaries of the film. Then, for normal incidence, Equation 37-8a describes destructive and Equation 37-8b constructive interference. Therefore $2nd = (m + \frac{1}{2})400$ nm and $2nd = m'(500$ nm$)$. These are consistent for $(m + \frac{1}{2})400 = m'(500)$, or $2m + 1 = 5m'/2$. The smallest integer values satisfying this are $m' = 2$ and $m = 2$. When either is substituted in the interference conditions, along with $n = 1.36$, one finds $d = 1.25(400$ nm$)/1.36 = 500$ nm$/1.36 = 368$ nm.

Problem

39. An oil film with refractive index 1.25 floats on water. The film thickness varies from 0.80 μm to 2.1 μm. If 630-nm light is incident normally on the film, at how many locations will it undergo enhanced reflection?

Solution

In a thin film of oil between air and water ($n_{air} < n_{oil} < n_{water}$), there are 180° phase changes for reflection at both boundaries. Therefore, for normally incident light, Equation 37-8b gives the condition for constructive interference, $d = m\lambda/2n = m(630$ nm$) \div 2(1.25) = (0.252\ \mu\text{m})m$. Varying thickness of $0.80\ \mu\text{m} \leq d \leq 2.1\ \mu\text{m}$ implies that $3.17 \leq m \leq 8.33$. Since m is an integer, $4 \leq m \leq 8$, or 5 bright maxima occur at locations corresponding to the allowed integers from 4 to 8.

Problem

41. Two perfectly flat glass plates are separated at one end by a piece of paper 0.065 mm thick. A source of 550-nm light illuminates the plates from above, as shown in Fig. 37-43. How many bright bands appear to an observer looking down on the plates?

Solution

Equation 37-8a applies to constructive interference for normally incident light on the thin, wedge-shaped film of air between glass surfaces (although in this case, the 180° phase change affects rays reflected from the bottom surface of the film). Thus, $d = (m + \frac{1}{2}) \times \lambda/2n_{air} = (m + \frac{1}{2})(550$ nm$)/2 = (m + \frac{1}{2})(275$ nm$)$. The

thickness of the film varies between 0 and 0.065 mm, so m varies between 0 and $[(0.065$ mm$/275$ nm$) - \frac{1}{2}] = 235$. Thus, there are 236 bright bands visible from above (since $m = 0$ counts as the first bright fringe).

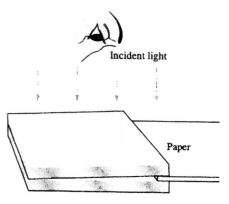

FIGURE 37-43 Problems 41, 42, 43, 72.

Problem

43. You apply a slight pressure with your finger to the upper of a pair of glass plates forming an air wedge as in Fig. 37-43. The wedge is illuminated from above with 500-nm light, and you place your finger where, initially, there is a dark band. If you push gently so the band becomes light, then dark, then light again, by how much have you deflected the plate?

Solution

The difference in the thickness of air in the wedge between a bright and an adjacent dark band is $\frac{1}{4}\lambda$ (one-quarter wavelength in air), so the upper plate was depressed by $\frac{3}{4}\lambda = 375$ nm.

Problem

45. What is the wavelength of light used in a Michelson interferometer if 550 bright fringes go by a fixed point when the mirror moves 0.150 mm?

Solution

Each bright fringe shift corresponds to a path difference of one wavelength. The path changes by twice the distance moved by the mirror. Thus, $550\lambda = 2 \times 0.15$ mm, or $\lambda = 545$ nm.

Problem

47. The evacuated box of the previous problem is filled with chlorine gas, whose refractive index is 1.000772. How many bright fringes pass a fixed point as the tube fills?

Solution

Since the wavelength of the light is different in a gas (e.g., chlorine or air) and in vacuum ($\lambda_{\text{gas}} = \lambda_{\text{vac}}/n_{\text{gas}}$), there is a difference in the number of wave cycles in the enclosed interferometer arm when the box is evacuated or filled with gas. The light travels the length of the arm twice, out and back, and each cycle of difference results in one fringe shift. Thus, the number of fringes in the shift is

$$\frac{2\times42.5 \text{ cm}}{\lambda_{\text{gas}}} - \frac{2\times42.5 \text{ cm}}{\lambda_{\text{vac}}} = \frac{(n_{\text{gas}} - 1)(85 \text{ cm})}{(641.6 \text{ nm})} \approx 1022,$$

where $n_{\text{gas}} - 1 = 7.72\times10^{-4}$ for chlorine gas, and we dropped approximately three quarters of a fringe.

Sections 37-6 and 37-7: Single-Slit Diffraction and the Diffraction Limit

Problem

49. For what ratio of slit width to wavelength will the first minima of a single-slit diffraction pattern occur at $\pm90°$

Solution

When $\theta = 90°$, in Equation 37-9, and $m = 1$ for the first minimum, then $a/\lambda = 1$.

Problem

51. A beam of parallel rays from a 29-MHz citizen's band radio transmitter passes between two electrically conducting (hence opaque to radio waves) buildings located 45 m apart. What is the angular width of the beam when it emerges from between the buildings?

Solution

Take the width of the diffracted beam to be the angular separation between the first minima. These occur at $\theta = \pm\sin^{-1}(\lambda/a)$ (see Exercise following Example 37-6). Thus, $\Delta\theta = 2|\theta| = 2\sin^{-1}[(3\times10^{-8} \text{ m/s})/(29 \text{ MHz})(45 \text{ m})] = 26.6°$.

Problem

53. Find the intensity as a fraction of the central peak intensity for the second secondary maximum in single-slit diffraction, assuming the peak lies midway between the second and third minima.

Solution

The second and third minima lie at angles $\sin\theta_2 = 2\lambda/a$ and $\sin\theta_3 = 3\lambda/a$. If we take the mid-value (as in Example 37-7) to be at $\sin\theta = 5\lambda/2a$, then the intensity at this angle, relative to the central intensity, is $\bar{S}/\bar{S}_0 = [\sin(5\pi/2)/(5\pi/2)]^2 = 4/25\pi^2 = 1.62\times10^{-2}$.

Problem

55. The movie *Patriot Games* has a scene in which CIA agents use spy satellites to identify individuals in a terrorist camp. Suppose that a minimum resolution for distinguishing human features is about 5 cm. If the spy satellite's optical system is diffraction-limited, what diameter mirror or lens is needed to achieve this resolution from an altitude of 100 km? Assume a wavelength of 550 nm.

Solution

The angle subtended by a human feature 5 cm across at 100 km is $\theta_{\text{min}} = 5 \text{ cm}/100 \text{ km} = 5\times10^{-7}$ (radians). The Rayleigh criterion for a diffraction-limited telescope, using light of wavelength $\lambda = 550$ nm, requires an aperture of $D = 1.22\lambda/\theta_{\text{min}} = 1.22\times(550 \text{ nm})/(5\times10^{-7}) = 1.34$ m (see Equation 37-13b). (Atmospheric turbulence would limit the resolution to no better than $\frac{1}{2}'' = 2.4\times10^{-6}$ radians.)

Problem

57. A camera has an $f/1.4$ lens, meaning that the ratio of focal length to lens diameter is 1.4. Find the smallest spot diameter (defined as the diameter of the first diffraction minimum) to which this lens can focus parallel light with 580-nm wavelength.

Solution

The diffraction limit for a lens opening of diameter D, focusing light of wavelength λ is $\theta_{\text{min}} = 1.22 \lambda/D$. The radius of a spot, at the focal length of the lens, with this angular spread, is $r = f\theta_{\text{min}}$ (the spot radius equals the distance between the central maximum and first minimum). The minimum spot diameter is, therefore, $2f\theta_{\text{min}} = 2(1.22)\lambda f/D = 2(1.22)(550 \text{ nm})\times 1.4 \simeq 2.0 \ \mu\text{m}$ (since f/D is the f-ratio).

Problem

59. While driving at night, your eyes' irises have dilated to 3.1-mm diameter. If your vision were diffraction-limited, what would be the greatest distance at which you could see as distinct the two headlights of an oncoming car, which are spaced 1.5 m apart? Take $\lambda = 550$ nm.

Solution

If we use the Rayleigh criterion (Equation 37-13b for small angles) to estimate the diffraction-limited angular resolution of the eye, at a pupil diameter of 3.1 mm, in light of wavelength 550 nm, we obtain $\theta_{\text{min}} = 1.22(550 \text{ nm})/(3.1 \text{ mm}) = 2.16\times10^{-4} \approx 45''$.

(Actually, the wavelength inside the eye is different, $\lambda' = \lambda/n$, because of the average index of refraction of the eye.) This angle corresponds to a linear separation of $y = 1.5$ m at a distance of $r = y/\theta_{min} = 1.5$ m/$2.16 \times 10^{-4} = 6.93$ km $\simeq 4$ mi. Although other factors determine visual acuity, this is a reasonable ballpark estimate.

Problem

61. Under the best conditions, atmospheric turbulence limits the resolution of ground-based telescopes to about 1 arc second (1/3600 of a degree) as shown in text Fig. 37-45. For what aperture sizes is this limitation more severe than that of diffraction at 550 nm? Your answer shows why large, ground-based telescopes do not produce better images than small ones, although they do gather more light.

Solution

The aperture satisfying the Rayleigh criterion (Equation 37-13b) for $\theta_{min} = 1'' = \pi/(180 \times 3600) = 4.85 \times 10^{-6}$ (radians), at the given wavelength, is $D = 1.22(550$ nm$)/4.85 \times 10^{-6} = 13.8$ cm, or about $5\frac{1}{2}$ in. The resolution of all larger-diameter ground-based telescopes is limited by atmospheric conditions at this wavelength.

Paired Problems
Problem

63. Find the total number of lines in a 2.5-cm-wide diffraction grating whose third-order spectrum has the 656-nm hydrogen-α spectral line at an angular position of 37°.

Solution

The grating condition for normally incident light (same as Equation 37-1a) and the given data imply a grating spacing of $d = m\lambda/\sin\theta = 3(656$ nm$) \div \sin 37° = 3.27$ μm, or a grating constant of $d^{-1} = 3.06 \times 10^3$ lines/cm. On a grating 2.5 cm wide, the total number of lines is $(3.06 \times 10^3/$cm$)(2.5$ cm$) = 7.65 \times 10^3$ ($=7645$, to within a hundredth of a line).

Problem

65. A 400-line/mm diffraction grating is 3.5 cm wide. Two spectral lines whose wavelengths average to 560 nm are just barely resolved in the fourth-order spectrum of this grating. What is the difference between their wavelengths?

Solution

The resolving power of a grating is $\lambda/\Delta\lambda = mN$ (see Equation 37-6). If the entire width of the grating is illuminated, $N = (400/$mm$)(3.5$ cm$)$ and $\Delta\lambda = 560$ nm$/4(14,000) = 0.01$ nm.

Problem

67. A thin film of toluene ($n = 1.49$) floats on water. What is the minimum film thickness if the most strongly reflected light has wavelength 460 nm?

Solution

Since $n_{toluene} > n_{water} > n_{air}$, there is a 180° phase change for reflection only at the air/toluene interface, and not at the toluene/water interface, of the film. Then Equation 37-8a applies for constructive interference (of normally incident rays) and $d = (m + \frac{1}{2})\lambda/2n = (m + \frac{1}{2})(460$ nm$)/(2 \times 1.49) = (2m+1)(77.2$ nm$)$. The minimum thickness is 77.2 nm, although odd multiples of this are also possible.

Problem

69. What diameter optical telescope would be needed to resolve a Sun-sized star 10 light-years from Earth? Take $\lambda = 550$ nm. Your answer shows why stars appear as point sources in optical astronomy.

Solution

The angular size of the sun, at a distance of 10 ly, is only $\theta = 2(6.96 \times 10^5$ km$)/10(9.46 \times 10^{12}$ km$) = 1.47 \times 10^{-8}$ (see Appendix E), so even a diffraction-limited space telescope would need an aperture of $D = 1.22\lambda/\theta = 1.22(550$ nm$) \div (1.47 \times 10^{-8}) = 45.6$ m to resolve it in visible light (see Equation 37-13b). (However, ground-based optical interferometers are currently being developed.)

Supplementary Problems
Problem

71. White light shines on a 250-nm-thick layer of diamond ($n = 2.42$). What wavelength of visible light is most strongly reflected.

Solution

If the diamond layer is surrounded by air (or material of lesser index of refraction) then Equation 37-8a is the condition for constructive interference for normally incident light. Thus, maximum intensity occurs for wavelengths $\lambda = 4nd/(2m+1) = 4(2.42)(250$ nm$) \div (2m+1) = 2420$ nm$/(2m+1)$. The only integer which gives a visible wavelength is $m = 2$ (i.e., $2420/700 < 2m+1 < 2420/400$), for which $\lambda = 2420$ nm$/5 = 484$ nm.

Problem

73. In Fig. 37-23 the mth Newton's ring appears a distance r from the center of the lens. Show that the curvature radius of the lens is given approximately by $R = r^2/(m + \frac{1}{2})\lambda$, where the approximation holds when the thickness of the air space is much less than the curvature radius.

Solution

As explained in the solution to Problem 41, there is constructive interference between rays reflected (normally) from the upper and lower surfaces of the film of air which separates the lens and the glass plate, producing a bright Newton's ring when $2d = (m + \frac{1}{2})\lambda$ (Equation 37-8a with $n_{air} = 1$). The thickness of the air film at the position of the ring (a distance r from the central axis of the lens) is $d = R - R\cos\theta$, where $\sin\theta = r/R$. If $d \ll R$, then $\theta \ll 1$, and the small-angle approximation gives $\theta \approx \sin\theta = r/R$, and $\cos\theta = \sqrt{1 - \sin^2\theta} \approx 1 - \frac{1}{2}\theta^2$. Then $d \approx R(1 - \cos\theta) \approx R\cdot\frac{1}{2}(r/R)^2 = r^2/2R$. Substituting this into the interference condition, one gets $R = r^2/(m + \frac{1}{2})\lambda$.

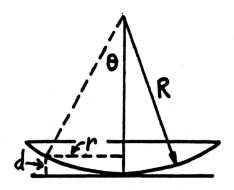

Problem 73 Solution.

Problem

75. How many rings would be seen if the system of the preceding problem were immersed in water $(n = 1.33)$?

Solution

When the interference pattern of Newton's rings, described in Problems 73 and 74, is generated by a thin wedge of water between two glass surfaces $(n = 1.33 < n_{glass})$, one need only replace λ by λ/n in the result in Problem 73. The maximum distance of a bright fringe from the central axis of the lens in Problem 74 is still $r_{max} = 1.25$ cm; therefore $m + \frac{1}{2} \leq nr_{max}^2/\lambda R = (1.33)(1.25 \text{ cm})^2/(500 \text{ nm}) \times (7.5 \text{ cm}) = 5.54 \times 10^3$. There is a bright fringe for each integer m from 0 to 5.54×10^3, provided the incident

light is sufficiently coherent. The small-angle approximation used in Problem 73 is barely justified here, since $\theta_{max} = \sin^{-1}(r_{max}/R) = 9.6°$. The more exact result is $m + \frac{1}{2} \leq 2nR(1 - \cos\theta_{max})/\lambda = 5.58 \times 10^3$.

Problem

77. The signal from a 103.9-MHz FM radio station reflects off a building 400 m away, effectively producing two sources of the same signal. You're driving at 60 km/h along a road parallel to a line between the station's antenna and the building and located a perpendicular distance of 6.5 km from them. How often does the signal appear to fade when you're driving roughly opposite the transmitter and building?

Solution

If we assume a constant phase difference between the direct and reflected waves, essentially a two-slit interference pattern is produced along the road traveled by the car, with minima (or maxima) spaced approximately $\Delta y = \lambda L/d$ apart, along the road and near the perpendicular bisector of the line between the sources. (A constant phase difference in Equations 37-2a and b cancels out in calculating the spacing.) The time between dead spots on this section of road, for a passing car with speed v, is $\Delta t = \Delta y/v = \lambda L/vd$. Using $\lambda = c/f$ and the numbers given, we find $\Delta t = (3 \times 10^8 \text{ m/s})(6.5 \text{ km})(3.6 \text{ s}/60 \text{ m}) \div (400 \text{ m})(103.9 \text{ MHz}) = 2.82$ s. (The actual positions of the maxima and minima would, of course, depend on the phase difference between the direct and reflected waves.)

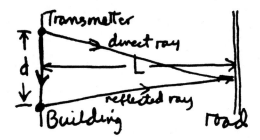

Problem 77 Solution.

Problem

79. The component of a star's velocity in the radial direction relative to Earth is to be measured using the doppler shift in the hydrogen-β spectral line, which appears at 486.1 nm when the source is stationary relative to the observer. What is the minimum speed that can be detected by observing

in first order with a 10,000-line/cm grating 5.0 cm across? *Hint:* See Equation 17-9.

Solution

The resolving power of this grating, in first order, if fully illuminated, is $mN = 1(10^4/\text{cm})(5 \text{ cm}) = 5 \times 10^4$ (see Equation 37-6). This means that two closely spaced wavelengths are resolvable if $|\lambda/\Delta\lambda|$ is less than the resolving power, or equivalently, $|\Delta\lambda/\lambda| > (mN)^{-1} = 2 \times 10^{-5}$. The Doppler shift from a light source moving along the line of sight (the radial direction) with speed v is $|\Delta\lambda/\lambda| \approx v/c$. (This approximate formula is valid if $v \ll c$.) Therefore, the Doppler shift is resolvable with this grating if $v/c > (mN)^{-1}$, or $v > (2 \times 10^{-5})(3 \times 10^5 \text{ km/s}) = 6$ km/s. (The resolving power and the Doppler formula both depend only on the relative shift, so this result is independent of the observed wavelength.)

Problem

81. In a double-slit experiment, a thin glass plate with refractive index 1.56 is placed over one of the slits.

The fifth bright fringe now appears where the second dark fringe previously appeared. How thick is the plate if the incident light has wavelength 480 nm?

Solution

Without the glass plate, the second dark fringe appears at an angular position given by $d\sin\theta = 3\lambda/2$ (Equation 37-1b with $m = 1$). The glass plate, with thickness Δ, introduces an additional optical path difference of $(\Delta/\lambda_{\text{glass}}) - (\Delta/\lambda) = (n-1)(\Delta/\lambda)$, where $n = \lambda/\lambda_{\text{glass}}$ is the refractive index of the plate. The fifth bright fringe occurs at an angular position for which the total path difference is five wavelengths, or $(d\sin\theta/\lambda) + (n-1)(\Delta/\lambda) = 5$ (this is a modified Equation 37-1a with $m = 5$). Since the angle is the same in both cases, we can substitute $d\sin\theta/\lambda = \frac{3}{2}$ to obtain $5 = (\frac{3}{2}) + (n-1)(\Delta/\lambda)$, or $\Delta = 7\lambda/2(n-1) = 7(480 \text{ nm})/2(0.56) = 3.00 \ \mu\text{m}$.

PART 5   CUMULATIVE PROBLEMS

Problem

1. A *grism* is a grating ruled onto a prism, as shown in Fig. 1. The grism is designed to transmit undeviated one wavelength of the spectrum in a given order, as refraction in the prism compensates for the deviation at the grating. Find an equation relating the separation d of the grooves that constitute the grating, the wedge angle α of the prism, the refractive index n, the undeviated wavelength λ_0, and order m_0.

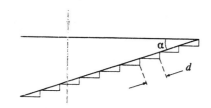

FIGURE 1 A grism (Cumulative Problem 1).

Solution

Consider the interference of rays of wavelength λ, from the same plane wavefront incident normally on the

upper surface of the grism in Fig. 1, which emerge from adjacent slits of the grating (grooves). The two rays will be in phase (producing an intensity maximum) when their path lengths, in wavelengths, differ by an integer, m. From the sketch, $|PQ/\lambda_n -$

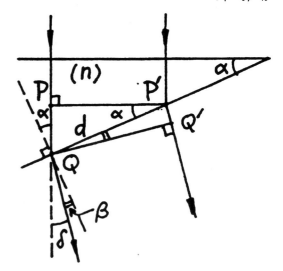

Cumulative Problem 1 Solution.

$P'Q'/\lambda| = m$, where $\lambda_n = \lambda/n$ is the wavelength in the grism, and n is its refractive index. Since $PQ = d \sin \alpha$, $P'Q' = d \sin \beta$, where $d = P'Q$ is the groove separation, and $\delta = \alpha - \beta$ is the deviation, this condition can be written as $|n \sin \alpha - \sin(\alpha - \delta)| = m\lambda/d$ (the grism equation). That a given wavelength (λ_0) be transmitted undeviated ($\delta = 0$) requires $(n - 1) \sin \alpha = m_0 \lambda_0/d$, which is the sought-for equation.

Problem

3. A closed cylindrical tube whose glass walls have negligible thickness measures 5.0 cm long by 5.0 mm in diameter. It is filled with water, initially at 15°C, and placed with its long dimension in one arm of a Michelson interferometer. The water is not perfectly transparent, and it absorbs 3.2% of the light energy incident on it. The laser power incident on the water is 50 mW, and the wavelength is 633 nm. The refractive index of water in the vicinity of 15°C is given approximately by $n = 1.335 - 8.4 \times 10^{-5}\, T$, where T is the temperature in °C. As the water absorbs light energy, how long does it take the interference pattern to shift by one whole fringe?

Solution

The interference pattern shifts by one fringe when the optical path length through the water (the distance out and back across the tube, divided by the wavelength in water) changes by unity. (The phase difference is the optical path length times 2π radians.) The wavelength in water depends on the temperature, through the refractive index, i.e., $\lambda(T) = \lambda/n(T)$, and $n(T) = a - bT$, with a and b given. Therefore, a shift of one fringe implies:

$$\frac{2\ell}{\lambda(15°C)} - \frac{2\ell}{\lambda(T)} = 1 = \frac{2\ell}{\lambda}(n(15°C) - n(T)) = \frac{2\ell}{\lambda} b\, \Delta T,$$

or $\Delta T = \lambda/2b\ell$, where ΔT is the change in temperature from 15°C, $\ell = 5$ cm is the length of the tube, $\lambda = 633$ nm, and $b = 8.4 \times 10^{-5}$/°C. From Equation 19-5, $\Delta T = \Delta Q/mc_W$, where $\Delta Q = \mathcal{P}_{abs}\Delta t = $ (power absorbed from laser)(time), $m = \frac{1}{4}\pi D^2 \ell \rho = $ (volume of tube) × (density of water), and c_W is the specific heat of water. Thus, the time required for a shift of one fringe is $\Delta t = mc_W \Delta T/\mathcal{P}_{abs} = \frac{1}{4}\pi D^2 \rho c_W \lambda/2b\mathcal{P}_{abs}$. Numerically,

$$\Delta t = \frac{\frac{1}{4}\pi (5\text{ mm})^2 (10^3\text{ kg/m}^3)(4186\text{ J/kg·K})(633\text{ nm})}{2(0.032 \times 50\text{ mW})(8.4 \times 10^{-5}/\text{ K})}$$

$$= 193\text{ s} = 3.22\text{ min}.$$

Problem

5. In one type of optical fiber, called a *graded-index fiber*, the refractive index varies in a way that results in light rays being guided along the fiber on curved trajectories, rather than undergoing abrupt reflections. Figure 3 shows a simple model that demonstrates this effect; it also describes the basic optical effect in mirages. A slab of transparent material has refractive index $n(y)$ that varies with position y perpendicular to the slab face. A light ray enters the slab at $x = 0$, $y = 0$, making an angle θ_0 with the normal just inside the slab. The refractive index at this point is $n(y = 0) = n_0$. (a) By writing $\sin \theta$ in Snell's law in terms of the components dx and dy of the ray path, show that that path (written in the form of x as a function of y) is given by

$$x = \int_0^y \frac{n_0 \sin \theta_0}{\sqrt{[n(y)]^2 - n_0^2 \sin^2 \theta_0}}\, dy.$$

(b) Suppose $n(y) = n_0(1 - ay)$, where $n_0 = 1.5$ and $a = 1.0 = \text{mm}^{-1}$. If $\theta_0 = 60°$, find an explicit expression for x as a function of y, and plot your result to give the actual ray path. Explain the shape of your curve in terms of what happens when the ray reaches a point where $n(y) = n_0 \sin \theta_0$. What happens beyond this point?

Solution

(a) Snell's law (Equation 35-3) relates the refractive index and the direction of the ray path, at any y, to the values at $y = 0$; that is, $n \sin \theta = n_0 \sin \theta_0$ (n and θ are both functions of y). The slope of the ray path (with the y-axis) is $\tan \theta = dx/dy = \sin \theta/\sqrt{1 - \sin^2 \theta}$, so substitution and separation of variables yields $dx = n_0 \sin \theta_0 [n^2 - n_0^2 \sin^2 \theta_0]^{-1/2}\, dy$. The given expression for x as a function of y follows immediately

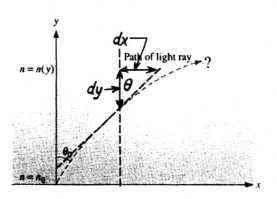

FIGURE 3 Cumulative Problem 5 Solution.

by integration from the origin ($x = 0 = y$). (b) If $n(y) = n_0(1 - ay)$, the integral in part (a) can be evaluated by using the last entry in the first column of the integral table in Appendix A. An intermediate substitution of $z = (1 - ay)/\sin\theta_0$ facilitates this, with the following result:

$$x = \int_0^y \frac{\sin\theta_0 \, dy}{\sqrt{(1 - ay)^2 - \sin^2\theta_0}} = \left(\frac{\sin\theta_0}{a}\right) \int_z^{1/\sin\theta_0} \frac{dz}{\sqrt{z^2 - 1}}$$

$$= \left(\frac{\sin\theta_0}{a}\right) \left[\ln\left(\frac{1 + \cos\theta_0}{\sin\theta_0}\right) - \ln\left(z + \sqrt{z^2 - 1}\right)\right].$$

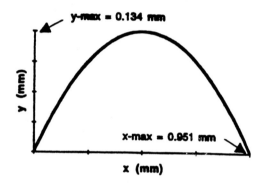

Cumulative Problem Part 5-5 Chart 1.

The given value $\theta_0 = 60°$ (or $\sin\theta_0 = \frac{1}{2}\sqrt{3}$) reduces this further to $x = (\sqrt{3}/2a)[\ln\sqrt{3} - \ln(z + \sqrt{z^2 - 1})]$, where $z = 2(1 - ay)/\sqrt{3}$. (Note that if the ln's are combined and the identity $1/(z + \sqrt{z^2 - 1}) = z - \sqrt{z^2 - 1}$ is used, the expression in the "Answers to Odd-Numbered Problems" is obtained, since

$$\frac{\sqrt{3}}{z + \sqrt{z^2 - 1}} = \sqrt{3}\left[\frac{2(1 - ay)}{\sqrt{3}} - \sqrt{\frac{4(1 - ay^2)}{3} - 1}\right]$$

$$= 2\left[1 - ay - \sqrt{\frac{1}{4} - 2ay + a^2y^2}\right].$$

However, this expression is not well suited for plotting.) At this point, it is convenient to exploit the relation between the natural logarithm and inverse hyperbolic functions, namely, $\ln(z + \sqrt{z^2 - 1}) = \cosh^{-1} z$, which allows one to express y(or z) as a function of x. The result is $z = \cosh(\ln\sqrt{3} - 2ax/\sqrt{3})$, or $ay = 1 - (\sqrt{3}/2)\cosh(\ln\sqrt{3} - 2ax/\sqrt{3})$, which is plotted below, for $a = 1$ mm^{-1}. Since $\sin\theta = (n/n_0)\sin\theta_0 \leq 1$, the above expressions are valid for $0 \leq y \leq (1 - \sin\theta_0)/a = 0.134$ mm (or $1 \leq z \leq 1/\sin\theta_0 = 2/\sqrt{3}$). The ray path is bent back towards the x-axis after reaching its maximum penetration, where $n = n_0 \sin\theta_0$.